'Dr Campbell's important field study concerns the bureaucratic processing of asylum applications from Ethiopians and Eritreans seeking asylum in the UK. While this excellent work describes the pertinent formal law, its striking originality lies in its ethnographic perspective. This includes detailed case studies of the peculiar workings of an overloaded, underprepared and understaffed government bureaucracy righteously turning down most such applications.'

Professor Sally Falk Moore, Harvard University, USA

'The processing of asylum claims largely takes place in conditions which exclude the voices of the people whose future is being decided. This important book offers rich anthropological insights into the operation of the refugee determination system and identifies the need for continued vigilance about failures to protect vulnerable individuals.'

Professor Werner Menski, SOAS, University of London, UK

'Dr Campbell's remarkable book provides deep insights into the UK asylum system and how it limits who is determined to be a refugee. Findings and conclusions are premised on extensive interviews and analysis of cases in the British asylum system. It will become a touchstone for future asylum system studies.'

Dr James C. Simeon, York University, Canada

AF694831

Bureaucracy, Law and Dystopia in the United Kingdom's Asylum System

The central concern of this book is to find answers to fundamental questions about the British asylum system and how it operates. Based on ethnographic research over a two-year period, the work follows and analyses numerous asylum appeals through the British courts. It draws on myriad interviews with individuals and a thorough examination of many state and non-state organizations to understand how the system works. While the organization of the book reflects the formal asylum process, a focus on specific legal appeals reveals the 'political' factors at play as different institutions and actors seek to influence judicial decision-making and overturn/uphold official asylum policy. The final chapter draws on the author's ethnographic findings in the UK's 'asylum field' to re-examine research on the Refugee Status Determination systems in the US, Canada and Australia which have narrowly focused on judicial decision-making. It argues that analysis of Refugee Status Determination systems must be situated and studied as part of a wider, political, semi-autonomous 'asylum field' which needs to be better understood.

Providing an in-depth ethnographic study of a national asylum system and of immigration law and practice, the book will be an invaluable resource for academics, researchers and policy-makers in the UK and beyond working in this highly topical area.

Dr John R. Campbell is a Reader in the Anthropology of Africa and Law at the School of Oriental and African Studies, London. He has undertaken fieldwork in Ghana, Tanzania, Ethiopia and the UK, and has undertaken development-related consultancies in Kenya, Ethiopia and Botswana. In addition to teaching the anthropology of development and the ethnography of Eastern Africa, he teaches courses on legal anthropology. His most recent book is *Nationalism, Law and Statelessness: Grand Illusions in the Horn of Africa* (Routledge, 2013).

Law and Migration

Edited by Satvinder S. Juss

King's College London, UK

Migration and its subsets of refugee and asylum policy are rising up the policy agenda at national and international level. Current controversies underline the need for rational and informed debate of this widely misrepresented and little-understood area.

Law and Migration contributes to this debate by establishing a monograph series to encourage discussion and help to inform policy in this area. The series provides a forum for leading new research, principally from the Law and Legal Studies area, but also from related social sciences. The series is broad in scope, covering a wide range of subjects and perspectives.

Other titles in this series:

Gender and Migration in Italy
A multilayered perspective
Edited by Elisa Olivito
978-1-4724-5575-8

Towards a Refugee Oriented Right of Asylum
Laura Westra, Satvinder Juss and Tullio Scovazzi
978-1-4724-5778-3

The Integration and Protection of Immigrants
Canadian and Scandinavian critiques
Edited by Paul Van Aerschot and Patricia Daenzer
978-1-4724-3654-2

Asylum – a Right Denied
A critical analysis of European asylum policy
Helen O'Nions
978-1-4094-0409-5

Regional Approaches to the Protection of Asylum Seekers
An international legal perspective
Edited by Ademola Abass and Francesca Ippolito
978-1-4094-4297-4

Immigration, Integration and the Law
The intersection of domestic, EU and international legal regimes
Clíodhna Murphy
978-1-4094-6251-4

Bureaucracy, Law and Dystopia in the United Kingdom's Asylum System

John R. Campbell

Routledge
Taylor & Francis Group
LONDON AND NEW YORK

First published 2017 by Routledge

2 Park Square, Milton Park, Abingdon, Oxfordshire OX14 4RN
52 Vanderbilt Avenue, New York, NY 10017

Routledge is an imprint of the Taylor & Francis Group, an informa business

First issued in paperback 2019

Copyright © 2017 John R. Campbell

The right of John R. Campbell to be identified as author of this work has been asserted by him in accordance with sections 77 and 78 of the Copyright, Designs and Patents Act 1988.

All rights reserved. No part of this book may be reprinted or reproduced or utilised in any form or by any electronic, mechanical, or other means, now known or hereafter invented, including photocopying and recording, or in any information storage or retrieval system, without permission in writing from the publishers.

Notice:
Product or corporate names may be trademarks or registered trademarks, and are used only for identification and explanation without intent to infringe.

British Library Cataloguing in Publication Data
A catalogue record for this book is available from the British Library

Library of Congress Cataloging-in-Publication Data
Names: Campbell, John (John R.), author.
Title: Bureaucracy, law, and dystopia in the United Kingdom's Asylum system / John Campbell.
Description: Abingdon, Oxon [UK] ; New York : Routledge, 2017. | Series: Law and migration | Includes bibliographical references and index.
Identifiers: LCCN 2016027206| ISBN 9781138214958 (hardback) | ISBN 9781315444802 (e-book)
Subjects: LCSH: Asylum, Right of—England. | Refugees—Legal status, laws, etc.–England.
Classification: LCC KD4142.C36 2017 | DDC 342.4208/3–dc23
LC record available at https://lccn.loc.gov/2016027206

ISBN: 978-1-138-21495-8 (hbk)
ISBN: 978-0-367-26637-0 (pbk)

Typeset in Galliard
by Swales & Willis Ltd, Exeter, Devon, UK

Contents

Boxes and tables

Boxes

Tables

Cases

1. *Eritrea/DA*: A 16-year-old Eritrean who applied for asylum in the UK in November 2006 with his sister. I attended and recorded his interviews with his caseworker, who took his claim. I also attended his appeal, took notes, and I possess his entire asylum file [38–9, 49–54].
2. *Ethiopia/DS*: He was born in Ethiopia in 1976. During the 1998–2000 war between Eritrea and Ethiopia his sister and brother were deported to Eritrea and he was harassed and beaten by the Ethiopian authorities, who seized his identity documents. He fled to the UK and applied for asylum in June 2000. I have his entire case file. I also interviewed him in November 2007 [40, 138–9].
3. *Eritrea/RY*: She was born in Eritrea in 1985, and applied for asylum in the UK in January 2008. I have the IJ's determination of her appeal, which was heard in July 2008 [40–1].
4. *Eritrea/TM*: He was born in Eritrea in 1971, and arrived at Heathrow airport in August 2006, at which point he was placed in the DFT. I possess the entire case file, and I interviewed the human rights activist who intervened on his behalf [36–7, 43–4, 128].
5. *Ethiopia/DY*: He was born in Ethiopia in 1977, and arrived in the UK, via Kenya, in July 2002. I have his entire case file, notes taken at his appeals and the final decision on his claim [82–8, 96].
6. *Ethiopia/TG*: I possess the skeleton arguments, and attended his final appeal. I attended and took notes on his 'application on the papers' in the CoA and the oral application in the CoA by his barrister [72, 77–80, 96, 102].
7. *Algeria/K*: A Lebanese national who appealed against his detention and was granted a bail hearing in January 2008. He was not represented by legal counsel. I attended his hearing while 'shadowing' a HOPO who assisted the IJ in this case. The HOPO provided me with basic information about the appeal, and I took notes of the hearing [90, 91].
8. *India/S*: An Indian national held in an immigration detention centre who appealed against his deportation following a criminal conviction. I attended his hearing while 'shadowing' a HOPO who assisted the IJ to decide the case. The HOPO provided me with basic information about the appeal, and I took notes of the hearing in January 2008 [64, 92–5].
9. *Gambia/LK*: I attended the permission hearing in the CoA, where I took notes of the proceedings [110–11].

10. *Zimbabwe/HS*: I attended the permission hearing in the CoA, where I took notes of the proceedings [111–13].
11. *Eritrea/GM*: I have the complete file. In addition, I interviewed the barrister several times during the course of this case, attended the oral application in the CoA with GM's barrister, and attended the appeal in the CoA, which was joined to two other Eritrean appeals [113–14, 115–18].
12. *Eritrea/GM, Eritrea/YT and Eritrea/MY*: I attended this appeal in the CoA and took notes. I also spoke to barristers representing two of the individuals, and to the instructing solicitors, who provided me with case files for the individuals [115–18].
13. *Albania/KJ*: An Albanian national in his early twenties who was held in immigration detention; he was appealing against the HO's initial decision to refuse his asylum claim. His appeal was heard in June 2008. I attended the hearing and took notes of the proceedings [128–9].
14. *Afghanistan/AH*: A young Afghani was caught by the police and interviewed in police cells before being transferred to a detention centre. I attended his reconsideration hearing and took notes [129–30].
15. *Burundi/K*: This was a disputed nationality case where the individual had been detained for 23 months. His bail application was heard at a London Tribunal in October 2008, and was refused. I attended the proceedings and took notes [130–1].
16. *Ethiopia/HT*: An Ethiopian national and her two sons. She was periodically detained at Oakington. I have her complete asylum file, and I interviewed her on 11 May 2007 [132–3].
17. *Eritrea/BH*: A 15-year-old Eritrean who was smuggled into the UK and claimed asylum. I possess his entire asylum file, and interviewed him on 7 December 2007 [134].
18. *Ethiopia/MT*: I possess her entire asylum file, and interviewed her on 20 August 2007 [135].
19. *Eritrea/MA*: I possess his entire asylum file, and interviewed him on 18 December 2007 [135–6].
20 *Eritrea/SK*: I possess his entire asylum file, and interviewed him on 23 July 2007 [137–8].
21. *Ethiopia/MB*: I possess his entire asylum, file and interviewed him on 7 December 2007 [139–40].
22. *R* v *Uxbridge Magistrates Court and Another, Ex Parte Adimi* [1999] EWHC Admin 765. This is a reported case heard in the CoA in 1999, the first to hear appeals against conviction for illegal entry into the UK [10, 153].
23. *R* v *Asfaw*: This case was heard in the UK House of Lords in 2008. Information about it comes from law reports and the House of Lords decision [10, 153–4, 155, 158].
24. *Eritrea/SH*. This concerns a 2014 prosecution and conviction of an Eritrean asylum seeker for illegal entry into the UK. Her appeal was heard at Chelmsford Magistrates' Court. I was an expert witness in this case, and I attended her criminal trial [154–5].

Case law, international legal conventions and other legal documents

British case law

AA (Zimbabwe) v SSHD [2007] EWCA Civ 149
AG (Eritrea) v SSHD [2007] EWCA Civ 801
Baiai [2008] UKHL 53
E v SSHD [2004] EWCA Civ 49
EB (Ethiopia) v SSHD [2007] EWCA Civ 809
FS (Treatment of Expert Evidence) [Somalia] UKAIT 00004
GM (Eritrea) v SSHD 2006
GM (Eritrea) and Ors v SSHD [2008] EWCA Civ 833
HB (Ethiopia) v SSHD [2006]
FI (Nigeria) v SSHD [2006]
EB (Kosovo) v SSHD [2006]
JL (Sierra Leone) v SSHD [2006]
HH and Others (Mogadishu: Armed Conflict: Risk) Somalia CG [2008] UKAIT 00022
HS (Zimbabwe) v SSHD [2008] EWCA Civ 915
IM (Risk – Objective Evidence –Homosexuals) Albania CG [2003] UKIAT 00067
JL (Sierra Leone) v SSHD
KA (Draft-related Risk Categories Updated) Eritrea CG [2005] UKAIT 00165
Karanakaran v SSHD [2000] EWCA Civ 11
Karanakaran v SSHD [2000] Imm AR 271
LK (Gambia) v SSHD 2008 (see 'List of cases')
LP (LTTE Area – Tamils – Risk?) Sri Lanka [2007] UKAIT 00076
MA (Draft Evaders – Illegal Departure – Risk) Eritrea CG [2007] UKAIT 00059
MA (Nigeria) v SSHD [2009] EWCA Civ 1229
MT (Algeria) v SSHD [2008]
MT, RB and U v SSHD [2007] EWCA Civ 808
Mohamed (Role of Interpreter) Somalia [2011] UKUT 00337 (IAC)
Muuse [2010] EWCA Civ 453
NM and Others [Lone Women – Ashraf] Somalia CG [2005] UKAIT 00076
R v Asfaw [2008] UKHL 31
R (Abdi and Ors) v SSHD [2008] EWHC 3166

R (Adam and Limbuela) v SSHD [2005] UKHL 66
R (Iran) and Others v SSHD [2005] Civ 982
R (On the Application of European Roma Rights Centre and Others) v Immigration Officer at Prague Airport and Another [2004] UKHL 55
R (On the Application of Frezghi Semere) v Asylum and Immigration Tribunal and the SSHD [2009] EWHC 335 (Admin)
R (On the Application of) Gudanaviciene and Others v The Director of Legal Aid Casework and the Lord Chancellor [2014] EWCA Civ 1622; [2015] 1 WLR 2247
R v SH (Eritrea) (see 'List of cases')
R v SSHD, Ex Parte Sivakumaran and Conjoined Appeals (UN High Commissioner for Refugees Intervening) [1988] AC 958, [1988] 1 All ER 193, [1988] 2 WLR 92, [1988] Imm AR 147
R v Uxbridge Magistrates Court and Another, Ex Parte Adimi [1999] EWHC Admin 765
SD (Expert Evidence) Lebanon [2008] UKAIT 00078
SM and Qadir v SSHD (ETS – Evidence – Burden of Proof) [2016] UKUT 229 (IAC)
SSHD v AH (Sudan) and Others [2007] UKHL 49
ST (Expert Evidence – Kurd – SM Confirmed) Iraq CG [2008] UKAIT 00094
YT (Minority Church Members at Risk) Eritrea CG [2004] UKIAT 00218
ZO (Somalia) EWCA Civ 442

International legal conventions

1951 Refugee Convention
European Convention on Human Rights

Other legal documents

AIT Practice Directions
AIT Procedural Rules
UK Court of Appeal Practice Directions
UK Court of Appeal Procedural Rules

Cases in the European Court

Metock v UK Case C-127/08
NA v UK (Application 25904/07)
Saadi v UK (Application 13229/03)

British legislation

Aliens Act 1905
Aliens Order 1920

Asylum and Immigration (Treatment of Claimants etc.) Act 2004
Asylum and Immigration Act 1996
Asylum and Immigration Appeals Act 1993
Borders, Citizenship and Immigration Act 2009
Commonwealth Immigrants Act 1968
Criminal Attempts Act 1981
Criminal Justice and Immigration Act 2008
Forgery and Counterfeiting Act 1981
Human Rights Act 1998
Immigration Act 1971
Immigration Appeals Act 1969
Immigration and Asylum Act 1999
Immigration, Nationality and Asylum Act 2006
Legal Aid, Sentencing and Punishment of Offenders Act 2012
Nationality, Immigration and Asylum Act 2002
Race Relations Act 1976
Terrorism Act 2006
Tribunal Courts and Enforcement Act 2007

Acknowledgements

The fieldwork on which this book is based was funded by a grant from the UK Economic and Social Research Council (RES-062-23-0296) entitled 'Refugees and the Law: An Ethnography of the British Asylum System'. The grant covered the cost of fieldwork in British courts, immigration firms, barristers' chambers and in Ethiopian and Eritrean refugee community organizations, churches and mosques and other organizations between January 2007 and January 2009. The grant also made it possible to employ Dr Solomon Afework as my research assistant. I owe Solomon a debt of gratitude as a colleague and a friend. He was responsible for the community-based research.

I am especially indebted to the individuals who give up their time to sit on the project advisory board, which was of immense help in strategizing research and finding key informants. In particular, I want to thank Eric Fripp (barrister, Lamb Building Chambers), Ravi Low-Beer and David Longe (both formerly with the Refugee Legal Centre), Professor Werner Menski (School of Oriental and African Studies) and Mrs Alem Gebrehiwot (Director, Ethiopian Community Centre in London, as it was then called).

Over the course of the project we were assisted by many individuals and organizations whose support made this study possible. I would like to thank the many asylum applicants who allowed me to follow their claims through the courts. I also want to thank the immigration lawyers/case workers who agreed to be interviewed, and the barristers who agreed to be interviewed and to let me follow their clients' cases through the courts. A final thanks goes to Alison Harvey at the Immigration Law Practitioners' Association for access to their archives, and to Roland Schilling and Peter Grady of the London office of the United Nations High Commission for Refugees for speaking to me about that organization's work in the UK.

I also want to thank the following individuals who carefully read and commented on draft chapters. Special thanks for their careful and critical comments on chapters in the book go to Barbara Harrel-Bond (formerly Director, Refugee Studies Centre, Oxford, Chapters 1–5), to Dr Claudia Tazrieter (University of New South Wales, Chapters 1, 7 and 8), to Eric Fripp (Chapters 5, 6 and the 'Conclusion and Postscript'), to Alison Harvey (Immigration Law Practitioners' Association), Roland Schilling and Peter Grady (United Nations

High Commission for Refugees, Chapter 8), and to James Ingram (Bail for Immigration Detainees, Chapters 1 and 2). Chapter 8 was presented at a seminar in the Department of Anthropology and Sociology, School of Oriental and African Studies, London in the spring of 2013. Needless to say, I take responsibility for any errors or omissions.

An earlier book, *Nationalism, Law and Statelessness: Grand Illusions in the Horn of Africa* (Routledge, 2013) followed one of five types of asylum claims I examined during fieldwork, namely claims by Ethiopian-born Eritreans who were made stateless by Ethiopia during the 1998–2000 border war between Ethiopia and Eritrea. Many of the debts incurred in the writing of that book remain, particularly to the Eritreans and Ethiopians who spoke to us about their experience of seeking asylum in the United Kingdom.

Most government officials refused to co-operate with my research. Their refusal can only be explained by a distrust of independent research. Exceptionally, however, the head of a London-based Home Office Presenting Unit allowed me to work-shadow five presenting officers during the course of a normal work day, following which I was allowed to interview these junior civil servants about their educational background, their training and how they saw their job. For this insight into the Home Office, I remain grateful.

Official distrust made it necessary to rely upon the United Kingdom's Freedom of Information Act (2000) to obtain basic information on government policy and policy implementation. This information should be in the public domain to allow the British public to understand and evaluate the work of government. It is important to note that where I report data that derives from a Freedom of Information request or where the source is an official UK Home Office or UK Border Agency report, *this data should be treated as provisional.* The provisional nature of official information arises because of (a) the late reporting of many cases/statistics (a proportion of which are not included when each report is published); (b) the results of 'data cleansing exercises'; and (c) the fact that subsequent publications do not adequately reconcile figures in earlier or alternative reports (UK 2012a: 17). In addition, the Home Office has changed the way it collects and reports data, which creates gaps in data coverage, and where statistics are reported differently by the Home Office and the Ministry of Justice, as is the case with the data in Tables 6.1–4, it is impossible to reconcile their data.

The research on which this book is based complied with the Economic and Social Research Council guidelines on informed consent. This means that we used consent forms which were written in Amharic, Tigrinya, Oromiffa and English. The purpose of the research was explained to all the individuals we sought to interview, where necessary through an interpreter, including the possible uses of the information they provided. A written consent form – in a language that was understood by the interviewee – was signed by the researcher and the interviewee, with one copy given to the participant and one copy filed with the project. We digitally recorded the majority of interviews, which were later transcribed. Given the reluctance of officials to participate in the research, it is notable that not one asylum seeker refused to participate. Where necessary, I have anonymized the interview data for the cases reported in this book, though there are some exceptions, notably where the Immigration and Asylum Tribunal or the English Court of Appeal has published a decision on a case.

In analysing asylum litigation, I have relied upon the following types of documents provided to me by applicants or their lawyers: witness statements; UK Border Agency Statement of Evidence forms, UK Border Agency screening interviews of asylum applicants; Home Office Reasons for Refusal letters; correspondence between the Home Office and the applicants' legal representatives; expert reports (when these were submitted); language analysis reports (when these were used to assess an asylum claim); medico-legal reports provided by medical experts on behalf of an applicant (when these were submitted on behalf of the applicant); the skeleton argument, or 'skellie', submitted by the applicants' legal representatives to the court prior to their appeal(s); the judge's decision on the claim (including decisions on previous appeals); and my own notes of appeal hearings. In many of the cases reported in this book I also interviewed the appellant and their lawyer.

An expanded discussion of the work of UN High Commission for Refugees in Chapter 8 was published as 'Asylum v. sovereignty in the 21st century: How nation-states breach international law to block access to asylum', *International Journal of Migration and Border Studies*, 2(1) (2016): 24–39.

I owe a special debt to my partner Sarah – and to my children Alex, Ellie and Nina, who did not see as much of me as they should have during my research and writing – without whose love and support this book would never have been completed. While I have many debts to countless individuals, many of whom must remain unnamed, I hope they will recognize their contributions to this study.

Finally, I dedicate this book to my mother, Dolores (who died in November 2014), and my father, Ray (who died in July 2015). They ensured that I was able to get the education they never had.

1 An anthropological approach to studying the asylum field

What happens to individuals fleeing persecution when they make an application for asylum in the United Kingdom? What role do government officials, lawyers and judges play in the asylum process? How is the asylum system organized? How are asylum applications argued and decided in British courts? Why is it that many more asylum applications are refused than granted? Is the process fair? These are the issues addressed in this book.

Research for this project was funded by a two-year grant from the United Kingdom's Economic and Social Research Council to undertake anthropological fieldwork into the British asylum system between 2007 and 2009. My research followed asylum claims (litigation) in the Immigration and Asylum Tribunal (IAT, or Tribunal; also known as Asylum and Immigration Tribunal, or AIT) and the Court of Appeal (CoA), to understand how the asylum system was organized and worked, how different actors and institutions saw and performed their roles, and why relatively few asylum applications are successful.

This study is the first ethnographically informed analysis of a national asylum system. Bohmer and Shuman (2008) have written a comparative study of asylum in the US and UK based on analysing the personal narratives of asylum seekers. However, their study did not address asylum law or policy, nor did it look at how asylum narratives are assessed and decided. Furthermore, their material pre-dates major changes in law and policy which came into effect after 2000. Travers (1999) published an ethno-methodologically oriented study of asylum claims heard in the UK's Asylum and Immigration Tribunal in 1997. While he interviewed key actors involved in asylum litigation, his principal focus was on 'talk', specifically how cases were argued and what different actors said about a case, legislation and so on. His findings also pre-date major legislative changes. Good (2007) has examined the role of expert country and medical evidence in asylum appeals in the UK, but he did not examine litigation or the wider context in which expert evidence is situated. Finally, Hamlin (2014) has undertaken fieldwork in the US, Canada and Australia to understand the similarities and differences between their respective Refugee Status Determination (RSD) systems. She argues that the differences between different national systems can be explained by the power exercised by the courts and the government, and by the extent to which administrative decisions on asylum claims are insulated from political interference and judicial review (JR).

Three of the aforementioned studies focus primarily on language/legal discourse, and they offer a fairly static picture of the asylum process. In contrast, Hamlin focuses on the relationship between the judiciary and the legislature without taking into account the wider political 'field' in which both operate. To address the limitations of the above studies, I have turned to the literature on the anthropology of law.

Anthropology, litigation and the state

In this study I focus on asylum-related litigation in British courts. In particular, I follow the trajectory of asylum claims as they move from the initial interview conducted by the United Kingdom Border Agency (UKBA), to a lawyer's office and then to court. This approach allows me to understand the specific facts of each asylum claim, and it provides a window into the wider social field where government/administrative institutions, the courts, non-governmental organizations (NGOs) and other actors attempt to influence judicial decisions. To accomplish this task, I attend to the language used by different actors, including how an asylum claim is 'translated', how a claim is argued in court, how judges decide and rationalize their decisions, and how officials alter the rules of the game to make it more difficult for applicants to obtain asylum. However, my interest is *not* with legal discourse. Though the power of law is expressed in and through language, in the field of asylum and immigration the state exercises its power to block, restrict, refuse and grant (some) asylum applications while simultaneously arresting, detaining and deporting individuals who are refused asylum.

I argue that the asylum system can be studied using Sally Falk Moore's (1973) concept of law as a 'semi-autonomous social field'. Moore coined the term to underline the importance of the wider social context in which 'law' is situated. She wanted to analyse the norms, procedures and rules of law, the various 'agencies' involved in the administration and adjudication of law and other organizations linked to the legal process. In her view, it is important to look at how government departments and the courts work, at the work of judges, lawyers and associated professionals, and at how the 'market' affects the delivery of justice. It is in this sense that I argue that immigration law and practice constitutes a 'semi-autonomous social field' which is both encapsulated by 'law' but is also semi-autonomous from it, in the sense that asylum litigation is influenced by organizations and processes 'outside' the law.

Each institution/organization, and the individuals who work in them, can usefully be seen as pursuing different objectives. For this reason, and following Long (2004), I argue that institutions need to be analysed as social 'actors' capable of pursuing a range of 'projects'/agendas. One way of thinking about the importance of actors in this field of study is offered by Conley and O'Barr (1998: 89), who observed that: 'the entity we call the law manifests itself in the behaviour of legal officials . . . . Because these are real people, their orientations and reactions are not uniform, but rather vary in interesting ways.'

It is therefore necessary to understand the perspective of both individuals *and* institutions whose actions and interests converge in 'a complex interplay of specific . . . strategies, "projects", resource endowments (material/technical and social/institutional), discourses and meanings' (Long 2004: 15). This approach allows me to understand how institutions and actors conceive of and act in the asylum field, where their actions converge in court to produce a legal decision.

Given the dominant role played by the state in the asylum field, it is necessary to sketch out my approach to it before describing the field. Studies of the state, and in particular the institutions responsible for immigration and asylum law and policy, have tended to follow the work of Max Weber by examining the formal, organizational nature of bureaucracy. Thus Heyman's (1995, 2004) work on the US immigration service points out the importance of 'bureaucratic thought work', the power of senior officials, and the impact of training and bureaucratic 'subculture' (Gilboy 1991; Jubany 2011) on the way that bureaucrats administer, regulate and control migrants and asylum applicants. This approach stresses the importance of understanding how bureaucracy works, the nature of work routines and workloads, and the 'local knowledge'/'thought work' of officials.

Another, complimentary, approach is to study 'the signature of the state'. Thus Veena Das has argued that the state can usefully be perceived as 'a form of regulation that oscillates between a rational mode and a magical mode of being' (Das 2004: 225). From the perspective of undocumented migrants and asylum seekers who stand at the margins of the state, the state is revealed in the way that officials invoke the law and make discretionary decisions. Here the written decisions and documents issued by officials directly affect the lives of individuals and, through their iterability and citability, documents take on a 'magical' significance because at its margins the state is powerful and illegible (Hoag 2010). This is a useful counterpart to Weberian approaches, especially when officials deliberately seek to remain 'invisible' and unaccountable (Jubany 2011; see below).

Das's notion of the 'signature of the state' can be stretched to include instances where officials fail to take a decision that falls within their discretionary power. Official failures/refusals to act affect asylum applicants who are refused status, deported or who are turned away at the border (Jordan, Strath and Triandafyllidou 2003). Instances of inaction or apparent failure to act in a reasonable or timely manner are rebuffed by officials who argue that all reasonable steps were taken and that complaints about inaction are unfounded. Typically, however, the underlying reason for inaction arises from 'lack of governance' within an institution, which leads to poor and/or unlawful decisions (UK 2012b: 2).

For instance, when an asylum applicant makes a fresh asylum application or files a judicial review against the decision of an official – which should suspend further state action against them – and the application is ignored or is not processed, the individual is left destitute or is deported. From the point of view of an asylum applicant who has complied with the law, it is not possible to understand why a petition succeeds or fails. In this context, official actions defy rational explanation. Both approaches outlined above – a concern with the state as a powerful bureaucracy and with how asylum applicants experience it – are pursued in this study.

There are a number of state institutions which directly shape the asylum field but which are normally seen as being distinct from or apart from 'law'. For instance, in parliament, elected politicians review, debate and pass legislation that fundamentally shapes asylum and immigration law and the way the entire field functions. At one remove from parliament is the Home Office (HO) (see Chapters 2 and 3), which I argue is the central institution in the asylum system. This department, overseen by the Secretary of State for the Home Department (SSHD), is part of the executive branch of the state. The Secretary of State, an elected politician, is responsible for immigration and asylum policy and the administration of the Home Office and its operational wing, the UK Border Agency. In addition to implementing legislation, the SSHD also creates law and policy by making formal policy statements and by 'laying statements' before parliament or the House of Lords (HoL).

Cabinet decisions and those of the SSHD are communicated to the HO/UKBA via discussions with senior officials in the Policy Development Group before being transmitted downwards to a plethora of officials who are expected to implement them (see Chapter 3). Crucially, policy-making in the HO/UKBA is an intensely insulated process which results in policies and decisions that are frequently in tension with the wider legal/statutory framework, including the 1951 Refugee Convention (Campbell 2013a; see Chapter 8 in this volume).

I focus on asylum litigation for two reasons. First, an asylum appeal is shaped in important ways by the way in which the HO/UKBA process and decide the initial claim for asylum. This 'pre-litigation' work is directly affected by HO/UKBA policies and instructions and by internal bureaucratic processes, e.g. the imposition of management targets requiring quick decisions, the quality of training given to caseworkers and so on, which gives rise to litigation, i.e. judicial reviews against official decisions and legal appeals. Thus HO asylum case workers interview asylum applicants at the beginning of the asylum process and make an initial decision on the claim. Typically, about 80 per cent of initial applications are refused by HO caseworkers, though 25–33 per cent of these decisions are overturned on appeal (Asylum Aid 2013; Amnesty International 2004; Smith 2004).

A second reason for focusing on litigation is that it provides a window into the key issues raised by the asylum claim and the work of state institutions and other institutional and individual actors in the asylum field. The work of a range of institutions is revealed in the legal and policy issues argued in an asylum claim, including behind-the-scenes work to influence how a claim is decided. Furthermore, the analysis of legal cases reveals that, contrary to official statements, litigation is a key element of HO policy and is used to secure HO policy objectives.

Courts are important institutional 'actors' which can be examined through an analysis of the decisions of immigration and appellate judges. In the UK the work of judges has primarily been analysed by scrutinizing written decisions (e.g. Harvey 1998; Yeo 2005). Indeed, only determinations promulgated at a specific point in time have been examined, even though many decisions are overturned on appeal. More problematically, researchers have not had access to all the relevant material – i.e. a record of court proceedings and individual case files – to accurately assess how cases are argued and decided.[1]

In the US and Canada, where statistics on judicial decisions are publicly available, researchers have provided a detailed analysis of judicial decision-making at all levels of the asylum process. For both the US and Canada, research has shown that a decision on an asylum claim 'depends in large measure on which government official decides the claims' (Ramji-Nogales, Schoenholtz and Schrag 2007: 296). Rehaag concluded his study of asylum adjudication in Canada in the following terms: 'outcomes in refugee adjudication appear to hinge, at least in part, on the identity of the adjudicator assigned' (2008: 335). These studies argue that the key problem is judicial decision-making. While this is certainly part of the answer, I argue that reliance on statistics is misleading unless it is goes hand in hand with in-depth, qualitative research that follows litigation and situates judicial decisions in a much wider political field.

Other important actors to understand are immigration caseworkers/solicitors and interpreters, who work in tandem to prepare an asylum application and the legal appeal. Due to the complexity of asylum law, applicants have little chance of obtaining asylum without legal assistance, and lawyers need interpreters to interview applicants. In effect, lawyers and interpreters (in the UK interpreters are barred from offering legal advice) function as 'gatekeepers' who can facilitate/block access to the legal system.

I draw on US-based research to set out my approach to these actors. Thus Mather and Yngvesson (1980–1981) look at the importance of language, lawyers and audience in the 'transformation' of disputes, and show how normative legal concepts and intervention by key individuals shape and influence the dispute process (cf. Conley and O'Barr 1998: chap. 5). Thus lawyers, judges, legal officials and interpreters use their skill in 'manipulating the discourse' of law to shape, redefine, redirect and argue a dispute. Indeed, Mather and Yngvesson argue that 'disputing be viewed as a bargaining process in which the object of the dispute, and the normative framework to be applied, are negotiated as the dispute proceeds' (1980–1981: 818). They note that is common to narrow the focus, restrict or exclude participation in the dispute beyond the immediate parties, and adopt a highly specialized form of discourse which the disputants are unfamiliar with and which prevents them from participating in the case. This aptly describes the trajectory of litigation in the UK's asylum system.

In a similar vein, Galanter has described lawyers as 'translators' in the sense that they fit a client's dispute into applicable legal categories and screen out claims they are not inclined to pursue (1983: 19). Indeed, Cunningham (1992) has argued that a lawyer's 'translation' of a case may misrepresent a client. More specifically, McKinley discusses a case in which an asylum applicant's narrative was substantially 'recast', initially against the wishes of the woman, 'into a persuasive and intelligible format for the judiciary to render a favourable decision' (1997: 70; see also James and Killick 2012).

The above observations raise three important concerns when examining the work of asylum case workers and interpreters. First, because the vast majority of asylum applicants do not speak English, lawyers require interpreters – who speak English and the language of the applicant – to help interview the applicant and translate their narrative of flight into a legal claim for asylum. The need for interpreters creates: (a) space for possible misunderstandings about the case (Gibb and Good 2014; Jacquemet 2009), and (b) given the ignorance of applicants about asylum law and the ignorance of the lawyer about what the interpreter tells a client, it is possible that interpreters (illegally) advise clients what to say and how to make a claim.[2] Second, the time available to an immigration lawyer to 'take the claim' from a client is shaped by financial pressures. At the time of my fieldwork, legal aid paid for five contact hours with a client (additional time had to be approved by the Legal Services Commission, or LSC). Given the time needed to interpret and answer each question and record the information on a form, misunderstandings about the claim can arise if lawyers focus on issues they consider important at the expense of listening to their clients (see Chapter 4).

The task of interviewing an individual to take their asylum claim may contribute to a third problem. The asymmetric structure of the interview (particularly interviews undertaken by the Home Office) introduces 'an elaborate set of [linguistic] constraints' which locate control over the process with the interviewer, who controls the topics to be discussed, the shift of topics, the amount of time the respondent has to answer, and whether the applicant is able to initiate a topic or explain their case (Corcoran 2004). In short, the asylum interview creates 'narrative inequality' and a one-sided interview which, when transposed into a written record, can create serious difficulties for an asylum applicant. The difficulty arises from the fact that the Home Office and the court rely upon a highly:

> complex set of discursive practices and language ideologies that are, in practice, being used as criteria for 'truth', 'trustworthiness', 'coherence' and 'consistency'. Such discursive practices require access to communicative resources that are often far beyond the reach of . . . asylum seekers.
>
> (Blommaert 2001: 414)

The situation is complex because asylum applicants are required to provide multiple statements – two interviews with the Home Office,[3] interviews with their legal representative which are submitted with their claim, written witness statements and oral testimony in court – which are assessed by an Immigration Judge (IJ). *Any* inconsistency between statements – in terms of chronology, names, 'evidence' of persecution, etc. – can undermine the applicant's credibility and lead an IJ to refuse the claim (see my analysis of *Ethiopia/TG* in Chapter 5). This situation arises because the asylum process relies upon:

> rules of evidence [which] stress textual consistency . . . linearity, logic, rationality and factuality; they require considerable attention to details: they rely on written language as the basic and most lasting format of declaring 'truth'; in short, *they are highly culture- and society-specific and reflect local ideologies of language.*
>
> (Blommaert 2001: 436; my emphasis)

Indeed, a recent study has argued that 'between 48 and 90 per cent of all asylum claims are rejected on the basis of adverse credibility' (Byrne 2007: 610; see also International Association of Refugee Law Judges 2013). Given the weight attached to credibility by IJs, it is surprising that the Tribunal has not adopted clear evidentiary principles to help IJs assess the credibility of asylum applicants.

Given the problems with Home Office interviews, limited access to a lawyer, and difficulties in bridging cultural and linguistic differences, the 'translation' of an asylum applicant's account and its transformation into a written document can be highly problematic. An examination of this issue requires research on lawyer–client interaction, which is frustrated by norms of confidentiality, yet without access we cannot understand how legal services are provided, how legal norms are transmitted to asylum seekers, or the nature of litigant (dis) satisfaction. In the US, Sarat and Felstiner (1986) observed and tape-recorded 115 lawyer–client conferences. They describe the central role played by lawyers, who attempted to persuade clients involved in divorce proceedings to negotiate a settlement, as an 'enactment of power'. Because lawyer–client interaction is hedged about with suspicion and doubt, their research describes interaction as a process of 'story telling' and interrogation in which the ultimate objective is to 'construct a mutually tolerable story that is likely to be persuasive' to the other party or to a judge (Felstiner and Sarat 1992: 1,455). In this context, power is involved in 'interpreting the past, defining the present, and setting an agenda for the future'; its objective is to 'negotiate a working definition of reality' that will advance a client's interests (Felstiner and Sarat 1992: 1,458).

Lawyer–client interaction is also problematic due to communication issues (e.g. involving the sifting and evaluation of a clients account), the need to translate gender/cultural differences, and a mutual aversion for confrontation that might result in the withdrawal or collapse of a case which occurs when, for example, a client fails to attend their appeal.

Even though interaction between an appellant and their legal counsel is fraught with tension and potential misunderstandings, it is important to note that asylum applicants who are represented by legal counsel have a significantly higher chance of securing status than individuals who are not represented (Ramji-Nogales, Schoenholtz and Schrag 2007: 340; Rehaag 2012).

The focus of fieldwork

Prior to undertaking this research I had worked on development in the Horn of Africa, and I had written 100-plus 'expert' reports for Eritreans and Ethiopians seeking asylum in the West (Good 2004). In this project I followed five different types of asylum claims:

1 the claims of unaccompanied asylum seeking children;
2 cases alleging 'sexual violence';
3 cases alleging forms of 'discrimination' recognized by s. IA(1) of the Refugee Convention;
4 cases submitted to the High Court seeking a judicial review of an official's decision on the basis that the decision was unreasonable, irrational or unlawful;
5 cases alleging that Ethiopia had violated international human rights conventions when, during 1998–2000, it arrested and deported 75,000 of its nationals (see Campbell 2013b).

My research officer, Dr Solomon Afework, also interviewed and studied Ethiopian and Eritrean refugee community organizations to learn how they were connected to the Horn and how they attempted to assist newly arriving refugees.

During 2007–2009, 76 organizations either provided us access to their institution and/or they allowed us to interview their staff, clients, professional associates, family and friends (see Table 1.1). Eleven law firms/NGOs, five barristers' chambers, two departments of the UKBA, the Treasury Solicitor's Office (TSol), eight national refugee organizations, 13 British NGOs, 27 Ethiopian RCOs and 11 Eritrean RCOs assisted the project in this way.

In addition to the interviews, I followed asylum appeals through the courts, attended three country guidance cases, seven judicial review applications in the High Court, four unrepresented asylum appeals for individuals held in the Detained Fast Track (DFT), 10 immigration appeals, 16 bail hearings for individuals held in immigration detention and six deportation hearings. At the Court of Appeal I attended eight 'permission' hearings (oral applications) and two full appeals; I also attended one asylum appeal heard in the House of Lords (now the Supreme Court).

The principle of 'informed consent' was followed in all meetings and interviews. The purpose of the research was explained to everyone, and signed consent forms were used. Where possible, we recorded the interview and transcribed it. When informants were reluctant to be recorded, we took notes which were later written up. If individuals did not wish to participate in the research, we left them in peace. Interview and consent forms were written in Amharic, Tigrinya and Oromiffa (the principal languages of Ethiopia and Eritrea) and English. We paid

Table 1.1 Interviews by type and number

Interpreters: 8	*Immigration caseworkers/solicitors: 18*	*Barristers: 15*	*Clerks in barristers' chambers: 3*
Other interviews: 39	Government officials: 10	Asylum applicants: 7	Immigration Judges: 4

a small fee for their time to the asylum applicants who were interviewed (some of whom were destitute). I employed and trained research assistants who spoke the relevant vernacular language to interview asylum applicants and to translate the interview into English. Finally, I have anonymized all the interviews and most of the cases discussed in this book; where cases have not been anonymized, either the asylum applicant granted me permission to identify them or the case is a matter of public record.

Methods, research access and the limitations of this study

At the outset of fieldwork in late 2007 I had made arrangements with immigration caseworkers in law firms to attend the first meeting they had with a prospective asylum applicant. At this meeting I was to introduce myself, explain the project and seek the person's consent to attend case meetings and follow their claim. My objective was to observe and record lawyer–client interaction, and to separately interview both parties at key stages of the legal process to understand their distinctive interests in and perceptions of the case, and the substantive legal issues raised by the case (Conley and O'Barr 1990: 29, *passim*).

However just as fieldwork began, the Home Office announced the creation of the 'New Asylum Model', which reorganized the procedure for interviewing, managing and processing asylum claims (see Refugee Council 2006). Immigration caseworkers panicked. They felt that the new procedure left them too little time to alert me about a case and that too much was being asked of their clients. I made alternative arrangements for identifying cases, which involved interviewing immigration caseworkers about their work and asking them to identify the barristers they instructed to represent their clients before the Tribunal. I then contacted barristers and asked for a meeting to explain my research. Barristers generously agreed to assist me. They introduced me to their clients, and after obtaining the person's consent, I was allowed to follow the case through the courts. I was also able to attend pre- and post-hearing conferences between barristers and their clients and to interview the applicants and their barristers.

Access to barristers – who litigate the case – proved invaluable because they briefed me about the case and they gave me access to their clients' case files. As my contacts with barristers expanded, I was able to pick up new asylum claims. In addition, I attended the Tribunal and the Royal Courts of Justice, where I identified and followed additional asylum claims.

At court I took interpretative notes to create a record of the hearing which, together with case files and information from an applicant's legal counsel, I used to analyse cases.[4] This proved invaluable in helping me to identify and analyse the 'the goals, strategies, and thought processes' of litigants, lawyers and judges and to identify the structural components present in legal judgments (Conley and O'Barr 1988: 478; Conley and O'Barr 1990).

Since legal cases are critical to this study, it is important to discuss the value and the limitations of the case method approach. Anthropologists' use of the 'case method' originates in Llewellyn and Hoebel's *The Cheyenne Way: Conflict and Case Law in Primitive Jurisprudence* (1941; see also Conley and O'Barr 2004). The method was put on a firm methodological footing by Max Gluckman (1955) in his work on Barotse jurisprudence, though the legitimacy of relying upon Western legal concepts for comparative study was challenged by Paul Bohannon (1957). Key debates emerged concerning the validity of analyses which use Anglo-American legal concepts (as opposed to analysing indigenous concepts) and the precise information which should be contained in case reports and the sociological value of 'cases'. However, as Conley and O'Barr (1990: 4) have noted: 'differences of opinion among legal anthropologists have never involved questioning the case as the basic unit of analysis'.

Indeed, a variety of cases have been collected over the years, including: observed cases, cases taken from court records, memory cases and 'hypothetical' cases. Each type of case brings with it somewhat different issues and considerations. Twenty-four cases are examined in this book, of which only two, *R* v *Uxbridge Magistrates Court and Another, Ex Parte Adimi* [1999] EWHC Admin 765 and *R* v *Asfaw* (see Chapter 7), were not observed. It is important to note, however, that not all the cases are used to explore litigation *per se*. Thus the cases cited in Chapter 7 are used primarily to explore the perspective and experience of asylum seekers.

Following the post-modern turn in the 1980s, a series of questions arose about anthropological claims to knowledge. Conley and O'Barr have summed up the challenges for legal anthropology (1990: 3–9; 1998: chap. 6). The first issue is whether the choice of 'cases' as a unit of study is appropriate. While this may be a concern in studying 'non-Western' societies, in Britain lawyers are trained using the case method and cases are an integral part of the British legal system. While reliance on cases has focused on specific questions, i.e. about winning and losing, the role of precedent, legal strategies, legal argument and the analysis of 'facts', in this study I also look at wider issues, including the perspective and work of lawyers and other actors and institutions attempting to influence litigation.

The second issue concerns how cases are selected and included in a study, and whether the cases selected are representative or atypical. I initially attempted to identify and follow Ethiopian and Eritrean claims because of my knowledge of the Horn of Africa. However, as a result of contacts with lawyers and the time spent in court, I followed asylum appeals involving individuals from other countries and cases concerned with bail, detention and deportation. It was never my intention to select cases for a random sample because, given the large number of asylum claims in the UK, such a sample was logistically impossible. Instead I have attempted to provide an in-depth, qualitative study of the 'field' of asylum by making use of a relatively small number of asylum cases to *explore the encounter between asylum seekers and the legal system*. As I hope this book will demonstrate, the issue is not the country which asylum applicants come from, but the legal issues and arguments raised by a claim which provide insight into how the asylum field works.

Third, most legal anthropologists have provided accounts of cases in the form of an abridged summary of the facts, the legal process and aspects of legal reasoning.

As Conley and O'Barr (1990: 4) have noted, this style of reporting is similar to that used by Anglo-Saxon legal institutions.[5] Seldom are verbatim accounts provided which allow readers to analyse cases for themselves. There are two reasons why this style of reporting has been relied upon: (1) a summary rather than a verbatim account may reflect the fact that the ethnographer does not speak/understand the language used in the proceedings, and (2) anthropologists have failed to question the adequacy of this type of report.

In the research reported in this book, officials and lawyers use English to interview asylum applicants, and they write case files and litigate in English. As a native English speaker, I followed, recorded and documented the process. I follow the methodological approach set out by A.L. Epstein (1967) regarding the collection and analysis of case studies. Epstein reminds us of the need for a verbatim or a sufficiently detailed account of the dispute which makes clear the (substantive legal) rules, the procedure of enquiry/adjudication and the modes of redress/enforcement. The record should also provide enough information about the parties involved in litigation to understand their 'aims, purposes and values' (Epstein 1967: 207). The account must be detailed enough to illustrate not merely the 'modes of legal thinking', but also the interplay between norms, standards and legal rules. In short, because litigation is seldom about the application of a 'single unequivocal rule', it is essential to adequately reference the 'arguments adduced' during the hearing to show the potentially dynamic application of law to new issues and to individual cases. I have relied on the case files, interviews and my observational notes of asylum hearings to provide what I hope will be a sufficiently detailed account of individual cases.

Sometimes I was refused research access to a state institution, and it is worth discussing why this occurred and what impact it might have had on my findings. In early 2006 I wrote to the Department for Constitutional Affairs (DCA) – later renamed the Ministry of Justice (MoJ) – seeking access to the courts and permission to interview Immigration Judges and High Court judges. My request was refused because I was not authorized to undertake research by the DCA. I therefore made my own arrangements, which involved attending court as a member of the public, listening to cases and taking notes.

In early 2008 I wrote to the Designated Immigration Judge (DIJ) in charge of the Tribunal at York House (London) seeking permission to 'work shadow' (observe) Immigration Judges. My request was forwarded to the Deputy President of the Tribunal, who requested a copy of my research proposal. Mr Ockleton took exception to my proposal and refused my request because 'your research is not based on a detailed and accurate knowledge of the system as it is and a genuine open-minded attempt to discover more about it'. The 'Catch-22' nature of this reply was somewhat ironic. Nevertheless, I was able to interview four part-time IJs about their training, caseload, work and the work of the Tribunal. I also interviewed former officials who had worked in the Tribunal.

In December 2009 I wrote to the Head of the Administrative Court at the Royal Courts of Justice asking for assistance to understand the work of the Administrative

Courts and for information about specific types of cases. In the absence of an answer, I wrote a second time, but once again did not receive a reply.

In late 2007 I sought research access to the Home Office, but I received no reply. Nearly a year later, while I was at court waiting for an asylum appeal to begin, I introduced myself to a Home Office Presenting Officer (HOPO) who subsequently asked his manager for permission to participate in the project. After explaining the nature of my research – I wanted to interview HOPOs about their training and career – I was granted the right to 'shadow' and interview five HOPOs at a London Tribunal. Access to HOPOs proved to be very helpful in understanding their work and perspective.

After completing research with HOPOs, I requested permission to meet with asylum case owners in Central London. I was granted a meeting, at which I requested permission to attend their interviews with Ethiopian and Eritrean asylum applicants (subject to the latter's permission and permission of the applicant's legal counsel). In March 2008, while I was waiting to attend the first interview, I was contacted by the head of the Home Office Research and Statistics Unit, who asked me to meet with him to discuss the progress of my research and 'how the Agency might assist me'.

The meeting occurred just as the Independent Asylum Commission (2008) issued a damming report on the Home Office and the asylum system. It became clear that HO staff were worried about my research. In an attempt to reassure them, I provided an assurance about confidentiality and explained the objectives of my research. However, the official sought to co-opt me without at the same time granting me research access. I waited two months without hearing from him, at which point I emailed him and asked for a decision. He replied that my request had been 'lost'. I was directed to a different official, who was very defensive, though he too failed to get back to me. I emailed my gatekeeper at Lunar House, but my emails went unheeded.

My inability to obtain research access to state institutions left me with one option, namely to make written requests for information by relying on the Freedom of Information Act (2000).[6] Obtaining basic, much less accurate information using Freedom of Information (FOI) Requests has proved to be a difficult task because FOI departments, particularly at the Home Office, deliberately misinterpret requests, delay providing information, deliberately alter the wording of requests and/or refuse to answer requests.

Official refusals/evasions in answering FOI Requests are illegal, but go unsanctioned. The extent of official efforts to mislead and/or refuse to comply with my FOI Requests became clear when officials copied me into their internal correspondence. These petty actions are clearly political and are well documented (Roberts 2005; Walby and Larsen 2011a and 2011b; Michener 2011). The practices reflect an awareness that the public has a right to access official documents, and show the elaborate steps which officials take to cover up/obscure their work by 'acts of self-censorship, the careful management of paper trails, and a tendency toward off-the-record kinds of communication' (Walby and Larsen 2011a: 37). Officials not only stonewall requests, they also institute different forms of 'governance mechanisms' in an effort to prevent disclosure (Walby and Larsen 2011a: 34).

A refusal to reveal information about how an institution operates speaks volumes about how officials perceive the public; nevertheless, such refusals make the state and their actions legible in ways that officials do not foresee. Thus a refusal by the Tribunal to answer a query about why certain asylum claims were chosen as Country Guidance cases reflects either an overly casual approach to an important issue or that the Tribunal wished to keep the issue secret. The same can be said for Home Office refusals to provide clear information about its work and policies.

When officials from the HO/UKBA and the Tribunal refused to provide information to my FOI Requests, I make this clear in the text. While the situation clearly creates gaps in my knowledge, particularly on policy issues, the problems are not irresolvable. It has proved possible to 'see through' policy (Shore and Wright 1977; Wedel et al. 2005) – a task facilitated by interviews with former officials and by analysing litigation.

The focus and organization of this book

This book has two principal objectives. First, given the absence of information in the public domain, I set out the political processes which structure and shape the asylum 'system'. Second, by following asylum litigation, I analyse how asylum claims were decided in a context in which different institutions and actors attempt to influence judicial decisions.

Each institution is explored using an actor-centred approach which looks at their 'work and perspective' as a 'social actor' whose 'understandings, interests and values are pitched against' other institutions in an 'inter-locking project' or political struggle (Long 2004). In the asylum field, this struggle occurs in a legal arena where actors – all of whom are constrained by recognized rules even as they draw upon quite different resources – converge to contest a case (Bailey 1969).

In Chapter 2 I trace the evolution and development of the British asylum system, notably the development of the Home Office and the accretion of tasks given it via legislation and by the Secretary of State. This process has given rise to a complex, massive institution which, despite having access to substantial resources, has been beset by major administrative problems that have given rise to a radical restructuring to bring it into the twenty-first century. The manner in which the Home Office, together with its legal advisers and the Treasury Solicitor's Office, assess and litigate cases is carefully examined.

Chapter 3 examines the structure and operation of the Home Office and its operational wing, the UK Border Agency. In particular, I look at how the SSHD creates and announces new policies and rules. Using a range of actual cases, I examine the work of Home Office immigration officers (IOs), case owners, HOPOs and legal officers to demonstrate why the Home Office is a flawed institution and why official decisions are frequently unlawful.

Chapter 4 examines and describes the work of immigration case workers/ solicitors and interpreters (in private law firms) and independent barristers.[7]

I outline the importance of legal aid in immigration law and the impact of successive cuts in the legal aid budget on the quality of legal representation. Using case material and interview data, I look in detail at how lawyers 'translate' an asylum seeker's narrative of flight into a legal claim, and how they prepare to litigate a case in court. Finally, I describe the role of barristers' clerks, who create and manage a market for barristers.

Chapter 5 analyses the Immigration and Asylum Tribunal and looks at the work of Immigration Judges. In particular, I discuss how IJs are recruited and trained, and the importance of the 'legal' and spatial architecture of the Tribunal which gives IJs the authority to control proceedings and speedily arrive at a decision. I then examine specific claims to show how asylum claims, bail applications and deportation cases are argued and decided by IJs.

Inevitably, many asylum applicants seek to appeal against decisions made by the Tribunal. Chapter 6 begins by examining legislative efforts to restrict asylum appeals. I then look at how applications for reconsideration – the term used to describe appeals against an IJ's decision – were assessed by the Tribunal in its role as a 'filter' for onward appeals to the Court of Appeal. This sets the scene for an analysis of the English Court of Appeal which focuses on 'applications on the papers' and 'oral applications' to a Lord Justice in the CoA. If the CoA finds that the Tribunal made a serious error of law in deciding a case, the case will be referred back to the Tribunal to be reheard. However, the CoA also hears cases. I examine three oral applications and one statutory appeal heard by a panel of Lord Justices (LJs) to understand the nature of judicial decision-making at this level. I conclude by asking whether, in view of the number of appeals granted by the CoA, the Tribunal adequately decides cases, and whether the Tribunal and the CoA provide an effective check on the power of the Home Office.

Curiously, most studies of asylum fail to ask asylum seekers about their experience of seeking asylum. Indeed, officially commissioned research assumes that asylum seekers rationally plan their flight and that they exploit the asylum process. In fact, most asylum seekers possess as little control over their flight from persecution as they exercise in their asylum claim. Chapter 7 explores the experience of individuals fleeing persecution in their country of origin, their reliance on agents to reach Britain, and the indifference of officials. I examine the Kafkaesque experience of individuals arrested at Heathrow airport and held in immigration detention, the experience of individuals applying for bail, the situation facing unaccompanied asylum seeking children and of individuals who made in-country asylum applications. It seems clear that the extensive state of confusion among asylum applicants about the law and their legal status reflects, in large part, the manner in which they are categorized, criminalized and processed by the state.

Chapter 8 analyses the work of three organizations – the Immigration Law Practitioners' Association (an NGO), the Office of the UN High Commissioner for Refugees (UNHCR, a specialized agency of the United Nations) and the Independent Chief Inspector (ICI) of the UKBA (a government body) – which in very different ways have sought to monitor, lobby and reform the work of the HO/UKBA. I argue that they have had a very limited impact on asylum policy and practice because, structurally speaking, they have no direct role in litigation and because the government finds it expedient to insulate the Home Office from criticism.

I conclude by asking what an anthropological analysis of asylum litigation reveals. First, a focus on the wider social field in which UK asylum law and practice is situated clearly shows why a focus on 'law' fails to explain the interplay between policy and judicial decisions because it overlooks the fundamentally 'political' nature of the entire asylum field. An actor-focused approach contrasts the way institutions represent their work with what they actually do; it also illustrates how very different interests bring a wide range of institutions to court. A focus on the wider field illustrates the tensions at play between institutions, and the fact that the asylum field is fluid, dynamic and driven forward by the power of the Home Office and by global events which create refugees.

An in-depth ethnographic analysis of the UK's asylum field also shows that research which is based solely on a statistical analysis of judicial decisions is deficient, not because the RSD system does not operate like a lottery, i.e. the quality of a judicial decision depends on the particular judge who hears the case, but because such an approach is too narrowly focused. Research on litigation needs to show how the courts and judges are one part of the wider asylum field. While it is partly the case, as Hamlin (2014) has argued, that administrative decisions on asylum claims may be insulated from political interference or judicial review by the state, this is unlikely to be a satisfactory explanation for observable differences between national asylum systems.

Notes

1 An analysis of judicial decision-making based solely on written determinations is problematic because 'there is potential for significant deviation between the ways in which judges make decisions under fire and the way they [subsequently] describe that process' (Conley and O'Barr 1988: 471).

2 In the US some refugee lawyers 'coach' applicants in how to shape their narrative of flight into a more persuasive narrative of persecution (see McKinley 1997).

3 Home Office interviews are poorly prepared, lacking in focus, and are conducted in a hostile manner which tends to create an account that is incoherent and difficult to reconcile with subsequent statements taken in a less aggressive and less pressured interview with their lawyer (UNHCR 2006).

4 My original intention was to use the record of the hearing as a basis for discussions with the presiding judge; however, the Tribunal refused my request to speak to judges.

5 It is precisely for this reason that studies which follow files through the administrative courts provide a limited view of the work of the law; see Latour (2010).

6 For information about the Act, see Information Commissioner's Office (n.d.).

7 The predominant approach to the study of lawyers reflects the normative view of lawyers themselves at the expense of careful, empirical research (Berends 1992: 5).

2 The evolution of the British asylum system

To understand the asylum field and the manner in which asylum claims are litigated, it is necessary to examine the evolution and development of the British Home Office. I begin by looking at the creation in the early twentieth century of the Home Office, which was given a mandate to regulate the entry of foreigners into Britain. The second section examines how the haphazard expansion of the HO created an increasingly dysfunctional, albeit powerful, bureaucracy. The third section looks at how the HO conceptualizes and pursues litigation to prevent challenges to its policies. I conclude by setting out the contemporary 'asylum field' and the structure and organization of the 'arena' in which litigation takes place. A detailed examination of the work/operation of the Home Office and UK Border Agency during 2007–2009 is taken up in Chapter 3.

Aliens, refugees and the British Home Office in the twentieth century

It was not until the passage of the Aliens Act (1905) that a statutory basis for regulating alien immigration came into being. Prior to the Act the Board of Trade assumed responsibility for immigration, whereas the Home Office was concerned 'about aliens either as a potential threat to political stability or as criminals' (Pellew 1989: 371).

At the end of the nineteenth century there was growing pressure on the government to restrict the entry of Jews, which culminated in a 1902 Royal Commission inquiry into alien immigration. Despite the lack of hard evidence, the commission recommended the creation of a department of immigration to control the entry of 'undesirable' aliens (all aliens were to be registered, and 'minor criminals' were to be deported). Though the recommendations were opposed by the SSHD – in part because it would have involved 'the reversal of our policy for the last two hundred years as to the right of asylum and the law of extradition' (cited in Pellew 1989: 372) – they were accepted by the Conservative Government and passed into law as the Aliens Act (1905).

The Act created a network of Immigration Officers who were stationed at major ports. Implementation of the Act fell to the newly elected Liberal Government, which was loath to take it forward. Nevertheless, a small unit in the

HO was created to oversee immigration at 13 ports, and 'immigration boards' staffed by local establishment figures were created to handle appeals against an Immigration Officer's refusal to allow an alien to enter (there was no right of appeal to a court of law). The government's antipathy towards the Act created enormous tensions and frustrations for HO officials, whose ability to implement it was frustrated by wider political concerns and the reluctance of the HO to incur expenses. An exception from the Act was made for aliens seeking to enter Britain as political or religious refugees (Pellew 1989: 377).[1] The vague terms of the 1905 Act, together with decisions taken by government ministers, seriously frustrated efforts to implement it (Shah 1999: chap. 3).

Electoral politics, two world wars, the unprecedented growth in air and ferry traffic, decolonization and the rapidly expanding global movement of population resulted in an accretion of new tasks being assigned to the HO. On the one hand the Aliens Order (1920) required all aliens to register with the police; but rather than updating the Act or introducing new legislation, parliament renewed the 1920 Act annually until it was finally replaced by the Immigration Act (1971). In the meantime the Second World War saw the government adopt emergency powers to control the entry of displaced people into Britain, which led to a new task being given to the Home Office, namely detaining and repatriating enemy aliens. As more individuals entered Britain, public concerns began to grow about illegal entry, the entry of 'coloured' people (many of whom were British overseas citizens), the threat to British jobs posed by immigrant labour and, following Britain's membership of the European Economic Community in 1973, the right of Europeans to enter, work and live in the UK.

Between 1948 and 1962 Britain had an open migration regime allowing all subjects of the Crown the right of residence in the UK (Geddes 2003). However, in 1962 the first of a series of restrictive pieces of legislation was adopted which re-defined British citizenship by distinguishing between citizens of the UK and its colonies and citizens of Commonwealth Countries (only the former had a right to enter Britain). In effect, new legislation excluded individuals on the basis of their national/cultural difference and/or because they were perceived to 'threaten' mainstream values and social cohesion (Bosniak 1991). The 1962 Commonwealth Immigrants Act was followed by legislation which gave the HO new enforcement tasks, e.g. the detection of fraudulent immigration/work documentation and controlling illegal entry. As new tasks were given to the HO, its inability to implement legislation was compounded by a failure to rethink management and organizational issues and a failure to commit adequate resources to accomplish the tasks assigned to it.

In 1969 an independent Immigration Tribunal was established on a statutory basis and was tasked with hearing appeals against the SSHD from Commonwealth citizens and 'aliens' regarding their right of entry, their right to an entry certificate/visa and the right to appeal against a revocation of permission to enter the UK (Hepple 1969). A two-tier Tribunal was created and staffed by 20 full-time and 30 part-time 'adjudicators' who heard initial appeals from the Home Office – estimated at 15,000–20,000 appeals per annum – while the upper tier heard appeals from adjudicators (there was no right of appeal beyond the Tribunal, but unlawful decisions by adjudicators could be judicially reviewed). The SSHD continued to exercise her authority to hear 'security cases' and deportations (an appeal against the latter was allowed only if the individual was outside the UK).

Legal aid, a means-tested government fund to assist individuals who could not afford to pay for legal counsel to represent them at court, was introduced in 1949, and became available for immigration and asylum claims in 1954 (though it was little used until the 1980s). The intention of the Immigration Appeals Act (1969) was to draw a line between 'justiciable issues and policy' (Hepple 1969: 670), though relatively quickly this line became quite blurred. For instance, the Commonwealth Immigrants Act (1968) was passed in an effort to exclude Asians of East African origin who held British/Commonwealth passports (Cohen 2003: 39; Juss 2007).

The 1971 Immigration Act introduced the notion of 'patriality' (the 'one grandparent rule'), which created three types of British 'citizen': full citizenship (with a right of abode in the UK), British Dependent Territories citizenship and British overseas citizenship. Individuals in the latter two categories did not have a right of abode in the UK, and could be deported if 'conducive to the public good' (Couper 1981: 440–442). Legislation introduced after 1993 has sought to correct 'problems' with the 1971 Act by imposing tighter frontier controls and more stringent controls on asylum applicants.

Whereas during the 1960s and 1970s the number of asylum applications was relatively limited, by the late 1980s the number of applicants overwhelmed institutional arrangements and the SSHD's ability to manage the process and justly decide asylum claims (Pirouet 2001: chap. 4). The realization that government policy and institutions were unable to manage growing flows of refugees and migrants led, unsurprisingly, to further legislation.

In the early 1990s, following the furore over the deportation – the official term is 'return' – of asylum seekers to Sri Lanka, where they faced possible persecution, legislation was proposed to provide a limited in-country right of appeal for individuals refused asylum. In 1993 parliament passed the Asylum and Immigration Appeals Act (1993), which granted asylum applicants (and individuals subject to deportation) the right of an in-country appeal to an independent adjudicator at the Immigration Appeal Tribunal (including a right to appeal against an adjudicator's decision to the appellate court). Since the passage of the 1993 Act, the law, procedures, appeal rights as well as the structure of the Tribunal have been continuously reformed (see Chapters 6 and 8).

Attempts to modernize the Home Office in the twenty-first century

Despite continuous asylum-related legislative reforms and policies intended to 'modernize' the immigration system (Duvell and Jordan 2003), a massive gap developed between the growing rhetoric to exclude foreigners/asylum applicants and the ability of the HO and the Tribunal to manage and fairly assess asylum applications.

To cite the most recent problems, between 2006 and 2007 the HO was hit by a succession of crises – lapses in the prison probation service, the failure to deport foreign national prisoners, inadequate capacity to handle a rising prison population, and the failure to process the records of British prisoners held overseas – which led to the resignation of two Secretaries of State. One SSHD famously referred to the HO as 'not fit for purpose' (Painter 2008).

Parliamentary scrutiny revealed serious underfunding of key departments, a lack of leadership, and poor senior management, numerous examples of departmental 'fragmentation and silos' characterized by the absence of communication between departments with other ministries, and a tendency by ministers and senior managers to impose arbitrary management targets on staff which exacerbated administrative problems (UK 2006b; see also Chapter 7 in this volume).

These failures led to major reforms in early 2007 in an attempt to define its strategic priorities and improve its operational management. First, responsibilities for criminal justice were removed from the HO and given to the newly formed Ministry of Justice, which also took over responsibility for constitutional matters, civil and administrative justice, the courts and legal aid (UK 2007c).

Second, the Immigration and Nationality Department (IND) was hived off from the HO and transformed into the quasi-independent UK Border Agency, which was tasked with implementing asylum and immigration policy. In addition, the Chief Inspector of Borders and Immigration (see Chapter 8) and an advisory committee on migration were created (UK 2007a). The rationale for this radical reorganization was to refocus the work of the HO by delegating to it the task of strengthening control over the UK's borders, fast-tracking asylum decisions, deporting greater numbers of 'failed' asylum seekers and foreign national prisoners and improving cross-sectoral co-operation with other agencies.

In April 2007 the government introduced the New Asylum Model (NAM) (Information Centre about Asylum and Refugees [ICAR] 2007b), which completely reorganized asylum procedures. A regional system of asylum processing and decision-making was introduced in which a named case owner was assigned to process asylum claims, and the totality of claims were divided up and processed in one of five 'segments' or pathways. The segments were: (a) third-country applications, (b) children, (c) potential 'non-suspensive' appeals, (d) late/opportunistic applications and (e) general case work. Cases in segments a, c, d and children whose age was disputed were to be detained and their asylum applications 'fast-tracked' and decided within 20 days. Unfortunately, the haste to modernize the Home Office failed: indeed, during 2007–2009 further failures occurred which led to further reorganizations and the elaboration of ever more immigration rules, management targets and legislation (see Chapter 3).

Why was the HO in perpetual crisis, and how did the above problems affect the wider asylum system and asylum litigation? Prior to the reforms of 2006–2007 the different government ministries/departments responsible for immigration control operated relatively autonomously from one another. Each department had its own agenda and objectives, which gave rise to tensions and problems of co-ordination between the IND, Work Permits (UK), Customs, benefits agencies and the police (who were responsible for identifying, arresting and deporting undocumented migrants; Duvell and Jordan 2003).

Home Office problems were/are due to a range of issues (Painter 2008). First, the accretion of tasks given to the HO meant that its responsibilities often overlapped with other departments and ministries, each of which had their own distinctive organizational culture. Second, overall, the HO's responsibilities were unwieldy and poorly integrated, and the failure of policy exposed officials to public scrutiny to such an extent that they reacted to criticism without carefully thinking through issues of management and strategic policy (Consterdine 2013). Finally, some of its key objectives and tasks were underfunded. Painter (2008) attributes these problems to limited civil service reform and over-centralization, but an equally valid explanation is that the 'extreme loose coupling' between senior management and junior staff who worked on quite discrete issues/policies contributed to a situation in which very different actor rationalities were at play, which made the HO unmanageable (March and Olsen 1989; Olsen 1983).

At the same time the external environment in which the HO operated also constrained its operations. On the one hand there were many political interventions by the 'New Labour' Government in the form of new legislation which, on the one hand, created immense legal complexity, and on the other hand, created more work for the HO. As Painter noted:

> The intensity of political intervention, manifest in constant administrative meddling and micro-management, compromised the ability of the civil service machine to perform to its potential. The sheer volume of ill-conceived initiatives and policy overload caused havoc at the Home Office.
>
> (Painter 2008: 279)

Furthermore, the government's pursuit of neo-liberal economic policies linking the UK firmly into the global economy in pursuit of investment and skilled migrant labour was seriously at odds with the 'control' orientation of the HO (Overbeek 2002; Fernandez-Kelly 2007). In the context of increasing globalization, the claim that a sovereign state can effectively control its borders and regulate immigration was inevitably going to be seriously challenged by the scale of international population movement. As if this were not enough, NGOs, refugee organizations, liberal interest groups and international institutions such as the European Union and UNHCR sought to influence British asylum and immigration policy (Sassen 2000; Morris 2002; Dauvergne 2004; see also Chapter 8 in this volume).

A further factor influencing the HO arose from political events in Britain. Since the late 1990s the press, political parties and politically conservative organizations have increasingly portrayed asylum applicants as 'economic migrants', and have blamed them for rising crime and terrorism. The situation deteriorated following the July 2005 bombings in London, which gave rise to allegations linking refugees to terrorism,[2] which in turn led to demands to reform the law and the asylum system. The government responded to these demands by announcing steps – e.g. the intention to expel suspected terrorists, to instruct judges how to interpret the Human Rights Act, to change British and European Union (EU) legislation to allow the deportation of terrorist suspects – which brought it into conflict with the judiciary and its international legal obligations.[3]

How, then, did the various crises in the Home Office affect the asylum process and asylum litigation? It appears that instead of carefully considering legislation and the ability of HO officials to carry out their expanding remit, the government pushed ahead with legislation to give new powers to a dysfunctional bureaucracy whose decisions could only be overturned at considerable expense through litigation, including publicly funded judicial review proceedings.

Between 1993 and 2007 seven pieces of primary legislation were adopted in an effort to make it difficult, if not impossible, for asylum applicants to reach Britain and obtain refugee status.[4] The most significant elements of this legislation included:

1. the introduction of a 'white list' of 'safe countries' from which asylum applicants would be barred from making an appeal;
2. certifying as 'unfounded' (thereby dismissing) the claims of asylum applicants who fail to produce a passport/valid travel document and/or who fail to explain its absence, and the claims of those who fail to apply for asylum while passing through a 'safe' country;
3. the introduction and expansion of 'fast-track' asylum determination procedures to reduce the time taken for an asylum decision and to speed up the removal of applicants whose claims are refused;
4. reduction in the availability of legal aid for asylum claims;
5. the repeated reorganization of the Immigration and Asylum Tribunal which adjudicates asylum appeals;
6. changes intended to restrict the right to appeal against decisions of the IAT;
7. adopting tougher immigration policies, more stringent border controls and supporting the creation of a new EU institution called Frontex to 'push back'/prevent asylum seekers and migrants from reaching Europe (Schuster 2000; Geddes 2003; Flynn 2005).

Thus the focus of recent asylum law and policy has been to prevent individuals from reaching the UK, from making an asylum claim and to fast-track appeals and/or restrict appeal rights. In 2003 the Prime Minister announced a radical plan to eliminate the appeal rights of asylum applicants and restructure the Tribunal. Rawlings referred to this plan as:

> a 'revenge package': one designed to pre-empt or drastically reduce a whole activity of formal legal challenge and by necessary implication to neuter the judicial role in the constitution. The chosen vehicle was the government bill that was to become the Asylum and Immigration (Treatment of Claimants, etc.) Act 2004.
>
> (Rawlings 2005: 378)

The Bill and the political struggle by lawyers, the judiciary and other institutions against the introduction of this Act, and the government's response to them, are discussed in Chapter 6. At the heart of this intense, short-lived debate was an argument over the appropriate way to manage and fund an asylum system that was being overwhelmed by the sheer numbers of applications.

The impact of this flurry of legislation – and of the growing number of immigration rules and regulations introduced by the SSHD (see Chapter 3) – was to substantially strengthen the power of the HO/UKBA without at the same time providing improved training and resources to front-line staff who are expected to implement the policies. The effect of this process is threefold: (a) front-line staff are given greater authority, but their ability to decide complex cases fairly is constrained by the growing number of HO rules and regulations; (b) senior staff impose management/work targets which constrain front-line decision-making by limiting the amount of time available to assess and decide claims; (c) pressure on caseworkers results in poor decisions, which are overturned – by judicial reviews in the High Court and/or by the Tribunal – which results in further ad hoc interventions by senior officials in the work of front-line staff (which disrupts the latter's ability to do their job).

Government litigation: the work of the Home Office Legal Adviser's Branch and the Treasury Solicitor's Office

Since the seventeenth century the British government has recruited lawyers into the civil service to provide legal advice to ministers and to litigate on its behalf, though it was not until 1933 that the Home Office appointed a specialist legal adviser (Drewry 1981). Prior to this date the HO and most other government departments received legal advice from the Treasury Solicitor's Office. By 1971 the Home Office Legal Adviser's Branch (HOLAB) was providing legal advice on many aspects of policy-making. In 1979, whereas TSol employed 132 legal staff, the HO employed 19 (making it the eleventh largest of 21 departments employing full-time legal staff).[5] Legal advisers move between TSol and government departments; indeed, there appears to be no clear division of labour between TSol and lawyers employed in government departments.

HOLAB functions in an advisory capacity to all HO departments, and it links Presenting Officer Units – which file reports on a database that summarizes every asylum and immigration appeal – to the Country of Origin Information Service (COIS) and the Onward Right of Appeal Unit (also known as the Appeals and Litigation Team, or ALT). The decision to litigate an asylum (or immigration) appeal is triggered by ALT, which looks at appeals granted by the Tribunal and decides whether to appeal against its decision (they must appeal within 10 days of an IJ's decision). If the HO appeals, a presenting officer is required to defend the SSHD's decision to refuse the application before the Tribunal. The majority of appeals brought against an IJ's decision are filed by appellants/asylum applicants. However, a much greater proportion of appeals brought by the SSHD are allowed (ICAR 2009: charts 8 and 9). Statistics on the outcome of these appeals suggest not merely an imbalance between the parties, but also that the Tribunal adopts a deferential role towards the SSHD (see Chapters 5 and 6).

In recent years there are two processes responsible for expanding the work of the HO and thus its need for in-house legal counsel: an increase in parliamentary legislation and the rapid expansion in the number of Immigration Rules and Instructions created by the SSHD (see Chapter 3).[6] HOLAB officials advise HO/UKBA officials and ministers on all areas of the department's work. In particular legal advisers are involved in taking legislative Bills through parliament, they instruct parliamentary (legal) counsel, who draft legislation, and they attend parliament during all stages of a Bill's passage. HOLAB officials draft subordinate legislation (e.g. European Union legislation), and they provide legal advice to HO officials on a wide range of legal issues (e.g. the Human Rights Act 1998, Freedom of Information Act 2000, etc.). In short, the services they provide blur any distinction between legal and policy advice.

HOLAB also advises HO officials how to conduct and handle domestic litigation, particularly if it is high-profile, politically sensitive, or if a case might require a change in HO policy. HOLAB decides whether to contract TSol to instruct senior barristers to litigate on behalf of the HO. Indeed, TSol acts on behalf of the HO/UKBA in a wide range of appeals, including: (a) asylum cases listed in the Upper Tribunal for Country Guidance; (b) applications for permission to judicially review HO decisions; (c) defending against applications for *habeas corpus* to release someone from detention; (d) defending against emergency injunctions seeking to prevent an individual from being removed from the UK; (e) defending against claims arising from poorly drafted legislation (as occurred in relation to Section 55 of the Nationality, Immigration and Asylum Act 2002);[7] (f) applications for permission to appeal to the High Court and the Court of Appeal; (g) litigating appeals in the High Court; (h) litigating appeals in the Court of Appeal (see Chapter 6); and (i) litigating appeals in the House of Lords (now the Supreme Court).

If the HO decides to litigate a case, HOLAB works with TSol to instruct barristers from 'government sets' to handle litigation. The solicitors or barristers work in teams headed by an experienced adviser. The Treasury Solicitor's Office employs over 350 solicitors/barristers and serves 180 departments. One of its largest clients is the HO/UKBA, to which it provides advice on policy, legislation, litigation and training (UK 2008c). TSol is organized into nine divisions which specialize in particular areas of law or work for specific government departments. Thus 'Division 2', with 100 to 120 staff, services the HO/UKBA. According to TSol's work plan:

> Our aim is to help the Home Office in relation to immigration, nationality and asylum issues. Our aim is to help the Home Office deliver its objectives by reducing delays, addressing obstacles to removal, managing the voluminous

> litigation in a practical and cost effective manner and responding to the legal challenges to regular government initiatives in this high-profile area.
>
> (UK 2008c)

At the time of my fieldwork this division was called the Immigration and Judicial Review Team,[8] and it handled all HO litigation. In 2008 the unit was divided into three teams (each with about 30 solicitors plus support staff). In addition to handling the litigation indicated above, the unit also handled national security cases,[9] third-country[10] removal and asylum support (this includes work for the Judicial Review Unit). Staff work consisted almost entirely of working on files and instructing counsel prior to a hearing. As the Head of the Division reiterated to me: 'all HO litigation revolves around the issue of removal', i.e. removing individuals from the UK who are in breach of immigration law.

Solicitors at TSol work with HOLAB officials to assess appeals and define a strategy for dealing with litigation. TSol staff look through the cases to differentiate between those which are 'totally fact-specific' and cases that raise legal issues which may have a wider policy impact. TSol will attempt to stay related cases behind what it perceives to be a key test case.[11] This assessment factors into TSol's litigation strategy. As the head of TSol's Immigration and Judicial Review Team told me:

> We'd say, do we think it's appealable? What were the chances of winning on appeal? What would be the down side of appealing and loosing? If we accepted it, what would the impact be? What would we have to do to comply with it? Would it cause difficulties? Is there a need to amend legislation?

In relation to losing a key appeal, he observed: 'That's the advantage of being government. You litigate, and if you win that's fine; if you lose, well, you change the law.'

When a case is listed for a 'permission hearing' in the CoA or the Administrative Courts (see Chapter 6), a TSol solicitor files an 'acknowledgement of service' and 'grounds of resistance' with the court. The head of division believed that TSol is successful in getting 80 per cent of permission applications 'knocked out of court', i.e. by convincing a Lord Justice to refuse the appeal on the basis that the claim is unfounded. However, the evidence does not support his claim (Bondy and Sunkin 2009; UK 2013d; see also Chapter 6 in this volume).

When an asylum claimant succeeds in getting a case listed for a hearing, TSol instructs barristers from the Attorney General's panel system, which provides access to experienced barristers working in prestigious private chambers called 'government sets' (see UK 2013a) (see Box 2.1). Once a barrister or barristers are instructed by TSol, a series of planning meetings are held with relevant departments to map out a strategy, review existing material, find new country of origin information (COI), identify ways of undermining the evidence and arguments by the claimant and prepare their legal arguments.[12] Inevitably, the barrister's role is to defend the decision of the SSHD to refuse the claim.

Box 2.1 The Attorney General's panel system

Panel A: 'Senior juniors' (barristers of at least 10 years' standing) handle the most complex litigation; they will often face Queen's Counsel ('silks').

Panel B: 'Middle juniors' (barristers with 5–10 years' advocacy experience) handle 'substantial cases', e.g. hearings in the CoA, applications for JR or *habeas corpus* applications.

Panel C: 'Junior juniors' (barristers with 2–5 years' experience) are responsible for permission hearings for JRs. They also assist in more important cases.

Though the objective of litigation is to test the interpretation and application of the law and the powers of the SSHD, it is notable that litigation is taken quite personally. For example, independent counsel invest considerable time, effort and expense (much of which is not paid for by legal aid) to secure their client's right to asylum. For its part, TSol and the HO view litigation as vexatious and lacking in merit. This perception is indicated by the head of TSol, who, in reply to a question about the high level of asylum litigation, replied:

> The difficulty is that we are dealing with people who do not want to go back [to their country of origin]. And therefore their legal advisers will use any avenue open to them to stop [them] going back or to delay that process. And judicial review, regrettably, is used by some of them simply as a tactic to put off the evil day in the hope that the evil day may never in fact come.

As Table 2.1 indicates, the HO relies heavily on litigating against all types of asylum (and immigration) claims in order to enforce its policies. Unfortunately, both TSol and the Ministry of Justice have failed to record significant amounts of data, and they have not differentiated between litigation on asylum cases and litigation on immigration cases, which makes it impossible to analyse asylum and immigration litigation separately.

Regarding the high and growing financial cost of litigation (see Table 2.2 below), the head of TSol told me:

> Government departments will want to achieve the right result . . . . So ministers will have a policy. The policy will be enacted in an Act of Parliament. BIA [the Border and Immigration Agency] will want to see that Act of Parliament properly enforced. And the cost of litigation is part of the cost of enforcing it the same way as having detention centres, it's a cost.

The very large sums paid by the HO/UKBA to TSol make it clear that litigation is a key strategy. However, the rising cost of HO litigation is not caused by litigious

Table 2.1 Litigation undertaken by TSol for the Home Office and UKBA, 1997–2011

Year	*Asylum Country Guidance appeals*	*Removals, judicial reviews and detention*	*Judicial reviews*	*Administrative Court*	*Court of Appeal*
1997	No records	No records	No records	1,743	No records
1998	—	—	—	1,696	—
1999	—	—	—	1,884	—
2000	—	—	—	2,189	7
2001	—	—	—	2,563	8
2002	—	—	—	3,563	61
2003	—	—	—	3,927	183
2004	—	—	—	2,271	268
2005	—	—	—	3,093	307
2006	—	—	—	4,201	393
2007	71	2,586	—	4,392	424
2008	72	n/a	—	4,528	478
2009	71	n/a	6,116	1,231 (to May)	2,501
2010	33	2,549	7,570	n/a	609
2011	14	2,969	8,448	n/a	757

Source: FOI Requests to TSol dated 8 May 2009, 20 March 2012 and 15 November 2012.

asylum applicants, it reflects (a) the rapid passage of successive, poorly drafted, legislative acts; (b) the tendency by the SSHD to rapidly create Immigration Rules to provide a quick fix for problematic asylum policies and procedures (see Chapters 3 and 8); and (c) the fact that all British political parties have adopted a conservative approach aimed at removing the right of 'failed' asylum seekers to appeal against Tribunal decisions.[13] Each of the above factors has contributed to a highly complex legal system in which independent legal counsel have felt compelled to take their clients' claims to the High Court or the Court of Appeal in an effort to clarify the intentions of parliament in passing a specific piece of legislation and/or to clarify the extent to which HO/UKBA policy and decisions are legal (see Chapter 8).

As Table 2.2 makes clear, not only has Home Office and UKBA expenditure increased exponentially year on year, so too has HO expenditure on litigation.

Regardless of the amount of resources expended by the HO on litigation – which dwarfs the meagre legal aid budget that pays the costs of independent counsel – the outcome of litigation is unpredictable. Cases which TSol believes are winnable when permission was initially sought in the High Court or the Court of Appeal are not infrequently decided in favour of asylum claimants (see Chapter 6).

Conclusion

This chapter has explored the evolution of the Home Office, which, via numerous legislative Acts, has been given wide-ranging and complex tasks and policy

Table 2.2 The cost to the Home Office and UKBA of instructing TSol to litigate, 2006–2011

In calendar year of Bill	*Client*	*Fees (£)*	*Charges(any manual adjustments to fees) (£)*	*Fees and charges + VAT (£)*	*Disbursements including VAT (£)*	*Total (£)*
2006	HO	1,142,320	24,750	204,237	1,049,179	2,420,487
	UKBA	9,400,807	0	1,645,141	4,014,740	15,060,689
2007	HO	1,661,347	58,500	300,973	2,143,943	4,164,764
	UKBA	13,171,410	0	2,304,997	5,086,478	20,562,885
2008	HO	1,301,044	16,750	227,389	1,875,992	3,421,176
	UKBA	12,609,674	6,060	2,179,646	5,104,952	19,900,332
2009	HO	1,054,162	67,805	168,174	1,914,032	3,204,174
	UKBA	14,384,589	52,167	2,165,652	5,627,313	22,229,721
2010	HO	1,391,169	358,026	306,336	2,348,186	4,403,716
	UKBA	16,175,526	65,000	2,842,211	6,301,641	25,384,378
2011	HO	1,224,624	34,167	249,956	1,488,437	2,997,184
	UKBA	16,055,920	–45,350	3,169,175	7,071,909	26,251,655

Source: FOI Request to TSol dated 22 September 2014.

objectives to meet. This process has created a complex, massive institution which, despite having wide powers and access to substantial resources, has been beset by serious administrative and managerial problems. A belated recognition of problems within the HO, namely its inability to implement its enforcement tasks, resulted in further legislation aimed at making it increasingly difficult for asylum applicants to secure refugee status, and it resulted in a radical restructuring which split the Immigration and Nationality Department off from the HO to create the UK Border Agency.

However, rather than addressing internal organizational problems, and without attempting to understand the complex political and economic processes behind growing population mobility, the government has relied upon legislation to criminalize asylum seeking and to reinforce border controls. This process has contributed to a situation in which the implementation of asylum (and immigration) policy has become increasingly problematic, dysfunctional (with respect to ability to effectively implement policy), contested and expensive.

As Chapter 3 will show, the SSHD's efforts to expand her authority to regulate and control the entire asylum field has *reinforced* the importance of litigation – by the HO/UKBA and independent counsel – in confirming/challenging asylum policy and the legality of HO/UKBA decision-making, particularly given the government's unwillingness to rethink its policies and engage in policy dialogue with its interlocutors (see Chapter 8).

Notes

1 For more information on the Aliens Act (1905) and what it gave rise to, see Silverman (2012).
2 E.g. T. Whitehead, '1 in 4 terror suspects are asylum seekers', *The Express*, 22 August 2005.
3 See: P. Wintour, M. White and A. Travis, 'Judges to be told to act on deportations', *The Guardian*, 12 August 2005; P. Johnston, 'Clarke urges EU to rethink rights laws on deportations', *The Telegraph*, 7 September 2005; E. MacAskill, J. Glover and V. Dodd, 'Expulsions illegal, UN tells Clarke', *The Guardian*, 25 August 2005; anon., 'Don't browbeat us, top judge tells PM', *The Express*, 12 October 2005.
4 By date of enactment: the Asylum and Immigration Appeals Act (1993); Asylum and Immigration Act (1996); Immigration and Asylum Act (1999); Nationality, Immigration and Asylum Act (2002); Asylum and Immigration (Treatment of Claimants) Act (2004); the Immigration, Asylum and Nationality Act (2006); and the UK Borders Act (2007).
5 By 2007 HOLAB employed 50 lawyers and 18 support staff at a cost of £3.4 million per annum.
6 Source: Home Office website pages on HOLAB at http://www.homeoffice.gov/uk/about-us/organization/directorate-search/lab/ (accessed 5 November 2007; the HO website was reconfigured in 2013, so this URL no longer works).
7 A major source of litigation prior to my fieldwork were Section 44 claims, as they came to be known, which concerned the right of the SSHD to refuse asylum support to individuals who made a late claim for asylum. See the lead case in this litigation: *R (Adam and Limbuela)* v *SSHD*, which is discussed at: http://www.escr-net.org/node/364787 (accessed 27 July 2016).

8 This discussion is based on an interview with the head of the unit, Simon Harker, conducted at 1 Kemble Street, London on 28 September 2008.

9 In particular, litigation initiated by the SSHD against suspected 'terrorists' who are detained and tried under the Control Orders.

10 This refers to individuals who have filed an asylum claim in the UK, but who have travelled here via a 'safe' third country where by law they should have made an asylum claim, e.g. individuals entering the UK from France.

11 TSol will make an argument to the court that a specific case should be considered as the test case, and that all other cases which raise the same issue should not be considered by the courts – i.e. they should be 'stayed' – until the lead case is decided. However, TSol's strategy is not always successful.

12 Interviews with S. Harker (see note 8 above), and with Mr Rob Kellar of One Crown Office Row Chambers on 9 October 2007; he had recently been instructed by TSol on a Country Guidance (CG) case on Ethiopia.

13 Despite the enthusiasm to return 'failed asylum seekers'/illegal immigrants, there is very little evidence about what happens to them on return. See the research reported by Rights in Exile Programme (2016).

3 The work of the British Home Office and the UK Border Agency

This chapter examines the work of Home Office and UKBA officials. Building on Chapter 2, the first section sets out the structure and organization of both institutions between 2007 and 2009 and looks at their policy objectives and the raft of 'internal instructions' issued by the SSHD which instruct her officials how to implement policy. I argue that the reforms and reorganizations discussed in Chapter 2 did not improve the way the HO/UKBA implemented policy.

The second section looks at Home Office policy implementation. In particular, I examine how Home Office immigration officers, asylum case owners and presenting officers dealt with different types of asylum cases. I conclude by asking whether the work of these officials represents the actions of a state bound by law.

The Home Office and the UK Border Agency

The HO is part of the executive branch of the British state. The elegantly designed façade of its headquarters in Central London obscures a complex bureaucratic organization[1] which, despite having key powers stripped from it in 2007, continues to be responsible for counter-terrorism, policing/public security, and asylum and immigration (Consterdine 2013; Clayton 2012: chap. 2). The SSHD, an elected member of parliament from the governing political party, is responsible for managing the HO/UKBA with the assistance of junior government ministers and a Parliamentary Under Secretary of State. Day-to-day work in the HO is supervised by a Permanent Secretary (a senior civil servant) who is assisted by five Director Generals in charge of nine departments/divisions. The HO employs just under 3,000 civil servants, and its operational budget is approximately £3.5 billion per annum (UK 2010–2011: table 6). In the asylum field, the HO is responsible for immigration, border control, for ensuring that asylum decisions are taken quickly and fairly[2] and for enforcing compliance with immigration law (i.e. the detection and removal of individuals who are in breach of UK law).

Policies are dictated by the Cabinet, and the SSHD discusses Cabinet decisions with senior officials in the Policy Development Group, which is responsible for implementing the 'four pillars' of Home Office policy: (1) asylum processes; (2) border enforcement; (3) managed migration; and (4) integration. In fact, and as the website for the Research, Development and Statistics Unit[3] of the

Home Office indicates, nearly all research is focused on asylum processes. The UKBA sees the value of research only in terms of facilitating, not informing, policy decisions.[4] Following these discussions, decisions are transmitted downwards to officials who are expected to implement them.

Though legal advisers, policy strategists and officials responsible for gathering and analysing intelligence attend policy discussions, decisions are not informed by research or an appreciation of the need to respect due process. The peculiar tunnel vision of the HO results in policies which have a limited chance of meeting policy objectives, which conflict with other government departments, and which bring the government into conflict with its international legal obligations.

The SSHD also exercises her prerogative under the Immigration Act (1971), s. 4(1), which allows her to introduce immigration rules that have the power of law. In recent years the rules have been focused on controlling the growing numbers of asylum applicants, excluding asylum applicants from benefits and reducing their right to appeal against asylum decisions (Clayton 2012: chap. 1; Campbell 2013b: chap. 6).

A senior civil servant has noted the 'defensive and cautious culture' that pervades the Home Office, and described it 'as politically driven . . . focused on short-term decision-making and tomorrow's headlines' (quoted in Consterdine 2013: 8). This 'culture of discretion' has arisen partly out of 'a constant state of crisis', high workloads and under-resourcing (Jordan, Strath and Triandafyllidou 2003). Though hierarchically organized, officers in the Immigration and Nationality Directorate were initially allowed limited discretion to decide individual cases (Vincenzi 1992). Official decisions are marked by an organizational culture that 'included a range of assumptions, stereotypes and myths' about particular nationals and communities, notably the myth that immigration is 'a threat to society' and that success can be measured by the number of individuals who are deported (Duvell and Jordan 2003: 315–316).

In 2006, and out of frustration with his officials, the SSHD famously stated that the HO was 'not fit for purpose', and announced an internal reorganization aimed at improving procedures, dealing with asylum claims and deporting foreign criminals.[5] In 2007 the SSHD made an executive decision to transform the Immigration and Nationality Directorate, a department in the HO, into the UK Border Agency (Clayton 2012: 25, 44).[6]

The crime/control orientation of the HO is indicated by the UKBA's mandate to work with HM Revenue and Customs, Special Branch and a variety of transport organizations and regulators. The emphasis on control is evident in the Home Office Business Plan (UK 2008d).

The HO pursues its objectives by briefing and advising ministers and parliament, drafting legislation intended to strengthen its role, and by devising new policies and introducing methods aimed at improving staff efficiency. The HO has pushed for legislation to expand its authority with respect to: (a) extending the grounds for deportation[7]; (b) expanding the grounds for depriving British citizens of their nationality (the Terrorism Act 2006, s. 56); (c) making it easier to prevent an individual with terrorist connections from obtaining asylum (e.g. ss. 54 and 55 of the Immigration, Asylum and Nationality Act 2006); and

(d) stigmatizing and criminalizing asylum seekers by creating new immigration offences which incur criminal sanctions (e.g. 'entering without leave' under s. 24(1)(a) of the 1971 Act, and 'refusing to co-operate' with the authorities in their efforts to re-document a person for removal under the Immigration Rules, Pt 9, paras 320–322; see also Clayton 2012: chap. 2).

Using the authority granted to her under ss. 3 and 4 of the Immigration Act (1971), the SSHD issues a growing number of policies, Immigration Rules[8] and concessions to instruct officials how to implement policy (McKee 2006). As Clayton has remarked, these rules 'are made by the minister pursuant to a statutory duty to do so, and are subject to the negative resolution procedure in Parliament' (2012: 30–33). A minister 'lays' a written statement before the House of Commons or the House of Lords which 'notes' the new rule; the 'rule' is *not* subject to discussion or amendment (only once has a rule been overturned). These rules have the force of law, and can *only* be challenged by judicially reviewing the decision of an official who fails to follow the rule or concession (see Chapter 6).

The SSHD also issues 'internal instructions' to officials to limit the discretion they have to decide a case.[9] These instructions first appeared on the HO website in 1998, and include: (a) policy statements (e.g. the *Operational Enforcement Manual*, which sets out guidance on dealing with illegal entry and deportation/removal); (b) Immigration Directorate Instructions (IDIs), which set out how to apply the rules; (c) Asylum Policy Instructions (APIs), which set out a policy and summarize how caseworkers should assess applications made under it; (d) Nationality Instructions, which provide guidance for handling applications for British citizenship; and (e) Operational Guidance Notes (OGNs), which synthesize country of origin information and case law to instruct caseworkers how to assess the asylum claims of individuals from specific countries. Finally, the HO periodically issues temporary 'concessions' which cover instances not directly addressed by the rules or policy and which allow officials to grant leave outside the rules (increasingly, these are incorporated into new Immigration Rules).[10] In fact, the HO amended existing and/or introduced new IRs *82 times* between 2003 and 2013.

The extent to which asylum and immigration have increasingly become subject to bureaucratic rules is indicated in Box 3.1, which summarizes the type and number of instructions/rules in effect in May 2013.

Box 3.1 Home Office asylum and immigration instructions and rules, May 2013

Type of instruction and number		*Type of instruction and number*	
Asylum Policy Instructions	39	European Casework Instructions	14
Asylum Process Guidance	18	Information Management Guidance	1

Contact Management Information	2	Nationality Instructions	101
Detention Service Orders and related Instructions	77	Non-compliance with biometric registration regulations	4
Immigration Directorate Instructions	35	Operating standards for pre-departure accommodation (return of families)	1
Enforcement Guidance and Instructions	6	Statelessness Guidance	1
Entry Clearance Guidance	18	Working in the UK Casework Instructions	3
Total: 320			

Several observations are in order. First, while the proliferation of instructions etc. is partly a response by the SSHD to prevent claimants from securing status (see Chapter 8), there can be little doubt that the sheer number of instructions/rules makes it difficult for officials to assess asylum applications. Second, the proliferation of rules undermines the UK's commitment to implement the 1951 Refugee Convention (Dunstan 1998). Even so, the tendency to publish policy instructions on the HO website is welcome because it ends a period during which policy was not disclosed, and it allows asylum seekers/immigrants to judicially review decisions which breach their 'legitimate expectations'.[11] What is also apparent is that in the face of rising numbers of judicial reviews and litigation (UK 2013d: fig. 2; Bondy and Sunkin 2009), the Home Office actively circumvents the courts by drafting new legislation to place official practices on a statutory basis to prevent further legal challenges (Campbell 2013a: chap. 6; see also Chapter 6 in this volume).

The UKBA, whose headquarters is a 20-storey cement edifice in south London called Lunar House, is responsible for implementing Home Office policy. Its operations are overseen by a chief executive, and it is composed of 14 divisions/departments.[12] In 2007 the UKBA had a staff of 13,000 persons and an operational budget of £2 billion. The UKBA also managed the UK Border Force, whose 5,000 staff are responsible for securing the UK border and controlling entry at 138 ports and airports.

The UKBA's objectives are set out in its *Business Plan* (UK 2008d) as follows:

- we will protect our borders;
- we will tackle border fraud, smuggling and immigration crime;
- we will implement fast and fair decisions;
- this will be enabled by strengthening our operational capacity for delivery.

The UKBA's strategic objectives in relation to asylum and immigration policy were to:

- deliver robust identity management systems;
- reduce the time to conclusion of asylum applications [during 2007 40 per cent of all asylum cases were to be concluded within six months, this will rise to 60 per cent in 2008 and 90 per cent in 2009];
- increase the number of removals year on year;
- increase the removal of 'harm' cases as a proportion of total cases removed;
- reduce the vacancy rate in shortage occupations; and
- secure our border and control migration for the benefit of our country.

In addition to the institutional changes discussed above, a new system of cabinet oversight over the HO/UKBA was created in 2008 which sought to better co-ordinate and oversee its work, improve co-operation with other ministries and reduce costs (UK 2007b).[13]

Through the work of entry clearance officers (ECOs) stationed at British embassies, the HO/Border Agency has a global geographic reach. However, it is only the discretionary decisions made by officials in relation to individuals residing *in* the UK which are potentially challengeable in the British courts.[14] It is for this reason that the Home Office/UKBA sees litigation against it as a challenge to its authority.

It is important to look briefly at the Country of Origin Information Service in the HO, whose reports are supposed to inform the decisions of front-line officials.[15] This unit was created in the late 1990s to collect and collate information on the countries where asylum seekers/migrants originate and from countries which receive asylum seekers/migrants. COI reports are supposed to be based on an assessment of all available 'objective evidence' (e.g. reports by Amnesty, Human Rights Watch, the US Department of State, academic research, etc.) as well as information provided through inter-governmental information exchange networks which link the Home Office to its counterparts in other countries. The two principal information networks used by COIS are Eurosur[16] and Intergovernmental Consultations on Migration, Asylum and Refugees.[17] In short, the unit has access to up-to-date information on policy and objective evidence on country policy and conditions from around the world which is supposed to be included in COIS reports.

COIS is tasked with producing reports on the top 20 countries of origin whose nationals are seeking asylum in the UK. Its reports are expected to provide accurate, balanced, relevant, impartial and up-to-date information on asylum seekers' countries of origin which are to be used by UKBA officials at all stages of the asylum determination process.[18] The initial reports were intensely scrutinized, and COIS was accused of exhibiting 'bias' via the selective use of information. In 2004/2005 COIS became an independent unit within the HO, which meant that it was no longer subject to pressure from the policy unit, and the quality of its reports improved noticeably. However, in 2008 the unit was merged with the policy unit, with the result that its reports blurred any distinction between 'objective evidence' and Home Office policy (Pettitt, Townhead and Huber 2008).

The reports produced by the unit's 20 officers are supposed to inform the decisions of front-line staff as they assess asylum claims. However, in 2007–2008 caseworkers were making an estimated 250 requests per year to the unit for additional, very specific information that was not contained in COIS reports. In effect, caseworkers were attempting to find a 'killer quote' made by an asylum applicant in their Statement of Evidence Form (SEF) interview that would enable them to refuse the asylum application. In Chapter 4 I discuss the asymmetric nature of HO asylum interviews which take the form of an aggressive search for ambiguity or gaps in the applicant's account of persecution. The hunt for a 'killer quote' is undertaken following the SEF interview, and clearly indicates that rather than using COIS reports to assess claims, caseworkers are attempting to find ways to refuse claims.[19] This biased approach to assessing asylum claims, which is part of the HO culture discussed earlier, continues today.[20]

It is important to note that immigration officers, asylum case owners and HOPOs are junior civil servants who have in common four attributes. First, the entrance requirements for these posts only require A-level qualifications (i.e. a high school diploma). Second, they are given five weeks of intensive training and a further four weeks of mentoring before taking up their responsibilities. Third, their work is heavily influenced by the culture of their institution. Fourth, the decisions they are required to take are expected to be informed by the myriad instructions issued by the SSHD. It should be clear that the decisions that officials take, albeit under pressure of time to meet their management targets, are vitally important to the life and death of individuals seeking asylum in the UK. Below I examine asylum cases in some detail to illustrate how these officials actually perform their work.

The work of immigration officers

IOs are responsible for conducting the initial screening interview with individuals seeking to enter the UK to claim asylum. The decisions they make depart considerably from published Home Office guidelines, which set out the categories of persons who should *not* be held in the DFT even if their account is found to lack credibility. Between 2007 and 2009 the HO *Best Practice Guide* (Immigration Law Practitioners' Association [ILPA] 2008: appendix 2, para. 38) stated that the following types of individual should *not* be detained:

- unaccompanied minors;
- age dispute cases;
- disabled applicants, except the most easily manageable;
- pregnant females of 24 weeks and above;
- any person with a medical condition which requires 24-hour nursing or medical intervention;
- anybody identified as having an infectious/contagious disease;

- anybody presenting with acute psychosis and requiring hospitalization;
- anybody presenting with physical and/or learning disabilities requiring 24-hour nursing care;
- violent or uncooperative cases;
- individuals with criminal convictions, except where specifically authorized.

However, there is documented evidence that a substantial number of individuals who fall into the above categories were wrongly detained and that their appeals were poorly, if not wrongfully, decided (cf. Bail for Immigration Detainees [BID] 2006 and 2009; London Detainee Support Group 2009; Human Rights Watch 2010).[21] Below I examine the case of *Eritrea/TM* who was placed in the DFT and scheduled for deportation.

The case of *Eritrea/TM*

TM arrived at Heathrow airport in August 2006 on a flight from Sudan. Interviewed at the airport, he claimed to have a student visa, but he was placed in the DFT. Shortly after he was detained, he claimed asylum. His entire case was heard in the DFT at Harmondsworth Immigration Centre.

He was refused legal representation at his appeal, presumably because his claim was believed to lack credibility, and he was compelled to defend himself. He testified that: (a) in Eritrea he was threatened by security officials because his office had reputedly leaked government information; (b) he had served in the military, but had never been demobilized; (c) he paid an agent to take him to Sudan, from where he flew to the UK using a valid passport; and (d) because he did not know how to claim asylum, he wrongly told immigration officials that he was coming to study.

At his appeal the HOPO argued that he was 'not credible', largely because of the discrepant information he had given to officials at the British embassy in Asmara (where he obtained a visa) and on arrival. The HOPO stated:

> It is that repeated assertion that the appellant intended to return to Eritrea, made at interviews after arrival in the UK, which caused the respondent [the HO] to disbelieve the appellant has, as he has claimed since, a fear of persecution.

The HOPO also disputed TM's claim that individuals who served in the army were not demobilized, despite evidence of his service in the mid-1990s and in 2004. The HOPO argued that TM:

had either exaggerated or fabricated many parts of his account . . . . Nor did the Secretary of State consider that the appellant would be perceived as a deserter on return to Eritrea, because he had completed the minimum requirement of 18 months' military service before leaving.

The IJ accepted the HOPO's submissions. He found[22] that: (a) while all Eritrean citizens have a duty to serve in the military, that service is limited to 18 months (TM had therefore completed his military service and would not be considered a deserter); (b) TM's evidence was inconsistent between the various interviews; (c) regarding his claim of having been suspected of leaking government information, the IJ concluded that '[i]t is impossible to believe that the authorities entertained any such suspicions' because TM was not politically active; (d) TM would not have been followed by the security forces because if they had 'real suspicions', they would have detained him; (e) 'I do not accept that it would have been possible for him to pass through ten check points and cross the border into Sudan without proper authority to depart. That alone renders the appellants account impossible to believe'; and (f) existing case law (*KA (Draft-Related Risk Categories Updated) Eritrea CG* [2005] UKAIT 00165) does not establish any real risk on return for having left the country illegally. Accordingly the IJ dismissed his appeal. TM's appeal against the IJ's decision was also dismissed. At this point the HO began the process of documenting him for return.

However, before TM could be returned, the HO was compelled to reconsider its decision following a successful Rule 39 application to the European Court of Human Rights (ECHR) filed by an unpaid and untrained human rights campaigner (see Box 3.2). The court required the HO to suspend deportation and provide Strasbourg with answers to two questions. First, did TM leave Eritrea without 'the requisite exit visa'? Second, would his removal expose him to a risk of treatment prohibited by Art. 3? TM was quickly released from detention and given Indefinite Leave to Remain (ILR).

Box 3.2 Rule 39 applications to the European Court of Human Rights against the UK, 2008–2012

The ECHR only issues an interim measure against a Member State where, having reviewed all the relevant information, it considers that the applicant faces a real risk of serious, irreversible harm if the measure is not applied.

(continued)

(continued)

It is noteworthy that the UK has had more Rule 39 applications granted against it than any other EU member state.

2008		*2009*		*2010*		*2011*		*2012*		*Total*		*EU-wide applications*	
TA	G	TA	G	TA	G	TA	G	TA	G	TA	G	TA	G
1,438	527	1,178	222	1,048	127	790	35	722	13	5,178	924	14,112	3,290

Notes: TA = total number of applications filed. G = applications granted.
Source: ECHR (2013).

Litigation as a window illuminating the work of case owners/caseworkers

The case of *Eritrea/DA*

DA was born in Eritrea in 1990. He entered the UK illegally in November 2006 with his younger sister, and applied for asylum. Shortly after entering the UK, he was arrested and taken to the HO for a screening interview (SI) with an IO. The first task of the SI is to obtain basic information about the nature of the intended asylum claim and determine how the individual travelled to the UK. Any documents which establish an individual's identity are seized, and individuals are photographed and fingerprinted (prints are scanned into the Eurodac database to see whether the individual has made a prior asylum claim in the EU; Broeders 2007). Though officers are given training in how to interview asylum seekers (see UK 2014a), their assessment of an individual's credibility, and thus whether they will be allowed to claim asylum or whether to detain them, is based on 'local knowledge' which categorizes individuals by country of origin, gender, family situation, demeanour, level of education, etc. (Jubany 2011: 82; Gilboy 1991).

Officers believe that they need only apply intuition and common sense to assess the credibility of an asylum seeker. However, the asymmetric structure of the interview in combination with procedures that are 'fraught with unexamined assumptions about language, national identity, and communicative competence' produces a problematic interview record which is used to assess the individuals claim (Jacquemet 2009: 528f.). The transcribed text of these interviews is used to assess the 'truthfulness' of the applicant, despite the fact that the transcribed text is unlikely to be an accurate record of the interview (because of the cultural assumptions of officials, attempts to reduce semantic ambiguities which arose in the interview, the problematic nature of translation and the distortion of meaning caused in transferring speech into a written text).

If an officer decides that the application can be 'dealt with quickly' – a euphemism for a claim they believe to be fraudulent – the asylum seeker is placed in the DFT process. If the individual's claim is not credible, but for specified reasons they cannot be detained, the person is supposed to be given 'leave to enter' the UK and is 'disbursed' (sent) outside southeast England to wait for a 'substantive interview' and a decision on their claim.

Eritrea/DA was given leave to enter the UK and was issued with an Application Registration Card which indicated that he had filed an application for asylum; the card carried his personal details and a photograph. As an under-age asylum seeker, he was released to live in London and assigned to a regional asylum team for a substantive interview. He was directed by a 'friend' to an Eritrean caseworker at a law firm in London who took his initial claim. However, after he and his sister were put into care, he ran away and lived rough on the streets for six months before making a second asylum application in a different name. At this point he went to a different law firm, which took over his claim, interviewed him and filed his Statement of Evidence Form with the Home Office (his interview is discussed in detail in Chapter 4).

In his substantive interview in November 2007 the HO case owner invoked Immigration Rule 352, allowing him to interview DA as an under-age child.[23] The basis of his claim was that he had converted to Pentecostalism at the age of 10 and that he feared mistreatment by the authorities because of his religion. The HO caseworker did not dispute his history or the means by which he reached the UK, i.e. his flight to Sudan, travel through Libya to Italy and France and illegal entry into the UK. Instead the official: (a) argued that DA had failed to apply for asylum in a safe third country (i.e. Italy or France); (b) disputed his knowledge of Pentecostalism;[24] (c) refused to offer him discretionary leave under the relevant API (because he was 17½ years old[25]); and (d) refused his claim on the basis that it lacked credibility.

At his April 2008 appeal against the SSHD's refusal of his claim, the IJ listened to DA's oral evidence, considered legal and oral submissions by both parties and assessed relevant objective evidence on Eritrea. The IJ found that DA had 'been through very difficult experiences . . . . I find that those experiences, coupled with his youth, provide a satisfactory explanation for those discrepancies' identified by the HOPO. The IJ found that DA had left Eritrea illegally and, according to established case law, he would be perceived as a deserter/draft evader. Accordingly, DA had a well-founded fear of persecution if he were to be returned to Eritrea, so he was granted asylum.

The case of *Ethiopia/DS*

DS was born in Ethiopia in 1976. He claimed to have suffered persecution by the Ethiopian authorities because of his Eritrean ethnicity. He was beaten by the local authorities, his identity document was seized, and he was unable to continue his education. His brother and sister were deported to Eritrea at this time (see Campbell 2013b). With help, he fled Ethiopia and arrived in the UK in June 2000, where he applied for asylum. The RFL disputed the fact that he was singled out because of his ethnicity, stating that official 'actions stemmed from failures of discipline and supervision rather than from any concerted policy'. The HO caseworker argued that, following the June 2000 peace treaty between Eritrea and Ethiopia, DS could safely return to Ethiopia (alternatively, he could be returned to Eritrea because he also had citizenship there).[26] In short, the HO argued that his 'removal would not be contrary to our obligations'.

DS's 2004 delayed appeal was refused. The IJ found that his nationality had not been removed and that he could return to Ethiopia (regardless of having been refused recognition as a national by the Ethiopian embassy in London). The decision was successfully appealed against, and the case was reconsidered in 2006, when his appeal was dismissed again. The 2006 decision was successfully appealed to the Court of Appeal, which listed DS's appeal together with four related cases for a hearing. In the CoA, counsel for DS and for the SSHD both consented (agreed) that the Tribunal should rehear the case.

A *de novo* hearing was convened by the AIT in March 2008, at which the key issue was: would DS be at risk of persecution if he were returned to Ethiopia because of 'difficulties arising over his nationality'. Evidence was accepted by the court regarding his inability to secure a travel document (TD) from the Ethiopian embassy (officials refused to recognize him as a national) and about the circumstances which led him to flee Ethiopia. The court concluded that: (a) DS's claim was similar to that of *EB (Ethiopia)* v *SSHD* [2007] EWCA Civ 809 with respect to how the Ethiopian authorities arbitrarily deprived individuals of 'mixed ethnicity' of their nationality and with respect to the continuing attitude of the authorities towards individuals of mixed ethnicity. Accordingly, the Tribunal granted his appeal.

The case of *Eritrea/RY*

RY was born in Eritrea in 1985, and applied for asylum in January 2008. She claimed to fear persecution in Eritrea on account of her religious beliefs as a Pentecostal Christian. Based on her screening and substantive interviews, the HO case owner disputed her nationality and her claim to be a Pentecostal Christian. RY was also compelled to take a language analysis test – a verbal test contracted out to a Swedish firm, Sprakab.[27] Sprakab's analysis of a short telephone interview with RY concluded that she 'understands some Tigrinya but does not speak it; [she] has knowledge of Ethiopia but not Eritrea and speaks Amharic of a variety with certainty not found in Eritrea'.

At her 2008 appeal RY testified that she had been born in Ethiopia to parents who were Eritrean; she therefore understood Tigrinya – one of the languages of Eritrea – but did not speak it. In December 2000, at the height of the war between Eritrea and Ethiopia, she was deported to Eritrea. She lived in Eritrea without being conscripted, and was introduced to Pentecostalism in 2005 by an uncle. The government banned her church in 2007, but she attended prayers at the house of another member of the church. Later that year soldiers raided the house and detained her for 20 days, during which she was beaten and asked to identify other prayer meeting locations before a relative bribed an officer to allow her to escape. She illegally left Eritrea for Sudan, from where she travelled to the UK.

In assessing her claim, the IJ found that she had provided correct answers to 18 of the 19 questions she was asked about her religion. Furthermore, a witness testified in support of her claim to be a Pentecostal. With respect to the language analysis, the IJ noted that she had correctly answered all the questions about Eritrea and that the firm contracted to conduct the language analysis had erred in its analysis. For instance, there was objective evidence that Amharic was spoken in Eritrea 'as recently as 1993 and that large numbers of people who would normally have spoken Amhara [*sic*] were subsequently deported to Eritrea'. The judge concluded that she was a 'credible witness and one who is a Pentecostal from Eritrea', and he allowed her appeal.

Analysis

Every asylum seeker is required to undergo an initial screening interview which is conducted by an IO. If the individual is permitted to enter the UK, a case owner conducts a substantive interview with the applicant and, following initial submissions on the claim by the applicant's legal representative, the case owner makes an initial decision on the application. These officers work under considerable pressure, created in part by management targets: between 2007 and 2009 case owners were required to assess 30 cases per month, undertake two substantive interviews per day and make four decisions a day. High workloads contribute to stress and high staff turnover – conditions which, according to the union, had 'fractured' the 'standard' required for the New Asylum case work programme.[28] Under the NAM, asylum case owners were also expected to defend their decisions in court, but this task always fell to a HOPO.

Despite extensive guidance about how to interview applicants and how to evaluate asylum claims, the cases discussed here make it clear that IOs and case owners consistently refuse to believe what asylum applicants tell them, and that officers do not consider relevant COI. In each case, the case owner issued an RFL which refused the claim on a narrow point of law without looking 'in the round' at *all* the evidence, including the SEF interview, the completed claim and relevant COI reports. This failure, together with staff scepticism about the validity of asylum claims, is evidenced by the fact that between 1999 and 2013 72 per cent of all initial asylum claims were refused (UK 2010–2011: table 5). In 2007 the Home Office introduced the New Asylum Model and promised that caseworkers would be university graduates who would receive substantially improved training; nevertheless, the tendency to disbelieve applicants has remained a permanent feature of decision-making.[29]

Some of the problems identified in the cases cited above arise from caseworkers' cursory assessment of a claim and their reliance on HO Operational Guidance Notes which are known to selectively and erroneously cite objective country information and case law (Immigration Advisory Services [IAS] 2009a and 2009b; see also Chapter 8 in this volume). In short, officials seize on minor details of a claim in an effort to undermine the applicant's credibility and refuse the claim. Rather than assess the claim in its entirety or against conditions in the applicant's country, officers apply their 'intuition'/local knowledge to refuse a claim, and use OGNs or APIs to justify their decision. How else are we to explain that 26–44 per cent of all HO initial refusals are overturned on appeal by the Tribunal?

Analysis of the work of HOPOs[30]

HOPOs are recruited in one of two ways: either (a) they must possess A-level qualifications and apply; or (b) as an existing civil servant, they must apply for a transfer to this post (all five of the HOPOs I interviewed had a university degree). Officers work in a Presenting Officers Unit (POU) which is attached to a Tribunal hearing centre; the volume of asylum and immigration cases heard at a centre determines the number of HOPOs in a POU.[31] HOPOs attend a two-week induction course introducing them to everything from the role of the HOPO to case law, the Refugee Convention, appeals, advocacy skills and procedural rules. They are then posted to a POU and mentored for four to five weeks; three months into their post, they are sent on a three-day consolidation training course. Periodic training is offered to refresh their skills and to update them about changes to the law. In 2007 the average pay for a HOPO was £24,000–29,000 per annum.

One HOPO I interviewed referred to himself as 'a pretend barrister'. The term aptly describes how they see themselves, namely as legal advocates whose job is 'to defend the decision of the SSHD'. Strictly speaking, they defend the decision of the ECO to refuse a visa application and decisions by IOs to refuse an asylum application.[32] The role of a HOPO is set out in the UKBA's training manual as follows:

- To assist the UK Border Agency in it's [*sic*] key objectives of securing our border and controlling migration for the benefit of the country and in particular to ensure that we implement fast and fair decisions.
- Represent the decision-maker in line with the law, the appropriate Immigration Rule and UK Border Agency policy.
- Ensure that each case is argued fully, responding to new evidence and issues raised by the Immigration Judge and the appellant's representative.
- Ensure the Immigration Judge considers all the relevant parts of the Immigration Rule.
- Support the decision under appeal but be mindful of the need to assist the court and the Immigration Judge to reach a just and fair decision: this may involve disclosing evidence and material to achieve a balanced determination of the case.[33]

Unlike legal representatives, HOPOs are not 'officers of the court',[34] nor are they bound by a professional code of conduct.[35] Indeed, the SSHD sets management targets for HOPOs: in 2009 they were required to make 'a positive contribution towards the objectives' of only 15 per cent of allowed asylum and deportation appeals and 20 per cent of Entry Clearance (EC) appeals. In 2013 HOPOs were expected to win 70 per cent of asylum appeals and 60 per cent of all other appeals. A HOPO's work rota consists of taking '11 lists a month', i.e. they represent the SSHD in cases listed for a hearing on alternate days, and they use their off-day to read case files and prepare for court. Prior to 2001 HOPOs had authority to concede an appeal; however, that authority was subsequently removed from them.[36] One senior presenting officer (SPO) told me that 'genuine appellants succeed at the first stage [at their initial interview], everyone else should be refused'. However, another HOPO told me: 'It sends out the wrong signals to asylum applicants if POs concede cases, each application should be looked at on its own. Now we leave the judge to make a decision on the issue.' If a HOPO encounters a problematic decision by an IO/caseworker, they rewrite and reissue the RFL before the hearing to better address the legal arguments. Nevertheless, many HOPOs are relatively young and the general ethos of POUs is to win cases, so it is not surprising that an unofficial competition exists between POUs to achieve the highest 'win ratio' (reflected in monthly statistics for each unit).

If we return to *Eritrea/TM*, we can see the tenaciousness with which HOPOs defend the case owner's decision. Indeed, the HOPO relied entirely on the RFL in his submission to the IJ. Disappointingly, the IJ relied on the HOPO's submissions and conducted a cursory review of existing case law, notably *KA (Draft-Related Risk Categories Updated) Eritrea CG* [2005] UKAIT 00165. However, he missed a key issue reported at paras 113(f), namely that men aged 18–50 are currently at risk on return to Eritrea if:

> they can be considered to have left Eritrea illegally. Regarding this subcategory, it must be borne in mind that an appellant's assertion that he left illegally will raise an issue that will need to be established to the required standard.

Instead of checking whether TM had been issued an exit visa by the Government of Eritrea, the IO and the HOPO focused on whether he had a valid visa to enter the UK. By concentrating on inconsistencies in his statements, it was easy to undermine TM's credibility, which in turn made it easy to disregard his oral evidence and the information he supplied in a seven-and-a-half-page Application Notice appealing against the Tribunal's decision. I examine the work of IJs and the Tribunal in Chapter 5, but it is worth noting that HOPOs place IJs on a continuum from 'tough' (conservative, pro-Home Office), to 'good' (conducts a balanced hearing) to 'allowers' (those who think the HO interferes too much in private life). Another term used to describe 'tough' IJs was 'dismisser', a term that aptly describes the judge who presided over TM's appeal.

Conclusion

The HO/UKBA is a massive, complex and powerful bureaucracy over which the SSHD exercises extensive authority which is reinforced by drafting and securing the passage of legislation and by issuing growing numbers of instructions and rules. However, the peculiar tunnel vision which characterizes HO policy runs into difficulties because officials fail to grasp the complex factors driving the global movement of population (see Chapter 8).

Policy implementation has consistently been poor due to poorly conceived policies, high staff workloads, poor training of front-line staff, under-resourcing of key areas of work and *ad hoc* organizational changes. The response of the SSHD to the inability of her officials to meet policy objectives has been to remove their discretion to decide cases and to create a proliferation of instructions and rules which makes their job more difficult.

The work performed by HO officials is poorly understood by senior staff, and is of highly variable quality. Rather than carefully assessing individual cases, IOs wrongly detain large numbers of individuals, and case owners – who consistently refuse to believe what asylum applicants tell them and who fail to examine all the evidence – unquestioningly support their colleagues' decisions to refuse asylum claims. The situation is compounded because HOPOs, whose role is to defend the SSHD's decision, rely on the original Reasons for Refusal Letter (RFL) without assessing the evidence. A disbelief of asylum applicants together with a failure to evaluate all the evidence results in expensive and unnecessary litigation before the Tribunal, which overturns upwards of 25 per cent of all HO initial decisions. It is astonishing that the failings of HO officials to adequately assess initial asylum claims, and the willingness of HOPOs to defend indefensible decisions, has been so easily brushed aside by the Home Office, which merely argues that asylum applicants are economic migrants (not *bona fide* refugees), and that asylum litigation is vexatious and without merit.

Notes

1 An organogram of the organization of the Home Office can be found at 'Organograms – Home Office', available at: http://www.data.gov.uk/organogram/home-office (accessed 4 August 2016).

2 In fact, decisions are not taken quickly, with the result that a spiralling backlog of cases has developed since 2007 which have still not been resolved (UK 2012c; Campbell 2013b: chap. 6).

3 The document was available at: http://rds.homeoffice.gov,uk/rds/. In March 2013 this and other data produced by this unit was moved to a new government website and can no longer be accessed. I interviewed the director of the unit on 12 September 2007.

4 The Home Office has a long history of burying/disregarding research critical of its policies. See R. Verkaik, 'Crime statistics "were distorted by politics"', *The Independent*, 13 February 2006, about how the Home Office suppressed commissioned research which did not support government policy, and A. Travis 'Warning on shifting asylum seekers to dangerous areas is revealed', *The Guardian*, 16 March 2007.

5 See anon., 'Immigration system unfit – Reid', *BBC News*, 23 May 2006, available at: http://news.bbc.co.uk/1/hi/uk_politics/5007148.stm (accessed 4 August 2016).

6 In 2013, and in light of subsequent widespread criticism of the UKBA, the SSHD issued an executive order and reabsorbed the UKBA back into the HO. See the SSHD's statement in A. Travis, 'UK Border Agency to be abolished, Theresa May announces', *The Guardian*, 26 March 2013, available at: https://www.theguardian.com/uk/2013/mar/26/uk-border-agency-broken-up (accessed 4 August 2016).

7 In 2007 one person was deprived of their nationality (while outside the UK); in 2008 none; in 2009 two persons (one while outside the UK); in 2010 five persons (all of whom were outside the UK at the time). The legislative basis for depriving these individuals of their nationality was said to be s. 40 of the British Nationality Act (1981) (as amended by s. 56 of the Immigration, Asylum and Nationality Act 2006; source: FOI Request 16378 to UKBA dated 29 October 2010).

8 Initially, concessions took the form of written letters from the HO to a solicitor and were not made public. This meant that it was impossible to know whether official decisions were 'fair' (McKee 2006). This situation resulted in considerable litigation.

9 For specific information, see 'Publications: guidance', available at: http://www.ukba.homeoffice.gov.uk/policyandlaw/guidance/ (accessed 4 August 2016).

10 Most of the concessions which have been granted concern immigrants, not asylum seekers. However, see the 2011 controversy surrounding the government's stated intention to withdraw the 14-year residence rule which allowed individuals illegally resident in the UK to normalize their status documented by Immigration Matters (2011).

11 'A procedural legitimate expectation arises where a public authority has induced in someone affected by a decision a reasonable expectation that he will be granted a hearing or that some other procedure will be followed before a decision depriving him of some benefit or advantage is taken. A failure to act in accordance with the expectation and provide procedural protection is challengeable on judicial review'; 'Legitimate expectation', *Oxford Reference*, available at: http://www.oxfordreference.com/view/10.1093/oi/authority.20110810105248783 (accessed 4 August 2016).

12 See 'Organograms – UK Border Agency', available at: http://www.data.gov.uk/organogram/uk-border-agency (accessed 4 August 2016).

13 Cost reduction was to be achieved by fast-tracking asylum appeals, reducing judicial reviews by 20 per cent and by reducing asylum support costs by £80 million (UK 2007c). Cabinet oversight ended when the Coalition Government was elected in May 2010.

14 The major exception occurred when the HO used entry controls in Prague to screen passengers intending to travel to the UK; see: *R (On the Application of European*

Roma Rights Centre and Others) v *Immigration Officer at Prague Airport and Another* [2004] UKHL 55. The House of Lords found that 'The entry clearance system did not violate the UK's obligations under the 1951 Refugee Convention and the 1967 Protocol. However, the entry clearance system unlawfully discriminated against Roma by subjecting them to longer and more intensive questioning and therefore was in violation of sec.1(1)(a) of the Race Relations Act 1976.'

15 The discussion of COIS is partly based on interviews with an official in the unit.

16 See 'Eurosur', *Frontex*, available at: http://frontex.europa.eu/intelligence/eurosur/ (accessed 4 August 2016).

17 See *IGC – Intergovernmental Consultations on Immigration, Asylum and Refugees*, available at: http://www.igc.ch/ (accessed 4 August 2016).

18 See 'United Kingdom: Home Office', available at: http://www.refworld.org/publisher, UKHO,COUNTRYREP,AFG,,,0.html#SRTop31 (accessed 4 August 2016).

19 These 'fishing expeditions' were also noted by the Independent Chief Inspector of the UKBA (UK 2011b).

20 The 'culture' of the HO is manifested in many ways. For example, in 2008/2009 caseworkers used a set of cards produced by COIS on which was printed basic information about the top 20 asylum-producing countries to play 'Top Trumps' – a children's game – in their offices, i.e. cards were traded by caseworkers. In 2010 a part-time caseworker revealed a 'culture of hostility and aggression' within her unit, marked in part by staff using 'a toy gorilla which was put on the desk of any officer who approved an asylum application. She said the gorilla was used as a "form of public ridicule"'; anon., 'Whistleblower's claims about Cardiff asylum office', *BBC News*, 3 February 2010, available at: http://news.bbc.co.uk/1/hi/wales/south_east/8496759.stm (accessed 4 August 2016). In 2015 COIS issued country reports which failed to disclose information which contradicted its conclusions that it was safe to refuse and return asylum applicants to Eritrea (Arapiles 2015). In my 2015 review of Home Office policy on Eritrea I was given 10 caseworker requests sent to COIS which sought to identify 'killer quotes' in applicants' SEF interviews (Campbell 2015).

21 See 'Fast track deportations from the UK unlawful', *BBC News*, 26 July 2010, answers to parliamentary questions on this issue reported at 'Parliamentary questions, debates and statements on detention', *The Detention Forum*, available at: http://detentionforum.org.uk/news/in-parliament/parliamentary-questions-on-detention/ (accessed 4 August 2016) and evidence of high levels of 'self-harm' among detainees reported at 'Immigration: detention. House of Lords written question – answered on 27th June 2012', *They Work For You*, available at: http://www.theyworkforyou.com/wrans/?id=2012-06-27a.71.4 (accessed 4 August 2016).

22 Arguably, an appeal in the DFT, particularly where an individual is not legally represented, should follow the Surendran Guidelines, which allow an IJ to ask questions of the appellant, but prohibits the IJ from descending 'into the arena' and appearing to assume the HOPO's mantle (Asylum and Immigration Tribunal 2003). In short, the IJ should assist the appellant to clarify their evidence. This does not seem to have occurred.

23 See Immigration Rule 352, available at: http://www.ukba.homeoffice.gov.uk/policyandlaw/immigrationlaw/immigrationrules/part11/ (accessed 4 August 2016).

24 The large number of Eritrean asylum applications alleging religious persecution on the basis of membership in a 'minority'/Pentecostal church led the Home Office to issue special COI reports addressing this issue (UK 2006a).

25 The 2007 version of the API 'Processing an asylum application from a child' was withdrawn in 2009, and the 2009 version was replaced in July 2016 (see UK 2016c).

26 Documented in the API on 'disputed nationality' (issued in 2005) at: https://www.gov.uk/government/publications/disputed-nationality-allowed-appeals (accessed 21 August 2014).

27 See the Asylum Process Guidance Note on 'Language analysis' at: https://www.gov.uk/government/uploads/system/uploads/attachment_data/file/345592/Language_Analysis_AI_External_v17.pdf (accessed 4 August 2016) and Campbell (2013a).

28 See 'Asylum: the war in NAM heats up', an undated public message issued by the Public and Commercial Services Union in 2007 to its members. The briefing stated that pressures had led to 'some regions taking all appeals work away from the asylum teams, others giving interviews or backlog cases to lower graded staff, other asylum teams have annexed presenting officers units, and other fragmenting the distribution and allocation of cases . . . . PCS is of the opinion that this drift away from the case-ownership model is affecting the consistency of asylum case working . . . ' (copy in my possession).

29 For this pledge and evidence regarding poor decisions by asylum case owners, see UK (2009).

30 Information on the work of HOPOs comes from observations made during fieldwork, from interviewing and work-shadowing four HOPOs and one SPO, and from FOI Requests.

31 The POU at Feltham had 70-plus HOPOs and 5 SPOs, the Angel (Islington) POU had 25 SPOs, 6 senior caseworkers and 85 HOPOs.

32 Sources: FOI Request to HO dated 23 March 2007; FOI Request 11577 to UKBA dated 21 May 2009; FOI Request 26714 to HO dated 8 April 2013.

33 The training manual can be found at *Presenting Officer Induction Course, Day One: Trainers' Notes*, available at: http://freemovement.files.wordpress.com/2008/12/presenting-officer-induction-course-day-one-v2.pdf (accessed 4 August 2016).

34 An officer of the court is 'any person who has an obligation to promote justice and effective operation of the judicial system, including judges, the attorneys who appear in court, bailiffs, clerks, and other personnel. As officers of the court lawyers have an absolute ethical duty to tell judges the truth, including avoiding dishonesty or evasion about reasons why the attorney or his/her client is not appearing, the location of documents and other matters related to conduct of the courts'; 'Officer of the court', *The Free Dictionary*, available at: http://legal-dictionary.thefreedictionary.com/officer+of+the+court (accessed 4 August 2016).

35 See 'Home Office Presenting Officers', *Free Movement*, 2 December 2008, available at: http://www.freemovement.org.uk/2008/12/02/home-office-presenting-officers/ (accessed 4 August 2016).

36 According to the Home Office, 'in general, we will seek to withdraw if, having reviewed the decision [to refuse] under appeal and all the facts and evidence now available, it is clear to the reviewing officer that the decision under appeal is fundamentally flawed or new evidence suggests it is no longer sustainable' (source: FOI Request 27659 to HO dated 12 September 2013). However, official actions and information provided by POs/SPOs indicates that the HO does not withdraw its decisions/RFLs.

4 Taking and making refugee claims

The work of immigration caseworkers, interpreters and barristers

To understand the work of refugee lawyers – i.e. solicitors, accredited caseworkers and immigration barristers – it is essential to understand how an asylum claim is taken, translated, prepared and litigated. Their work is made possible by the government's provision of legal aid, a fund managed by the Legal Services Commission (LSC), which pays a lawyer for a pre-defined number of hours to take and make an asylum claim (with assistance from an interpreter). If a claim is refused by the HO, legal aid is also available to pay an advocate/barrister to argue the appeal before the Tribunal/CoA.

The first section looks at how immigration solicitors/caseworkers in private law firms translate a claim of persecution and file asylum applications with the Home Office. I look at one case in considerable depth to show how caseworkers and interpreters jointly interview an asylum applicant to co-produce an asylum claim. If the claim is accepted, the caseworker assists the asylum applicant to complete government forms to finalize their status. If the HO refuses the initial application, the applicant's lawyer prepares the client's case for an appeal to the Tribunal and instructs a barrister to argue it. The second section looks at the key role performed by clerks in barrister sets, namely creating a market for barrister services, and at how barristers prepare to litigate an asylum claim.

Translating a story of flight into a claim of persecution

When an individual arrives at a UK port and declares an intention to claim asylum, they undergo a screening interview, following which the IO decides either to allow them to enter the UK to claim asylum or to detain them at an immigration detention facility where their asylum claim is fast-tracked. An exception to this procedure occurs when individuals who enter the country illegally are apprehended by the police, at which point they are taken into police custody and their asylum claim may be taken in the cells (this is called a 'notebook' interview). If the illegal entrant is a child who wishes to claim asylum, they are taken to the Home Office for a screening interview. Below I examine how the asylum claim of a child who entered the UK illegally was taken, translated and transformed into a claim of persecution by an immigration caseworker working with an interpreter.

The case of *Eritrea/DA*

DA, whose asylum appeal was examined in Chapter 3, and his younger sister were smuggled out of Eritrea to Sudan, from where they travelled to Libya, to Italy and to the UK, arriving in England in 2006. The lorry carrying them was stopped by the police, and they were taken to the HO for a screening interview before being placed in the care of social services. During his interview officials discovered from the Eurodac fingerprint database that he had entered Italy prior to entering the UK. At this point he overheard officials say that he would be removed to Italy; he became frightened, and fabricated his claim. DA was put in touch with a caseworker at a London law firm who took his claim, following which he ran away and lived rough. Five months later he returned and, using a different name, attended a second HO screening interview. At this point an Eritrean refugee referred him to a (second) law firm.

At the second law firm he was interviewed three times (for a total of three-and-a-half hours), during which a caseworker took his statement via an interpreter and transformed his account into a recognizable asylum claim which was sent to the HO. I attended and recorded all of DA's interviews. In what follows I draw upon training given to caseworkers (which I attended[1]) and my training as an anthropologist to analyse the way DA was interviewed.

Prior to examining the interview process, it should be noted that asylum interviews can produce a very problematic written record (Jacquemet 2009). While perhaps less asymmetric and certainly less aggressive than Home Office interviews (Crawley 2010a), lawyers rely on the same problematic assumptions about language, national identity and communicative competence in the way they conduct an interview and 'entextualize' a written record of it for submission to the HO and the Tribunal. The key difference appears to be that a lawyer is not searching for ambiguity or gaps in an individual's account, but rather gives an applicant the benefit of the doubt by listening to and carefully probing what is often an incoherent, creolized account of persecution and flight. This is not an easy task. A good interviewer must understand the difficulties involved in taking an account, which in turn requires them to control the interpreter, who is not formally trained or accredited and who may not provide 'an exact interpretation' (as required by law). Indeed, the interpreter may not fully comprehend why an applicant is being asked certain questions or what the applicant is trying to say (Gibb and Good 2014), which means that parts of the interview, and its resulting entextualization, are likely to be inaccurate.

DA's interviews followed a standard pattern. First, the caseworker's knowledge of refugee law – notably Art. 1(A)2 of the Refugee Convention, which sets out the basis of a 'well-founded fear of persecution' – framed the way he assessed and re-presented DA's testimony in the statement that was submitted to the HO. Second, the caseworker had to address possible credibility issues. In DA's case, this meant discussing and correcting the statement taken by the first caseworker who interviewed him (and who had sent DA's statement to the HO). Any errors, omissions or inconsistencies between an applicant's written statements are seized upon by the HO and IJs to question the truthfulness and credibility of the applicant and to refuse the application.

Each interview addressed different topics. Thus, the first interview addressed four issues:

1 Introductions were followed by a request for DA to sign new forms giving the caseworker authority to handle his claim, etc. (this took 5 minutes).
2 DA's first statement was reviewed to determine how he fled Eritrea and reached the UK. In addition, a means test was performed to see if he qualified for legal aid, followed by an explanation of HO procedure. This was followed by a brief discussion about his screening interview, an effort to clarify why he ran away and lived rough on the street, and finally he was asked to identify members of his family (1 hour 13 minutes).
3 He was asked whether he had any outstanding needs in the UK, e.g. for medical treatment, from social services, etc. (5 minutes).
4 Finally, it took some time to agree the date of the next meeting (16 minutes).

The second interview addressed three issues:

1 The original statement was revisited, revised and rewritten specifically in relation to the conversion of DA and his siblings to Pentecostal Christianity, with regard to incidents of persecution which DA and his family suffered due to their faith, his sister's asylum claim, his release from police cells in Eritrea, and events in Libya prior to crossing the Mediterranean (2 hours 10 minutes).
2 Arrangements were made for the next interview (8 minutes).
3 They clarified whether he had any questions (2 minutes).

The final interview addressed two issues:

1 Following a discussion about his release from jail and his fear of returning to Eritrea, his statement was completed and signed (21 minutes).
2 He was briefly told what to expect at his HO substantive interview and how to prepare for it – e.g. 'read your statement' (he could not read English)! The issues discussed included the importance of ensuring his oral evidence was consistent with his statement, and the need to listen to and answer questions about his claim. The caseworker confirmed that a paralegal and the

firm's interpreter would attend the interview with him to ensure that he was treated fairly (15 minutes).

During DA's interviews five people were present: DA, the (English) caseworker, a Refugee Council Children's Panel worker, a female Eritrean interpreter and myself. It was notable that, due to time constraints, the caseworker simultaneously asked questions and word-processed DA's answers. The caseworker failed to monitor and control the interpreter. Thus, throughout the second and most of the third interview the interpreter was asked to read entire paragraphs from DA's statement for him to confirm or change. Furthermore, the interviews were constantly interrupted: the caseworker received nine phone calls, twice the caseworker walked out of the interview for several minutes and/or someone walked in. On several occasions the caseworker and the panel worker entered into extended conversations which were not translated for DA.

Below I provide excerpts from the interviews to give readers a sense of their rambling nature and the difficulties involved in asking and answering questions through an interpreter. At the beginning of the first interview DA was asked to sign three forms: confirmation that the firm would act on his behalf, a form allowing the firm to secure medical reports and his file from the first law firm, and a legal help form to secure funding to represent him. Very little explanation was offered about the forms. The italicized numbers in the interview text indicate the timing of verbal exchanges in minutes:seconds; the absence of text for Daniel and the interpreter indicates that they were conversing in Tigrinya, a language which the caseworker did not speak. The interview began with DA being asked a series of questions to ascertain whether he met the 'means test'.

CASEWORKER (CW): Okay, they ask whether you consider that you have any kind of disability, so some kind of physical disability, mental disability, learning disability, something like that. Just as a monitoring thing.

INTERPRETER (I): *6:18* Sorry physical, mental, and . . . ?

I:

DA:

CW: Learning disability, any kind of disability.

I: *6:37* Not really disabilities.

CW: Okay, that's good. Right, do you have any other names apart from ——? Middle name?

(continued)

(continued)

I:	*6:59*
DA:	
CW:	Do you want to write it for me?
I:	*7:09* At the moment he doesn't have a middle name.
CW:	Okay, okay, alright then.
PANEL WORKER (PW):	*7:22*
CW:	Just in case. Okay. And you're not married, right?
I:	*7:35*
DA:	No.
CW:	Okay. Where were you born in Eritrea?
I:	*7:41*
DA:	
CW:	Okay, I've got it here, [. . .] yeah?
DA:	Yeah.
CW:	Right. And your current . . . what's your current address . . . where you're living in the UK?
I:	*8:08*
DA:	[replies in English]
CW:	Excellent.
PW:	That's the one there.
CW:	Thanks. Okay. Who are you living with there?
I:	*8:41*
DA [in English]:	Social Service.
PW:	It's Social Services Housing, sharing with other people.
CW:	Okay. And which Social Services is it?
DA:	Lambeth.
I:	Lambeth.
CW:	Lambeth, okay. Do they give you any money?
I:	*9:00*
DA:	No.
CW:	Okay. You don't have any capital, you don't own a house? Have savings, valuable items that you haven't told anybody about?
I:	*9:24*
DA:	No.
CW:	Okay. Good. Did you have a letter from Lambeth that you showed me before . . . ?
I:	*9:50*
CW:	You had something from the social workers?
I:	*9:52*

PW: A letter that says that they're helping you, I think it's this one.
CW: Well, just one so that I can write to them and ask them.
PW: This one.
CW: That's the one, excellent.

The above four-minute segment illustrates how the means test was administered. It also illustrates the general, unspecific and poorly expressed nature of many of the questions asked of DA (which confused him) and the four-way verbal interaction which occurred in every interview. The time-consuming nature of relying upon an interpreter is illustrated when DA was asked to identify all the members of his family – his parents and nine siblings – which required a nine-minute discussion during which names were spelled out syllable by syllable.

In the three-and-a-half-minute segment below the caseworker attempts to clarify the specific dates when DA's aunt, with whom he was staying, was arrested by the authorities:

CW: *32:15* Okay. Do you remember sort of specific dates, or specifically when your auntie was arrested? What happened?
I: *32:38*
DA: *33:02*
DA: [in English] I remember the date of her last arrest.
CW: Okay. Was that the September 2006 one?
DA: Mmm . . .
I: Yeah, 17th of September.
CW: Okay, so before then, how many times would you say that she had been arrested before that last one?
I: *33:22*
DA:
I:
DA: *33:34*
I: Before that she has been arrested many times. They arrest her; they let her go. But I don't remember exactly how many times.
CW: Okay. And where were they arrested, do you remember, they were coming to the house, or to the hotel, or . . . ?
I: *33:48*
DA: *33:55*
I: They go and check everywhere, they would come to the house, they would go to the hotel. And um . . .
CW: But you can't remember exactly how many times, I mean are we talking like, tens of times, are we talking sort of four or five times?

(continued)

(continued)

I: *34:17*
DA:
I:
DA: *34:27*
I: About four times.
CW: So between 2001 and 2006 it was about four times?
I: *34:34*
DA: *34:42*
I: Yeah.
[*34:44* Silence. Phone call. The caseworker leaves the room.]

Caseworkers are advised to avoid long, convoluted questions and questions using double negatives; they are told to speak in short, grammatically correct sentences (IAS 2007). Caseworkers are instructed that they should only use open-ended questions to get clients to tell them their story, use closed questions to obtain specific information, and never use leading questions which suggest a particular answer lest their client assumes or supplies 'facts' which have not been established. This guidance was intermittently followed in DA's interviews. For instance, the caseworker did not establish a clear chronology of events during the interview; he failed to consistently flesh out events by asking appropriate who/what/why questions, and he did not use country-specific information to interrogate DA's account. Indeed, the caseworker's questions jumped back and forth between topics.

Just as worrying was the fact that the caseworker did not monitor the interpreter.[2] For instance, there were numerous times when the interpreter and DA had an extended conversation which ended with the interpreter providing a simple, short answer to the caseworker's question. This situation arose because the caseworker delegated key tasks – reading and confirming large segments of the statement – to the interpreter while the caseworker word-processed the form. It is notable that neither the caseworker nor DA seemed to be concerned about possible misunderstandings despite the high cost of getting the statement wrong and having the application refused.

The poorly organized and at times unstructured interview was nevertheless entextualized into a coherent seven-page statement spelling out DA's claim in consecutively numbered paragraphs. The statement was written in short, simple sentences and provided a clear chronology of events against which key elements of DA's story of persecution were linked to documented violations of human rights (i.e. conversion to Pentecostal Christianity; the compulsory conscription of his older siblings; life as a Pentecostal Christian in Asmara, where churches were closed down; and the arrest of an aunt and of DA and his sister) which culminated in their flight from Eritrea.

The interview reflects the effect of a tight time schedule (the statement was filed just in time for DA's substantive interview with the HO) and the pressure on caseworkers to take asylum claims quickly (due to limited legal aid funding) to cover their salary and the firm's overheads.[3] In short, caseworkers demonstrate varying abilities to manage the interpreters who help them take the asylum claim. Indeed, because interpreters are not qualified or accredited it is important to control the interview, to carefully articulate questions and to listen carefully to what the applicant says (by attending to gaps/lapses in communication which may indicate a problem that needs to be understood). Asylum applicants do not understand the purpose of the interview, they may resent being asked certain questions, and they rarely come away with a clear understanding of asylum procedures. While good caseworkers listen to their clients and give them the benefit of the doubt as they tease out an individual's narrative of flight, the process of taking and entextualizing an asylum claim is difficult – a task that is not made easier by pressure to take a claim quickly because of limited legal aid funding.

Preparing for the appeal: the work of caseworkers, barristers' clerks and barristers

As often occurs, the HO rejected DA's initial asylum claim. When this occurs, applicants must attend a further interview with their caseworker to address issues raised by the HO RFL. The caseworker then puts together a bundle of evidence to support an appeal to the Tribunal. In DA's case, the bundle consisted of: (a) a witness statement by a member of the church he attended in London (which spoke to his faith); (b) a report by a country expert which documented political conditions in Eritrea and the possible risk to DA should the HO return him there (cf. Good 2004); (c) a copy of relevant case law (*MA (Draft Evaders – Illegal Departures – Risk) Eritrea CG* [2007] UKAIT 00059); and (d) a copy of the HO's most recent Country of Origin Report summarizing the objective evidence on Eritrea. These tasks must be completed within five days.

Government legal aid payments, which reflect longstanding status differences between solicitors and barristers, have cemented into place a division of labour between the two types of legal practitioner. Even as legal aid has become the norm in asylum and immigration work, differential payments have ensured that, from the point of view of the appellant, legal representation is discontinuous: caseworkers who are in direct contact with the applicant and who prepare the initial application to the Home Office hand over – instruct – the appeal to a barrister, who litigates the case before an IJ in the Tribunal (barristers also handle appeals in the High Court and the CoA). The principal reason for this division of labour is that legal aid reinforces structural features found in many private law firms, where case preparation is relegated to secondary importance and litigation is seen as the role that wins the appeal (cf. McConville et al. 1994). This is, of course, nonsense because cases that are poorly prepared by a caseworker tend to be refused by IJs. Even so, under legal aid it costs less to instruct a barrister than for the firm to litigate the case itself. The result is that appellants and their barristers have little contact prior to the hearing; also barristers may be instructed late in the day, which can be fatal to the success of an appeal.

To understand how caseworkers prepared their clients' cases for appeal I interviewed 17 solicitors/caseworkers employed in 11 law firms/NGOs. The information they provided, which was confirmed in interviews with barristers and clerks in barristers' chambers, indicates that caseworkers/solicitors do *not* prepare their clients' appeals in the same way. Firms with large asylum/immigration teams (e.g. 20+ caseworkers) had a fairly strict division of labour between the work of Level I caseworkers (responsible for taking an applicant's narrative of flight and transforming it into an asylum claim) and Level II caseworkers/solicitors (who prepare the appeal). The appeal team meet with the applicant to help them understand the appeal process (and to take an additional statement if needed); they also identify and instruct medical and country experts to prepare reports (if required), prepare the bundle and instruct a barrister to litigate the case. However, if the team is small (e.g. one to eight caseworkers), this division of labour becomes blurred, with one caseworker handling a client's initial asylum application *and* any appeal (with limited oversight by a solicitor or Level II caseworker). Some firms informed their clients that if the HO refused their initial application, the firm could not represent them and that the applicant had to find another lawyer (this advice was wrong, and left applicants without legal representation; see Asylum Appellate Project 2009).

It is also the case that many small firms did not commission[4] expert reports (certainly, most did not consult/instruct an expert until after the initial application was refused). Caseworkers in larger firms, however, are more likely contact an expert and ask for advice on the assumption that the claim will be refused.[5] Firms which fail to instruct expert medical or country reports can jeopardize their client's chances of obtaining asylum (though some applications may not raise issues that require expert evidence).

To reiterate a point made earlier, barristers are sought by caseworkers to litigate their client's appeal because most law firms do not possess the expertise to litigate and because it is cheaper to instruct an independent barrister (who is paid by legal aid, not by the firm). I use the term 'instruct'[6] to refer to the way that solicitors or caseworkers approach a barrister for legal advice and request them to litigate their client's appeal. Once again there are wide variations in the ways that barristers are approached and asked to litigate claims.

Solicitors and caseworkers come to know about a barrister in a variety of ways. For instance, the decision to instruct a barrister is partly a reflection of the collective wisdom of members of the asylum team, though information may be picked up at training events held by the Immigration Law Practitioners' Association and from attending seminars at a barristers' chamber.

The decision regarding which barrister should be instructed seems to reflect: (a) the preference of senior members of the appeal team to instruct an individual from a prestigious chamber; (b) the desire to instruct a barrister with a reputation for winning specific types of cases; (c) a decision by the firm to instruct someone they know and trust, e.g. a former caseworker who has become a barrister (the head of one firm instructed his sister, who was struggling to develop her practice); and (d) a decision to save the firm money (resulting in litigating in-house or instructing an independent barrister based on a fixed-fee contract).

Newly qualified barristers acquire clients by taking over cases from their pupil-master at the chamber where they complete their pupillage. Only later and with perseverance does a barrister establish their own client base. Some barristers might be in the fortunate position of absorbing surplus work coming into a large immigration set which is allocated by the set's clerk.

An example shows how barristers are instructed. A number of barristers were litigating claims which raised the issue of draft evasion and illegal departure from Eritrea (i.e. leaving the country without an official exit permit). In late 2006 several sought permission from the Tribunal for their case to be listed as a Country Guidance case (see Chapter 5). The case selected was *MA (Draft Evaders – Illegal Departure – Risk) Eritrea CG* [2007] UKAIT 00059,[7] and it was heard by the Tribunal in March 2007. Against the odds and the direction of prior litigation on this issue, the barrister representing the asylum claimant won. The case consolidated her reputation, and led to numerous firms instructing her to litigate their Eritrean cases.

Independent barristers work out of a chamber or set. The term reflects a continuation of the tradition when barristers rented 'a set' of rooms – initially near the Royal Courts of Justice – from which they practised law. While originally a set might have been used by a single barrister and their clerk, over time barristers have joined together to share rooms and clerks. It is necessary to appreciate the work of clerks and the organization of sets to understand contemporary legal practice.

Since 1970, and due largely to the growing market for legal services, the number of practising barristers rapidly increased: in 1970 there were a total of 2,518 practising barristers; by 1994 the number grew to 7,986 (Blacksell and Fussell 1994). By the mid-1990s about 70 per cent of barristers practised in London.

Table 4.1 The average size of barristers' sets

Inn/location	*1970*	*1980*	*1991*
Lincoln's	8.6	12.4	14.9
Gray's	7.0	12.4	21.3
Temple	11.8	17.5	23.0
Rest of London	1.0	10.0	9.4
London (total)	11.0	15.9	19.9
Provinces	8.5	12.4	15.5

Source: Blacksell and Fussell (1994): table V.

Legislation has directly affected the size, organization and work of barristers and their chambers (see Table 4.1).

Statistics from the Bar Council indicate that in 2010 the number of barristers had grown to 15,387, and that the number of sets located outside London (387) was now slightly greater than in London (347) (Bar Council 2016). The reason for this increase reflects the growing status of the profession, and increasing regulation which, for reasons of efficiency, requires barristers to join together to meet the needs of a diverse range of clients and comply with legal regulation. In recent years there has been a tendency for small chambers to amalgamate, and as sets increase in size they develop a more varied, multi-disciplinary practice – i.e. immigration and asylum, crime, family law, human rights, etc. – to attract a larger client base.

Responsibility for managing the day-to-day running of a chamber falls on barristers, who form a general management committee, and on clerks, who service specific sets – e.g. immigration, crime – and who secure work for its members. When I asked a senior immigration clerk about his relationship to barristers in his set, he said: 'I run their life.' This was not hyperbole. While clients are attracted to a set by the reputation of its barristers, the ability of barristers to successfully represent clients is due to the work of clerks, who are *the* key link between law firms (who employ relatively few administrative staff) and the set. While a certain amount of the work that comes to a set is 'named' – i.e. a firm wishes to instruct a specific barrister – a large percentage of the work is negotiated with clerks over the phone or via email. Because an immigration set tends to be relatively large, the clerk plays a pivotal role in managing and distributing work to members.

Each set is serviced by one or more clerks who are recruited out of secondary school, from other chambers or from the government. While clerks have no legal training, they are expected to possess GCSEs (i.e. a high school diploma), especially in mathematics and English, to be literate (in order to take messages and use the computer system) and to have a good telephone manner. In the past clerks were paid a percentage of a barrister's income (Flood 1983: 6ff.), but today all clerks are salaried. The starting salary of a clerk is £10,000–12,000 per annum. In comparison, first-year barristers (tenants) might expect to earn £30,000 per annum and 'senior' juniors (experienced barristers who have not taken 'the silk' to become a QC) might earn £100,000 per annum.[8]

Clerks control a barrister's diary, which today is an electronic system into which *all* their work is inputted or booked (including a great deal of their social life) as well as all the case-related material. Barristers cannot enter information into their diary. The system lists all of a barrister's work commitments, stores all electronic material sent to the chambers, and contains a record of all correspondence, evidence and other material relevant to their work. Just as importantly, it is from the data stored in this system that clerks bill barristers' clients for their work.

Clerks play an essential role in the work of a set. In addition to booking a barrister's clients and ensuring that those clients are billed, they service existing clients and seek to attract new ones. Thus, when 'named' work comes in for a barrister whose calendar is full, clerks refer the solicitor to another barrister whose calendar is 'quiet'. Clerks ask solicitors what the case is about, to identify the practice area, etc., then, relying on their knowledge of members of the set – e.g. acquired from their involvement in the annual appraisal of barristers, etc. – they suggest several options. For instance, they might refer the solicitor to a junior barrister who worked with the solicitor's preferred barrister on a similar case. Some firms have an understanding that a chamber will handle all of its standard work, e.g. entry clearance appeals. If the preferred barrister is unavailable to take this work – because they are on holiday or engaged in an important case – then, with the firm's permission, a more junior barrister will be instructed to take on the overflow. In the end, however, it is the solicitor's decision regarding who should be instructed.

In large sets clerks organize seminars (where solicitors meet barristers), they liaise with clerks in other teams to 'cross-market' the chamber, they organize the production and distribution of newsletters, and they network with 'friends' in other chambers. Clerks use their own networks or contacts made in the Institute of Barristers' Clerks to 'pick my friends' brains' about how to deal with the LSC, to find a barrister to cover for an absent member or to learn how other chambers are dealing with specific legislative changes, e.g. the shift from fixed to graduated fees, etc. Though clerks begin their day at 8:30 a.m., as one noted: 'There is never a quiet moment.' One could also say, with little hyperbole, that much of the work they do goes unrecognized.

It is worth contrasting the work of independent barristers with barristers in government sets. Whereas all large sets offer a range of legal services, independent chambers tend to be fairly new and espouse an ethos of independence from government (as reflected in the motto of Garden Court: 'Recte faciendo neminem timens', 'Do right, fear no-one'). In at least one independent chamber the ethos of independence extends to a refusal to employ Queen's Counsel (QCs), or 'silks',[9] unless they were involved in establishing the chamber. Barristers from these chambers only undertake litigation on behalf of asylum seekers.

Sets or chambers which specialize in civil and public law are usually situated in government sets. Typically, senior members in such sets eventually join the judiciary, often at a very high level, which means that government sets evince a different ethos and relationship with government than is found in independent chambers. Many barristers in government sets serve on the Attorney General's panels (see UK 2013b) and are instructed, via the Treasury Solicitor's Office, to represent government departments. Barristers may be taken on as pupils in government sets, or they may join a set in mid-career. Typically, once they are accepted onto an Attorney General's panel they find that the volume of their work expands dramatically and that a *very* high percentage of work comes from one or two government departments, e.g. the HO/UKBA or the Ministry of Defence. As these barristers acquire experience, they tend to apply for inclusion in a higher panel group; each panel undertakes a particular type of litigation (see Box 2.1).

An experienced barrister in a government set described the ethos of her chamber as 'a weighty obligation to be fair when you are acting for the government' and 'helping the court to reach the right conclusion'. She saw a huge difference between the ethos of government and independent chambers, and she believed that independent barristers saw their duty to their client as over-riding their professional obligation to the court.

A barrister's specialization in government work is supposedly mitigated by the 'cab rank rule', which requires that all barristers:

> must take a case that is within their knowledge and expertise provided they are free to do so, no matter how unpalatable the case. Although there are practical exceptions, it means that everyone has the chance to be represented by a barrister of their choice, which in turn ensures a fair trial.[10]

In reality, the cost of securing the services of senior barristers in government sets is prohibitive, and barristers on the Attorney General's panels will be so tied up with government work that they will be unable to accept publicly funded asylum and immigration work.[11]

The changing market for legal services created by legislative reform has contributed to the constant disintegration and re-amalgamation of chambers and the movement of barristers back and forth between sets as individuals seek to consolidate their practice by joining a set where they can find like-minded individuals and secure sufficient specialized work. This means that there are wide variations in barristers' legal practice, type of work and caseload. Such differences are a reflection of an individual's seniority/reputation, their area of work and their political orientation and ambitions.

Independent barristers encounter difficulties which do not affect barristers in government sets. For instance, caseworkers who instruct independent barristers may not adequately prepare a case for litigation. Prior to 2003/2004 junior barristers not infrequently found that they were instructed late (and thus had little time to prepare) and that the cases prepared by small firms contained inconsistent statements and gaps in evidence which meant that they found themselves in front of a judge with a case they could not win. While poor case preparation continues to be a problem, particularly in deportation cases, it has declined because many small law firms lost their legal aid contracts (there was an 18 per cent reduction in the number of firms receiving legal aid in London between 2006 and 2009; see Table 4.2).

Table 4.2 Number of law firms/NGOs with legal aid contracts in Greater London, 2006–2009

2006/2007	*2007/2008*	*2008/2009*
191	165	156

Source: Adapted from FOI Request L&G/FOI-09/CH/3792 to Legal Services Commission dated 17 November 2009.

Table 4.3 Expenditure on legal aid, 1997–2009 (£million)

	1997/ 1998	*1998/ 1999*	*1999/ 2000*	*2000/ 2001*	*2001/ 2002*	*2002/ 2003*	*2003/ 2004*	*2004/ 2005*	*2005/ 2006*	*2006/ 2007*	*2007/ 2008*	*2008/ 2009*
Community Legal Services												
Civil and family representation	634	659	565	560	476	483	514	490	547	548	584	650
Civil and family legal help	121	131	144	144	138	162	188	184	182	180	180	176
Immigration and asylum	36	54	54	87	120	168	196	171	102	81	81	87
Total Community Legal Services	791	844	768	791	734	813	898	846	831	809	844	913
Criminal Defence Services total	734	779	783	873	982	1,096	1,179	1,192	1,197	1,171	1,179	1,187
Total legal aid expenditure	1,525	1,623	1,551	1,664	1,716	1,909	2,077	2,038	2,028	1,980	2,023	2,100

Source: FOI Request 66157 to MoJ dated 2 August 2010.

The second problem confronting independent barristers is that the reduction in legal aid fees together with changes in the type of litigation they undertake have reduced their income. Barristers have responded to this situation by diversifying their caseload, e.g. by undertaking deportation appeals (which command lower fees than asylum claims) and taking up privately paid immigration work (e.g. visitor visa appeals and work permit applications). Indeed, between 2002 and 2008 the five junior barristers I interviewed reported that their caseload had shifted dramatically away from asylum to deportation and immigration work.

In 2000 the Legal Services Commission was established with a mandate to control and disburse the legal aid budget, estimated at £2 billion per annum, which paid for legal representation in civil and criminal cases in England and Wales (see Table 4.3).

The data in Table 4.3 indicate that legal aid expenditure for immigration and asylum matters – only one part of the work funded under Community Legal Services – was consistently the smallest spend, particularly in comparison to criminal defence. Furthermore, the rise and fall of expenditure on asylum and immigration probably reflects changes in the number of asylum applications, a reduction in the number of funded hours and the decline in the number of law firms franchised to provide legal aid services.

At about the same time the government created three types of publicly funded franchise/licence: (a) legal help for basic legal advice, including taking an asylum claim; (b) Controlled Legal Representation (CLR) for representing a client before the Tribunal; and (c) certificated work for appeals to the CoA and for judicial review (Singh and Webber 2010). In 2004 the LSC, under pressure from the government, imposed cost limits on asylum and immigration work by capping the number of notional hours available under legal help and CLR to five hours, regardless of the complexity of the case.

In 2004, again under pressure from government to reduce costs and create a competitive market for legal services, the LSC introduced further changes that would eventually undermine legal aid-funded work. First, it introduced staged billing, whereby bills contracted by a firm would only be reimbursed by the LSC every six months. The very slow pace at which the LSC reimbursed firms led, in 2010/2011, to the collapse of Refugee and Migrant Justice (formerly Refugee Legal Services) and Immigration Advisory Services,[12] whose clients were left without representation. Second, the LSC introduced a requirement that legal aid providers must have an overall success rate of 40 per cent on their appeals. Third, it progressively reduced the hourly rate payable for asylum and immigration work below actual costs, which resulted in a drastic reduction in the number of lawyers willing to undertake legal aid work (see Chapter 8).[13] Fourth, it introduced a market for legal services by compelling firms to bid for contracts (inevitably forcing some firms to merge while others were forced out of the market).[14] In 2010 the LSC's administration of the scheme was so poor that it was abolished.[15]

The continued reduction in legal aid has had several effects on the quality of legal practice which are quite separate from reducing the fee a barrister obtains for litigating an appeal. Law firms reacted to cuts in legal aid by relying on in-house advocates (where they had them) to litigate cases, by agreeing a fixed-fee arrangement with barristers to reduce the firms costs, and where an independent barrister is instructed, firms do not fund a conference between the barrister and the appellant. Pre-hearing conferences are important because they enable a barrister to discuss the case with the asylum applicant and help to ensure that the applicant's oral testimony is consistent with their written statements. Because funding is no longer available for these conferences, barristers meet their clients, together with an interpreter, at court just before the case is heard. In short, government efforts to drive down the cost of legal aid have ensured discontinuous legal representation which has not necessarily improved its quality (cf. McConville et al. 1994).

In firms with in-house advocates, the advocate will review the case file (especially the HO RFL) and perform a merits test to assess whether the case has a 51 per cent or greater chance of success. The merits test is assessed in light of the client's case, available objective evidence relating to an applicant's country of origin and existing case law, e.g. relevant country guidance cases or reported Tribunal decisions. If the case passes the merits test – and most do[16] – counsel undertakes a series of preparatory tasks shown in Box 4.1. In-house advocates routinely undertake steps 1–4 and 6–10.

Box 4.1 Preparation for an asylum appeal

1. Draft and write an application to the LSC to secure funding for the appeal.
2. Take instructions from the client.
3. Take instructions from witnesses.
4. Finalize the client's statement with the interpreter.
5. Instruct medical and/or country experts to write reports and read through their reports.
6. Research and prepare the client's bundle.
7. Write the skeleton and a chronology which highlights key elements of case law and objective evidence.
8. Take additional steps to progress the case, including advising the client and witnesses about the appeal process.
9. Submit the bundle and skeleton to the court within the deadline.
10. Meet the client at court prior to the hearing.

When independent barristers are instructed, the sequence of actions can vary. In the first place, they review witness statements to see if they address the HO RFL; if they don't, they may require the instructing solicitor/caseworker to insert additional statements. Barristers are expected to have a better grasp of the objective evidence, including information about specific countries, and they will add new material to the bundle as appropriate. If absolutely necessary, barristers may seek to adjourn the case to allow time to obtain new evidence (though IJs rarely permit adjournments).

Barristers write the grounds of appeal, and the instructing solicitor always makes the funding application. Once the grounds of appeal are filed, barristers usually have a few days to prepare, if they receive the clients bundle in time. Finally, barristers mark up (with Post-its and highlighter) the bundle and cross-reference it to a written skeleton which summarizes key legal arguments, case law and the objective evidence.[17]

The extent to which barristers rely on a skeleton to argue the case varies considerably. What is important about the skeleton is that if a judge decides a case without taking into consideration the barrister's key arguments – outlined in the skeleton which is in the bundle – then it is easier to overturn the decision and obtain a reconsideration of the case. While submitting a written skeleton is a basic step in litigation, some counsel fail to write one; indeed, some individuals completely fail to prepare their client's case (see the case of *India/S* in Chapter 5). Finally, all good counsel meet their client prior to the hearing, to take them through the evidence and remind them what to expect. Just before the time appointed for the hearing, counsel and client enter the hearing room together.

Conclusion

An applicant's often incoherent and incomplete story of flight is pieced together by a caseworker and interpreter and translated into a coherent claim for asylum which is indexed against objective evidence of human rights violations. The actual process of taking a claim is, however, fraught with cultural misunderstandings as well as linguistic and practical problems involved in taking and translating the story.

When the HO rejects an asylum application, it falls to the asylum applicant's caseworker to prepare the case for an appeal to the Tribunal, though case preparation varies with the size and organization of the asylum team and is affected by cuts in legal aid which have led law firms to cut costs. Increasingly, firms have sought to rely upon less experienced in-house advocates, and many do not instruct medical and/or country experts.

The growing market for legal services created by recent legislation has had a decisive impact on legal practice, including the operation of law firms and barristers' chambers: increasing cuts in legal aid and growing regulation have squeezed the income of refugee lawyers, driven many firms out of the market, and pushed remaining firms and chambers to dissolve and re-amalgamate to survive. The government's embrace of neo-liberal market reforms of legal services has focused exclusively on driving costs down; reforms have not addressed professional legal standards nor initiated reforms to legal practice. While cost cutting is clearly restructuring legal services, it will not improve the quality of legal practice.

In this climate of uncertainty, economic concerns rather than considerations about justice tend to determine whether a law firm instructs an in-house advocate or an independent barrister. It is for this reason that barristers' clerks have become so important in creating a demand for their chamber by constantly marketing its barristers, planning and organizing their work, ensuring that barristers have time to prepare a case for litigation and by billing firms for their work.

Notes

1 In October 2007 I attended a week-long training course provided by the Immigration Advisory Services for individuals seeking to pass the LSC accreditation Level I examination.
2 The training course for Level I caseworkers did not provide practical training in interviewing or managing interpreters. It did, however, provide the following advice: 'You are not a scribe. The task is not simply to write down their answers to your questions. Rather you must add value to the entire process.' The examinations which Level I and II caseworkers must pass require candidates to possess basic practical skills in interviewing.
3 Caseworkers had to process a sufficient number of cases to cover three times the value of their gross salary, which was £24,000 per annum. Caseworkers were under considerable stress: one caseworker told me she cried in the bath every night; others spoke of nervous breakdowns and staff 'burnout'.
4 Caseworkers must formally request funding from the LSC for permission to instruct an expert, which requires filing a case plan that summarizes the case, assesses its merits, provides a summary of relevant objective evidence/case law, a cost breakdown of planned work, and the steps that will be taken.
5 The decision about which expert to commission is largely the result of advice from team members and/or soliciting the views of other refugee lawyers via the Refugee Lawyer Google network.
6 The task of instructing a barrister can only be undertaken by a solicitor or caseworker. An instruction establishes a contract between the two parties and has specific connotations for the delivery of a service. See Law Society, 'Instructing a barrister: New standard contractual terms', 24 January 2013, available at: https://www.lawsociety.org.uk/support-services/advice/practice-notes/instructing-a-barrister/ (accessed 8 August 2016).
7 See 'MA (Draft Evaders – Illegal Departures – Risk) Eritrea CG [2007] UKAIT 00059', 26 June 2007, available at: http://www.refworld.org/cgi-bin/texis/vtx/rwmain?docid=46822c3f2 (accessed 6 August 2016).
8 Barristers rent their offices and pay 10–15 per cent of their annual income to their chambers.
9 The title was awarded by the sovereign in recognition of the work of a barrister, who was given a special right of audience in the higher courts where only QCs can argue a case. In 2005 the secrecy surrounding the appointment of QCs ended, and individuals were allowed to apply to a public commission to be appointed a 'silk' (so called for the special silk robes they wear in court).
10 The quotation is from Bar Standards Board, 'Removal of the "cab rank" rule a major threat to justice', available at: https://www.barstandardsboard.org.uk/media-centre/press-releases-and-news/removal-of-the-%E2%80%98cab-rank%E2%80%99-rule-a-major-threat-to-justice/ (accessed 26 March 2013).
11 For an interesting insight about the effectiveness of the cab rank rule, see the blog of an anonymous barrister's clerk, *Clerkingwell*: http://jezhop.wordpress.com/.
12 See: 'Collapsed charity unable to manage its affairs', *The Guardian*, 17 June 2010, available at: http://www.theguardian.com/law/2010/jun/17/rmj-kenneth-clarke (accessed 6 August 2016), and O. Bowcott, 'Tens of thousands lose support as Immigration Advisory Services closes', *The Guardian*, 11 July 2011, available at: http://www.theguardian.com/law/2011/jul/11/immigration-advisory-service-closes-blames-government (accessed 6 August 2016).
13 There were voluminous submissions to the LSC and to parliament on this issue, e.g. White Ryland Solicitors (2006), Refugee Legal Centre (2006) and evidence before Parliament on 12 July 2007 reported in *Hansard*, 12 July 2007: col. 487WH.
14 When the LSC put civil legal aid contracts out to tender in 2010, only 252 of over 400 applicants secured a contract. See J. Robbins, 'Legal aid lawyers facing fight to survive after tendering shakeup', *The Guardian*, 14 July 2010, available at: http://

www.theguardian.com/law/2010/jul/14/legal-aid-lawyers-immigration-shake-up (accessed 16 August 2016).

15 See A. Hirsch 'Ministers axe Legal Services Commission to wrest back control of legal aid budget', *The Guardian*, 2 March 2010, available at: http://www.theguardian.com/uk/2010/mar/03/legal-services-commission-abolished (accessed 16 August 2016).

16 I have been told of firms which accept money for the appeal, only to inform their client that their case fails the merits test. In such cases individuals are left without legal representation and abandon the appeal, or seek to represent themselves, or in a very few cases obtain assistance from an individual who files a 'McKenzie's friend' brief to support their appeal.

17 Practice Direction 52A states: 'The purpose of a skeleton argument is to assist the court by setting out as concisely as practicable the arguments upon which a party intends to rely'; see Gexall, 'Skeleton arguments: If you don't do them properly you won't get paid!', *Civil Litigation Brief*, 11 May 2014, available at: https://civillitigationbrief.wordpress.com/2014/05/11/skeleton-argument-if-you-dont-do-them-properly-you-wont-get-paid/ (accessed 16 August 2016).

5 The Immigration and Asylum Tribunal and the work of Immigration Judges

An asylum applicant whose claim is refused by the Home Office has a right to appeal against that decision to an Immigration Judge who sits in the Asylum and Immigration Tribunal. This chapter examines how appeals were argued by barristers and HOPOs and decided by IJs. Any attempt to understand why some asylum applications are granted while many others that raise similar grounds are refused can only be answered by examining how due process operates in the Tribunal.

The Tribunal system was created in 1957 when, following a public scandal (Gibbard 2002), the government realized that its legitimacy hinged on the right of citizens to appeal against official decisions. While the original idea was to enhance public confidence by creating procedures that were accessible, informal, fair and impartial, this rationale has been undermined by the growing number of cases heard by tribunals and by contradictory demands for justice and higher standards of adjudication and efficiency (Sayers and Webb 1990; Young 1990; Leggatt 2001). The result of these tensions and of government reforms has been to create an adversarial process in which asylum applicants have virtually no chance of success unless they are legally represented.

I begin by looking at the recruitment and training of IJs and their competence and ability to manage hearings, assess legal argument and decide appeals. I then examine the legal architecture of the Tribunal in the form of its Procedural Rules and Practice Directions, which are intended 'to ensure that all citizens receive timely access to justice according to their different needs'.[1] Next I consider the impact of the spatial architecture of the Tribunal on due process. Finally, I look at how IJs decide asylum, bail and deportation appeals. I conclude by considering the effect of the legal and spatial architecture on the manner in which IJs determine asylum appeals.

The work of the Tribunal

The IAT/AIT was created by an Act of Parliament in 1969. Its 20 full-time and 30 part-time 'adjudicators' were expected to decide an estimated 15,000–20,000 appeals per year (Hepple 1969). Today there are 500 immigration judges (including part-time salaried judges) sitting in 14 hearing centres, two magistrates' courts and two immigration detention facilities. The statistics provided in this chapter do *not* provide an accurate measure of its work, for two reasons. First, official statistics combine data on asylum and immigration appeals together, and they include appeals against the decisions of IJs by asylum applicants and the Home Office (i.e. reconsiderations; see Table 6.1). It is therefore impossible to disaggregate asylum from immigration appeals, or initial appeals from reconsideration hearings. Second, because of my focus on asylum, I do not examine immigration appeals. The cost of running the Tribunal in 2010–2011, the only year for which operational costs are available, was £108 million (see UK 2011a, col. 3).

Box 5.1 Principal legislation regulating the work of Immigration Judges

1 The Immigration Act (1971)
2 The Race Relations Act (1976)
3 Section 84 of the Immigration and Asylum Act (1999)
4 The Nationality, Immigration and Asylum Act (2002)
5 The Asylum and Immigration (Treatment of Claimants, etc.) Act (2004)
6 Section 12(2)(a) of the Tribunal Courts and Enforcement Act (2007)

The legislation which the AIT must take into account is voluminous and complex; large sections of key Acts have been repealed by subsequent legislation, which means that lawyers and judges are dependent on computer-mediated systems to ascertain which passages of a statute remain in force and which have been repealed or amended. Unfortunately, the government failed to introduce a Bill to consolidate the various asylum and immigration laws and regulations, which would make it easier for judges, lawyers and officials to navigate the law. When combined with the SSHD's power to issue new Rules and Directions, it should be clear that asylum law is complex.

The work undertaken by IJs is made more difficult by the manner in which they are recruited[2] and trained: most IJs were solicitors with *no* prior knowledge of asylum and immigration law. The Judicial Appointments Board which recruits IJs requires applicants to meet fairly general criteria.[3] Applicants must be:

1 advocates or solicitors of at least five years' standing;
2 a member of the Bar of Northern Ireland, or a solicitor of the Court of Judicature of Northern Ireland of at least five years' standing;
3 someone who, in the Lord Chancellor's opinion, has legal experience which makes them suitable for appointment.

However, the Lord Chancellor can also appoint applicants with non-legal experience.

There is no upper or lower age limit for candidates apart from statutory retirement at the age of 70. Applicants may be a national of the United Kingdom, another Commonwealth country or the Republic of Ireland. Finally, an applicant must be 'of good character', i.e. have no criminal convictions.

While substantial information exists about judges in other jurisdictions in the UK, there is little reliable information about the background – i.e. the gender, age, ethnic identity or training – of IJs. Personal observation suggests that IJs were predominately male, white, middle-aged former solicitors (though a growing number of young immigration lawyers/barristers were recruited as part-time IJs). In 2010 full-time salaried IJs in the first chamber of the AIT earned a salary of £103,921 (plus £4,000 London travel allowance, i.e. four times the salary of caseworkers and twice that of many barristers).

Once they are recruited, IJs receive limited legal training. The annual reports of the Judicial College contain no information about the content of training for IJs, though it is clear that most training takes place in events lasting one day or less. Interviews with part-time IJs indicate that newly appointed IJs were provided with a three- to five-day intensive training programme that introduced them to asylum and immigration law and legislation, case law, 'primary purpose' and family law, aspects of 'judgecraft' (i.e. how to conduct oneself in court), procedural matters, demonstrating impartiality, how to write determinations, and how to handle appeals relating to work permits, visitors, marriage, etc. Annual training is in the form of a one-day 'refresher' or update and two-day training events. Training is provided by Senior Immigration Judges (SIJs) and is said to be very good. When new legislation comes into force, additional courses are provided to bring everyone up to speed.

However, the intensive and condensed nature of training leaves many IJs reeling. The difficulty of getting every IJ up to speed has been met in part by: (a) introducing a system of mentoring whereby an experienced IJ – now the Designated Immigration Judge at a hearing centre – 'shares' a list with a newly appointed IJ and assists them to identify relevant case law, assess the arguments and write a determination; (b) by providing internet resources that provide weekly updates of law, legislation and cases; and (c) by a system of informal networking (with other IJs, but also with lawyers outside the Tribunal).

Interestingly, despite the intense pressure on IJs to decide appeals, the Tribunal had only recently introduced individual performance assessments. However, the assessment, which is conducted by a DIJ, focuses primarily on whether an IJ feels they have mastered the statutes and case law etc. and their behaviour in court. Performance assessment looks cursorily at two or three past decisions to see how their decisions have stood up against appeals. One part-time IJ with 17 years' experience told me that he had never been 'carpeted' for poor decision-making because, he thought, the DIJ simply didn't have the time to examine his work. IJs possess considerable autonomy and exercise an unrivalled authority to decide appeals – despite evidence that not all are up to the job – which helps to explain why the individuals I interviewed enjoyed being an IJ.

A judge in the Upper Tribunal described the work of IJs in the following terms:

> There is far more legal interpretation and less fact-finding[4] when you progress from the first-tier Tribunal to become a Deputy Judge of the Upper Tribunal. This makes the role more intellectually challenging. There is still fact-finding – determinations can be set aside and remade from scratch – but there is more interpretation of what the law, rules and policies mean.
>
> Some appeals can take up to five days, but generally you are hearing between two and four cases per day. Appeals can be very quick because frequently there is no oral evidence, merely legal submissions. And the cases are as wide-ranging as you see in the first-tier Tribunal – visa issues, settlements, adoptions, deportations and asylum.[5]

The authority exercised by IJs is set out in the AIT's Procedural Rules (PRs) and Practice Directions (PDs), which are summarized in Boxes 5.2 and 5.3. Despite the expansion of asylum-related legislation and the volume of appeals decided by the Tribunal, the task facing IJs – to determine appeals against the decision of the SSHD – has not substantially changed. The principal exception to this is the 'specialization' of Upper Tribunal Judges.[6]

As defined by PR no. 4, an IJ's overriding objective is:

> to secure that proceedings before the Tribunal are handled as fairly, quickly and efficiently as possible; and, where appropriate, that members of the Tribunal have responsibility for ensuring this, in the interests of the parties to the proceedings and in the wider public interest.
>
> (Pt I, 4)

Efficiency is sought primarily in terms of preventing possible disruption in the flow of appeals. A notable omission from the Rules and Directions is that little is said about ensuring that justice should be achieved or that judicial decisions should be sustainable. Indeed, it appears that the key role of the Rules and Directions is to regulate appellants, their lawyers and experts.

The Directions and Rules make it very clear that the Tribunal exercises control over all procedural issues and questions of determining law and fact. For this reason it is surprising that the Tribunal has argued that counsel is responsible for delaying legal proceedings given that the biggest source of delay is caused when HOPOs fail to turn up at hearings or because they withdraw at the last minute from the initial decision.[7]

Box 5.2 The Tribunal's legal architecture: Procedural Rules (2011)

1 Citation and commencement
2 Interpretation
3 Scope of these Rules
4 Overriding objective
5 Appeals to the Tribunal
6 Special provisions for imminent removal cases
7 Service of notice of appeal on respondent
8 Filing of documents by respondent
9 Variation of grounds of appeal
10 Method of determining appeal
11 Certification of pending appeal
12 Withdrawal of appeal
13 Abandonment of appeal
14 Hearing appeal in absence of a party
15 Hearing two or more appeals together
16 Adjournment of appeals
17 Giving of determination
18 Special procedures and time limits in asylum appeals
19 Application for permission to appeal
20 Bail
21 General Provisions/Conduct of appeals and applications
22 Directions
23 Notification of hearings
24 Adjournment
25 Representation
26 United Kingdom Representative
27 Interpreters
28 Summoning of witnesses
29 Evidence
30 Language of documents
31 Burden of proof
32 Admission of public to hearings
33 Filing and service of documents
34 Address for service
35 Calculation of time
36 Signature of documents
37 Errors of procedure
38 Correction of orders and determinations

Source: *The Asylum and Immigration Tribunal (Procedure) Rules 2005*, available at: http://www.justice.gov.uk/downloads/tribunals/general/consolidated-ait-rules-191211.pdf (accessed 2 February 2009).

Box 5.3 The Tribunal's legal architecture: Practice Directions

1 Interpretation, etc.
2 Standard directions in fast-track appeals
3 Procedure on appeal
4 Evidence
5 Pursuing appeal after grant of leave
6 Form of notice of appeal etc.
7 Case management review hearings and directions
8 Trial bundles
9 Adjournments

(continued)

(continued)

10 Expert evidence
11 Citation of unreported determinations
12 Starred and Country Guidance determinations
13 Bail applications

Source: UK (2010c).

Unlike in other jurisdictions, the Tribunal exercises wide discretion regarding the evidence which can be submitted to it. PD no. 28 states that:

> (1) The Tribunal may allow oral, documentary or other evidence to be given of any fact which appears to be relevant to an appeal or an application for bail, *even if that evidence would be inadmissible in a court of law* [my emphasis].
> (2) The Tribunal may not compel a party or witness to give any evidence or produce any document which he could not be compelled to give or produce at the trial of a civil claim in the part of the United Kingdom in which the hearing is taking place.

This Practice Direction is double-edged. On the one hand, 'it is for the appellant to prove that the fact asserted is true', i.e. the burden of proof (PR 31), though low, lies with the appellant. However, while the burden of proof may be low, it is nevertheless the case that a very large percentage of asylum applicants have been refused because their evidence is deemed by the Home Office and IJs to lack credibility. In this regard, the UNHCR has argued that:

> In assessing the overall credibility of an applicant's claim, the adjudicator should take into account such factors as the reasonableness of the facts alleged, the overall consistency and coherence of the applicant's story, corroborative evidence adduced by the applicant . . . consistency with common knowledge or generally known facts, and the known situation in the country of origin. *Credibility is established where the applicant has presented a claim which is coherent and plausible, not contradicting generally known facts, and is, on balance, capable of being believed.*
>
> (UNHCR 1998: 3; emphasis in the original)

However, no agreed approach to assessing credibility exists – a situation that results in the rejection of 'somewhere between 48 and 90 per cent of all asylum claims . . . [by IJs] on findings of adverse credibility' (Byrne 2007: 6; see 'The asylum appeal of *Ethiopia/TG*' below).

A further, complicating factor is that the Tribunal believes that it possesses: 'its own level of expertise as a specialist tribunal, not only in the legal issues for its determination, but also in its knowledge of country situations and, to a lesser extent perhaps, in consideration and evaluation of medical reports' (Barnes 2004: 349). The Tribunal's claim of possessing expertise is disputed by country and medical experts. Country experts argue that lawyers, medical experts and social scientists are 'trained professionally to think' in different ways, and that the Tribunal needs social scientists to assess 'the cultural significance of "facts"' (Good 2004). Medical experts, on the other hand, have shown that the manner in which individuals are questioned affects their recall/memory and that 'memory is affected by the need to cope with emotional and traumatic experiences' (Cohen 2002: 300). Indeed, Cohen argues that 'current research on memory shows that stories can change for many reasons and do not necessarily indicate that the narrator is lying'. To the extent that this is true, then a key assumption of HO officials and IJs is undermined, namely that when an applicant's memories are vague and inconsistent, the individual is lying. Once again we see the central and problematic nature of the asylum interview in obtaining key facts about an applicant's claim.

The decisions listed in Box 5.4 indicate how the Tribunal has sought to control the evidence submitted by interpreters and country experts (Good 2004). PD no. 10 reiterates the Civil Procedure Directions (CPDs) (see UK 2014b), which state that expert reports 'should be the independent product of the expert uninfluenced by the pressures of litigation' and that experts should provide 'objective, unbiased opinion on matters within his or her expertise, and should not assume the role of an advocate'. The decisions in Box 5.4 reflect the asymmetric power of the Home Office in asylum proceedings: the HO is not required to produce its own evidence (instead, HOPOs attempt to discredit experts who are instructed by counsel for appellants), and experts must report adverse judicial decisions on their work and reveal their confidential sources.

Box 5.4 Case law and the Tribunal's regulation of 'experts'

1. 'Failure of the respondent [the Home Office] to adduce her own expert evidence cannot imbue expert evidence submitted by an appellant with any greater merit than it deserves' (*ST (Expert Evidence – Kurd – SM Confirmed) Iraq CG* [2008] UKAIT 00094).
2. Experts must 'refer the Tribunal to any cases which he is aware of and which may detract from what is said about him in the cases he has referred to' (*SD (Expert Evidence) Lebanon* [2008] UKAIT 00078).
3. 'Immigration Judges have a duty to consider all the evidence before them when reaching a decision . . . . It may on occasions be appropriate to reject the conclusions reached by an expert. What is crucial is that a reasoned explanation is given for so doing' (*FS (Treatment of Expert Evidence)* [Somalia] UKAIT 00004).

(continued)

(continued)

4 'It is not our view that . . . interview notes can properly be required before the expert evidence is considered, but if they are not . . . that may well result in less weight being put on that source because there is no possibility of testing it . . . it serves to underline the need to properly assess the expert, his or her qualifications and experience to give expert opinion, and the extent to which the data provided can be relied upon as independent, objective and reliable, and to have been impartially sifted' (*LP (LTTE Area – Tamils – Risk?) Sri Lanka* [2007] UKAIT 00076).

5 'The function of a court appointed interpreter is to interpret on behalf of the Tribunal what is said at the hearing . . . It is no part of the interpreter's function to be drawn into a position where he or she has to give 'evidence' at a hearing of anything, including the language being spoken by a witness' (*Mohamed (Role of Interpreter) Somalia* [2011] UKUT 00337 (IAC)).

If expert evidence carried significant weight in the Tribunal, as it does in criminal proceedings, one might understand why IJs regulate experts. As Good (2004) notes, however, the status of experts in the Tribunal is limited: experts provide only hearsay or opinion evidence. This means that IJs decide how much weight, if any, to attach to their evidence. Seen in this light, IJs' efforts to regulate experts illustrate the 'professional vision' of immigration judges, i.e. the *habitus* or situated perspective which emerges from their professional socialization, training, and courtroom practice (cf. Goodwin 1994; Bourdieu 1987).

The issue is not merely, as Good puts it, that the Tribunal's efforts to regulate expert evidence reflects an age-old attempt by the English judiciary 'to maintain its hegemony over the scientific and technical professions from which experts are drawn' (2004: 363). Nor is it simply the case that judicial efforts are informed by a specific vision of 'science' which is an 'empiricist, value-free caricature of the real nature of science', whereas 'disagreement among scientists is normal and natural' (Good, quoting Jones 1994).

The power of the judiciary is reflected in their vision and in the power delegated to them by the Tribunals' legal architecture which authorizes them to regulate and control legal proceedings and all the actors appearing before them *except* representatives of the Home Office. IJs possess the authority to impose their 'vision' by defining the legal issues, deciding which evidence and which submissions to accept and how to decide a case. Their 'perspectival vision', as Goodwin (1994: 626) calls it, is accomplished through the use of a 'complex of situated practices' which are linked to specific discursive procedures 'which structure what kinds of talk can and cannot be heard, who is qualified to speak the truth, and the conditions that establish the rationality of statements'. The 'vision' and authority of IJs is, however, highly contested despite the power vested in them. The cases examined below illustrate how they exercise their power.

The spatial architecture of the Tribunal

The spatial architecture of courtrooms has, since the nineteenth century, partitioned and segregated the parties involved in litigation and, together with the legal architecture, reinforced the power of the judiciary and limited public access to trials (Mulcahy 2007 and 2011). Most asylum appeals are heard in purpose-built hearing centres constructed between 1972 and 1996 (Mulcahy 2007: 389). Considerable space is dedicated for the use of judges (who have offices, a shared library and a dining room), ushers, clerks and administrative staff. In addition to hearing rooms (the number of which depend upon the size of the centre), centres have a small number of secure courtrooms (to hear bail applications) and temporary detention facilities, a large room for HOPOs, and a small number of rooms for counsel to meet their clients.

Mulcahy (2011) notes that while the design of courtrooms has remained 'frozen in time', the exterior design of courts demonstrates varying degrees of 'architectural creativity'. While this is certainly true for magistrate's and criminal courts, and for nineteenth-century 'legal cathedrals' like the Royal Courts of Justice (Brownlee 1983), it does not apply to asylum hearing centres. Hearing centres are purpose-built, modern office blocks of two to six storeys whose exterior is bereft of the symbols of power; indeed, it is impossible to differentiate hearing centres from other buildings.

Centres open their doors to the public shortly before 9 a.m. IJs, court officials, individuals arriving for a bail hearing and asylum applicants (with their counsel and witnesses) all use different entrances. Applicants and legal counsel pass through a metal detector and security check; once inside, they go to the main hall – a large room containing chairs and a few desks – to peruse bulletin boards on which are pinned lists of the cases to be heard. The list is a sheet of paper on which is typed the name of the judge, the number of the hearing room they will be hearing cases in, the name of the HOPO servicing the judge, and the appeals scheduled to be heard. The length of a list reflects the volume of daily case work; most IJs hear one asylum appeal and three to five immigration appeals.[8] Judges and HOPOs are allocated a set number of lists to process each month. Normally, judges complete their lists by early afternoon, after which they retire to write up notes on each hearing, read the submissions and case law, and write a decision.

As Mulcahy notes: 'it was in the mid-19th century that the modern court room was born' through a design which 'sought to reconcile the requirements of authority with those of humanity and publicity'. Courtroom design was increasingly centralized and specified by the judicial authorities. Thus, according to the government's design specification for Crown and magistrates' courts (and by default, asylum hearing centres):

> The courtroom layouts are the result of careful consideration by numerous user groups. They incorporate specific and well-defined relationships between the various participants by means of carefully designed sight lines, distances and levels. It has been found that attempts by individual designers to improve on these layouts have rarely been successful and consequently these layouts are to be adopted in all cases.
>
> (Mulcahy 2007: 389)

The layout of courtrooms reflects a historical process of spatial 'enclosure' which influences how appeals are organized, heard and decided (Mulcahy 2011; Spaulding 2011–2012). The courtroom layout prevents interaction between the various parties and symbolically reinforces the authority of the judge.

The same layout is found in all court houses. Asylum courts reflect a managerial but formal and distant positioning of the IJ – who make their own record of the appeal – who sit on a raised podium that is partitioned from the rest of the courtroom. Immediately opposite and facing the IJ, legal counsel for the state and for the claimant are seated to their right and left. When an appellant or their witnesses give evidence, they and an interpreter sit at a small desk facing the IJ which is located between opposed counsel. Immediately behind these desks are a small number of chairs for the public (which were nearly always unoccupied). The typical size of hearings rooms is small (e.g. a minimum of 6 by 10 metres). While pronounced physical segregation is minimal, nevertheless the spatial architecture clearly reinforces the procedural rules defining who has the right to speak, the forms of speech recognized by the court, and the power of the IJ.

Appeals and the Tribunal

Asylum and immigration appeals resemble criminal trials. The parties assemble in court prior to the arrival of the IJ. As the IJ, dressed in a suit, enters via a side entrance the usher asks everyone to rise. Once the IJ takes their seat, the proceedings begin. Appeals are orchestrated affairs: first, procedural issues are clarified, including whether the evidence/bundles have been served on all the parties. Second, the presence of all the parties (including the interpreter) is confirmed, together with their readiness to proceed. At this point the IJ determines the order in which the appeals will be heard. Third, notions of fairness mean that participants speak by taking turns. Fourth, if the appellant or a witness provides testimony, they are examined in chief by counsel for the appellant and cross-examined by the HOPO (the IJ may also ask questions). Fifth, both parties make a final oral submission. Finally, the IJ reserves their opinion and the hearing ends. The best way to understand how asylum litigation is spatially and legally 'enclosed' is to examine different types of appeals.

The asylum appeal of *Ethiopia/TG*

This case illustrates the many hurdles placed in the way of applicants, the effect of legal enclosures, and the ease with which cases can be dismissed on the basis of adverse credibility findings.

TG claimed asylum as a child. Because of his age, the HO granted him Exceptional Leave to Remain until his 17th birthday, and did not interview him. When TG applied to the HO to extend his leave to remain, the HO refused. That refusal triggered a delayed 2005 appeal which was dismissed by the Tribunal. A reconsideration hearing in 2007 was also dismissed. At this point the case was taken over by a new legal representative who successfully appealed on the papers to the Court of Appeal (see Chapter 6), which ordered that 'there were good and sufficient reasons for allowing the appeal' (i.e. serious errors of law had been made by the IJ who decided the appeal), and another reconsideration hearing was scheduled in November 2008.

The hearing began at 10:15 a.m., at which time the IJ (who was sitting with a DIJ) released the other parties waiting for a hearing and released the interpreter (because, having lived in the UK for six years, TG spoke good English). The IJs checked the bundles and obtained copies of missing material (PD 8); at this point TG's counsel submitted the case law he would be relying upon – *EB (Ethiopia)* v *SSHD* [2007] EWCA Civ 809 – and indicated that he would be making an argument under Art. 8 of the ECHR regarding 'the right to respect for his private and family life, his home and his correspondence'. Counsel indicated that he would argue that the Ethiopian authorities had discriminated against TG on the basis of his ethnicity/race and that TG had been deprived of his nationality by Ethiopia. In response to a question from the IJ, counsel confirmed that a key issue was statelessness arising from persecution. However, the background evidence of ethic/racial discrimination and the arrest and deportation of ethnic 'Eritreans' was not explored during the proceedings, nor was the current situation facing ethnic Eritreans in Ethiopia.

At 10:39 a.m. TG was called to give evidence by his counsel, who took him through the four statements that he had submitted and which were adopted into his evidence. The HOPO cross-examined TG for one hour, focusing on all aspects of his written and oral evidence. Below I look at five issues explored by the HOPO.

HOPO: In your first statement you say you established contact with an uncle. When was your last contact?

TG: About four years ago.

(continued)

(continued)

HOPO: Were you unable to speak to your mother?
TG: Yes.
HOPO: You spoke to your uncle about five times. Did you ask if the authorities were looking for you?
TG: No.
HOPO: For what reason? It never occurred to you to ask?
TG: It was not necessary to ask that question.
HOPO: Were you not concerned that the authorities were still looking for you?
TG: I was happy to be here.
HOPO: Did you not ask whether he had any problems given that he stood surety for you?
TG: No.
HOPO: Did you ask whether your mother had further problems?
TG: No.
HOPO: Can I draw your attention to the earliest statement. It says your brother is 16. Do you remember filling in this form?
TG: Yes, when I arrived.
HOPO: In 2001. It says there was 1½-year difference [in age] between you.
IJ: But you were 16 then, weren't you?
TG: When I was making [writing] that I was about 17.
IJ: Be he couldn't have been 16. So that was a mistake, was it?
TG: That was a mistake.

Questions were then raised about the restaurant owned by his (Eritrean) father which had been raided by Ethiopian security in June 1998 (following which his father had been arrested), about whether 'secret meetings' of Eritreans had occurred there, whether and when it was closed, and TG's work there after he had been expelled from school due to his ethnicity. A few questions were also asked about a subsequent raid on the restaurant when TG and his (Ethiopian) mother, the only family members present, were arrested and taken for questioning.

HOPO: You were detained for some time?
TG: Yes.
HOPO: You said you were released on 31 June 2000?
TG: Yes.
HOPO: There are only 30 days in June.
TG: There are discrepancies between the Ethiopian[9] and the European calendar. In Ethiopia each month has 30 days except the 13th month which has six days . . .

IJ: What day of the week were you arrested on?
TG: I don't remember.

Questioning then focused on his treatment in detention and what occurred when he was transferred to a 'transition camp' where he was detained to await deportation to Eritrea. It was at this point that his Ethiopian mother (who had been released from detention) and her brother secured his release and took him to hospital by offering themselves as sureties.

HOPO: They [the authorities] released you for treatment?
TG: Yes.
HOPO: Were any bail papers given to your mother or uncle?
TG: I don't know.
HOPO: Were any conditions attached to your release?
TG: I have no idea.
[. . .]
HOPO: Who stood surety for you?
TG: I guess my mom and uncle?
HOPO: Don't guess. Were they the sureties?
TG: Yes.

The HOPO's cross-examination was unusually thorough, relentless and sometimes off the mark (e.g. the HOPO assumed that TG, then 13 or 14 years old, would know why many things occurred, when in fact Ethiopian children are not confided in by their elders). Unsurprisingly, the HOPO's key submissions focused on TG's credibility.

When the IJ issued his decision seven days later (PR 17), there was a sharp disparity between the way he set out the background to the claim and his assessment of the facts. He started by noting that TG had to show 'that there was a real risk of persecution as a person who falls within Art. 1(A) of the Refugee Convention'.

The IJ's decision, however, focused entirely on issues of credibility. Thus the IJ began by arguing, following *Karanakaran* [2000] Imm AR 271, that it was the Tribunal's obligation to 'evaluate everything material which has been put before it relating to the appellant' (para. 35). Each of the subsequent nine paragraphs focused on discrepancies in TG's evidence, and there was little attempt to look at TG's evidence in the round against the background of events in Ethiopia in 1998, his age at the time or the fact that at the hearing TG was asked to recall events that had occurred a decade earlier.

Thus at para. 38 the IJ picked up on an apparent discrepancy between the date given in TG's original SEF completed in 2001 that his brother

(continued)

(continued)

was 16, which contradicted TG's oral evidence that he was 16 and that his brother was 1½ years older than him. The IJ concluded that '[T]he appellant has at no stage provided either documentary, or medical, proof of age and the Tribunal is not satisfied that a truthful age on entry was claimed.'

Paragraph 39 argued that TG was unable to explain how his brother 'came to escape the attention' of the authorities and was not arrested, even though he too was of 'mixed ethnicity'. In fact, TG's evidence was that his brother and his uncle were not present at the restaurant during the second raid when TG and his mother were arrested.

Paragraph 40 pursued the same issue: 'The Tribunal was further troubled by the apparent lack of adverse interest that other relatives of the appellant attracted from the Ethiopian authorities.' The IJ noted that the appellant's mother was arrested and released after three days, whilst the uncle was not arrested at all. The IJ went on to argue that '[T]he explanation offered was that these relatives were both Ethiopian and therefore were not of interest. This explanation lacks plausibility.' However, as TG's written evidence and oral testimony pointed out, and as the background evidence indicated, the Ethiopian authorities did not deport Ethiopian nationals: TG's mother and uncle were Ethiopian nationals.

At para. 41 the IJ noted 'a substantial departure in the appellant's story of the goings-on at the family restaurant from the given account at previous hearings'. Whereas at a previous appeal he had said he was involved in 'the collecting of monies at the restaurant', at the 2008 hearing he said that 'he had absolutely no involvement in the collection of funds at any time'. The apparent discrepancy in the date of his release was also picked up, i.e. that June only has 30 days (para. 42), as was his failure to account for a period of two months between his release from the transit camp and his departure to the UK.

The IJ 'concluded that the apparently accurate chronology and dating of claimed events could not be relied upon'. The IJ also presumed that TG would not have been released to sureties from the transit camp (para. 43). Finally, at para. 47 the IJ concluded that 'the evidence of the appellant is riddled with implausibilities and inconsistencies' and he dismissed the appeal.

Shortly after the Tribunal's decision, TG's counsel submitted an application to the Tribunal to reconsider its decision (PR 19) on the basis of a numerous factual errors, the IJ's failure to take account of the age of TG at the time he was arrested, and for failing to consider the expert report. However, the Tribunal refused to reconsider the appeal. TG's counsel made an 'application on the papers' to the CoA, which was refused (see Chapter 6), followed by an 'oral application' to the

CoA which lasted 23 minutes. The Lord Justice took 22 minutes to dismiss the appeal by noting that the case had been heard twice, that he had identified 16 different credibility issues in the claim, that counsel should insist on shorter reports from experts, and that fact-finding fell to the Tribunal.

The Tribunal's approach to credibility (summarized in Box 5.5) consists in a fairly mechanical assessment of the evidence submitted by an asylum applicant in a search for inconsistencies. It is clear that for the Tribunal, credibility consists of 'a complex set of discursive practices and language ideologies that are, in practice, being used as criteria for "truth"' (Blommaert 2001: 414).

Box 5.5 The Tribunal's approach in assessing credibility

Step One: Determination of the material facts
Step Two: Assessment of credibility of the material facts:

a consideration of the internal credibility of an applicant's statements, taking into account level of detail, inconsistencies, and mitigating circumstances that may affect these indicators;
b consideration of the external credibility of the applicant's statements with COI;
c based on the above, asserted 'facts' must be declared 'accepted', 'rejected', or uncertain (those facts that are internally credible ('a', has been satisfied) but lack any external evidence to confirm them ('b', a bit satisfied), these deemed 'unsubstantiated' or 'uncertain' or 'doubtful';
d for 'uncertain' facts, consideration of the benefit of the doubt principle under 339L of the immigration rules, which includes 339L(v), consideration of behaviour stipulated in Section 8 of the Asylum and Immigration (Treatment of Claimants, etc.) Act (2004);
e where all criteria of 339L of the immigration rules are not fulfilled, further consideration on whether the benefit of the doubt should be granted to 'uncertain' facts is required;
f final stage – list of 'accepted' and 'rejected' facts.

Source: UNHCR (2013): 225.

Byrne (2007) has identified barriers to communication which impede the effective assessment of credibility by Tribunals. The barriers include errors in translation, problems of interpretation in an oral hearing, mistakes in transcription of serial interviews, and cultural issues which impede translation and evidentiary barriers. Evidentiary barriers include the weight accorded to preliminary interviews and variations in recall, inconsistency between statements, and limited attempts by an IJ to adequately elicit the applicant's full account.

Byrne argues that:

> The mechanical application of the four traditional criteria of credibility (demeanour, corroboration, consistency and accuracy) to asylum proceedings will inevitably misguide the fact-finding process . . . they also can easily lead to an inaccurate evidentiary record depending upon the fact-finding approach and skills of the interviewer.
>
> (Byrne 2007: 20)

Citing Anker's (1992) study of US immigration courts, Byrne (2007: 20) notes that immigration judges tend to view asylum claims with 'presumptive skepticism' and that 'skepticism is confused, or seen as a component of, rigorous scrutiny by decision makers'. She argues that decisions which rely on findings of adverse credibility fail to adequately elicit a full account from the applicant, and tend to confuse conclusions about core and peripheral issues in the claim. This failure occurs because a skeptical IJ fails to adapt questions to make them 'more culturally accessible or by adequately reframing or following up questions where vague or irresponsive answers may be more the result of culture and education than an indicator of truthfulness' (Byrne 2007: 17). A tendency to rely upon inconsistencies in an applicant's evidence to refuse an appeal is very clear in this case.

The asylum appeal of *Ethiopia/DY*

This case illustrates the effect of architectural and legal enclosures and the work of different actors in shaping its eventual outcome. DY, who was born in Addis Ababa in 1977, fled from Ethiopia to Kenya, and in July 2002 he reached the UK and applied for asylum. However, although the HO issued two RFLs refusing his claim,[10] his initial appeal was not heard for six years. Furthermore, the appeal was adjourned four times (PR 24 and PD 9) because: the instructing solicitor filed the appeal late; the PO Unit lost the file; a key witness failed to attend; finally, the HOPO failed to attend. The decision of the IJ at the first hearing was overturned because he failed to consider the expert report. Below I examine DY's September 2009 reconsideration.

The hearing began at 11 a.m. because DY's counsel had been scheduled by the Tribunal to attend another hearing at the same time. The key issue was whether the HO was right to refuse the appellant under para. 336 of the Immigration Rules, and specifically whether:

> refusing his application would result in him being required to go . . . in breach of the Geneva Convention, to a country in which his life or freedom would be threatened on account of his race, religion, nationality, political opinion or membership of a particular social group.
>
> (Phelan and Gillespie 2007: 761)

When the hearing began, the IJ checked that the bundles were complete (PD 8), whether all the witnesses were present and whether both parties were ready to proceed. He then confirmed that it was to be a *de novo* hearing, and agreed to hear the appellant's witnesses' so that they could be released early.

IJ: Good morning, Mr DY. I expect that you undoubtedly speak English by now. But it is important that you understand everything. Though you may get impatient at points, it is better to have everything interpreted. That means you can use your first language; there is no worries about anything you don't understand. I did my best to pronounce your name, if I made a mistake, I apologize. You applied a long time ago for political asylum. The history of your appeal, you know. The Tribunal is starting all over again . . . . I will not take note of what happened at previous hearings. First thing, it is understandable that you may be nervous today. It doesn't help for me to say, please try to relax. But please try to. You are probably aware of what happens at a hearing, but I'll run through it. First, we will hear from your witness. Then you will give evidence. Then we will hear the evidence of Mrs S. Then Mr A from the Home Office will talk to me about your appeal. Finally, Mr F [DY's counsel] will talk to me on your behalf. After all that, it is my job to decide your appeal on the basis of the evidence. I will not make a decision today. At the end I will explain the procedure. Have you understood what I am saying?

DY [speaking through an interpreter]: Yes.

The first witness, a friend and Ethiopian refugee, testified on oath[11] that he had accompanied DY to the Ethiopian embassy where DY attempted to apply for an Ethiopian passport. However, the embassy refused to assist DY because he did not possess valid Ethiopian documents. The witness was taken through his statement, cross-examined by the HOPO, following which DY's counsel sought further clarification from him regarding his answers to the HOPO. The entire process took 30 minutes. A second witness, an Ethiopian refugee and the appellant's common-law wife and mother of his new-born child, testified on oath about their relationship, their desire to marry and the birth of their son. It was made clear that as an Ethiopian refugee she would not be able to go with the appellant if he were returned to Ethiopia. Her testimony took 30 minutes, and was structured in a similar fashion as occurred with the first witness.

At 12:25 DY was called to give evidence. His counsel took him through his witness statement, which involved confirming events at the Ethiopian embassy.

(continued)

(continued)

F: What did you tell the embassy staff about your family situation in Ethiopia?

A: Mr S asked me . . .

INTERPRETER [in English]: It is the name of the visa counsellor, sir?

A [continues]: . . . the whereabouts of my parents? Where did they come from? I told him my father is Eritrean and my mother was Ethiopian. He asked me whether they are alive. I informed him that I don't know the whereabouts of my two brothers and father and that my mother had passed away. I was not asked beyond that about my family background.

F: In your first witness statement (. . .) you told the embassy official that your birth certificate was with the Home Office and that other documents had been taken by the authorities in Ethiopia?

A: Yes, I did.

F: You say, Mr S [the official at the embassy] said (. . .) that a paper [birth] certificate was not useful. 'Now it's very different'?

A: That's correct.

F: I want to ask you about something [inaudible] in the second witness statement by Ms S . . . about your relationship to your child. In your supplementary witness statement that was submitted soon after N's birth . . . what is your relationship with N? Has it developed . . . ?

A: Yes, it has developed much.

F: Can you describe this development?

A: We have developed a relationship between father and son; it is of intimacy and love.

F: You are not residing full-time with Ms S and your son?

A: That's correct.

F: Why is that?

A: My life is restricted. The HO doesn't allow me to stay with her [. . .]

F: How much time do you spend with the child and the mother?

A: Most of my time.

The HOPO then cross-examined DY for two hours (excluding a break for lunch) regarding (a) his claim to have a 'family life'(clarifying his claim under Art. 8 of the ECHR); (b) his fear of being returned to Ethiopia and the possibility of being deported to Eritrea from Ethiopia (as a Jehovah's Witness); (c) about his family in Ethiopia (his siblings were arrested and had disappeared, his mother was beaten in detention and died shortly after her release, his mother's brother had initially assisted him to leave for Kenya, but had since died); (d) his visit to the Ethiopian embassy; and (e) his treatment by the authorities in Ethiopia (set out below). DY's testimony was in Amharic, and was translated by a court interpreter.

HOPO: You said earlier you arrived with a birth certificate, but other documents were taken off of you?
DY: Correct.
HOPO: How were you able to prevent the authorities taking your birth certificate?
DY: It was found by chance; it was in a book.
HOPO: You refer to a book in your mother's house after being searched?
DY: Yes, sir.
HOPO: Before leaving Ethiopia, did you try to get a replacement Ethiopian ID card?
DY: It was so difficult and frightening to apply. Most of the time I stayed hiding with my uncle. I was unable to approach them.
HOPO: You were released from detention on 20 December 2001 and stayed with your mother in Addis Ababa?
DY: Correct.
HOPO: It was at this time that you discovered that documents were missing from the house?
DY: It was my mother. I was in prison when the documents were taken away, and the birth certificate was found by my mother.
HOPO: She told you when you were released that documents had been taken?
DY: Correct. ID cards, school certificates, prescriptions . . . all were taken away.
HOPO: Those were documents needed to live in Ethiopia?
DY: These are very important to live in Ethiopia.
HOPO: My question is: the authorities didn't want to deport you, though they could have done. They sent you to your mother with reporting instructions. So why didn't you bother replacing essential documents?
DY: When I reported it to the police where I was [inaudible] and discouraged. That was to show . . . I am under their authority through reporting. They can take action against me at any time. I had no right to ask.

(continued)

(continued)

In his cross-examination, DY's counsel confirmed the whereabouts of his birth certificate (it had been given to the HO) and a 1998 medical certificate stating that he had refused a blood transfusion because he was a Jehovah's Witness (the authorities had missed both documents; the latter was accepted as evidence by the IJ under PR 29).

The IJ attempted to limit the length of oral submissions by both parties by invoking PR 4 (to ensure 'that proceedings are handled as fairly, quickly and efficiently as possible'), but he failed to curtail the HOPO's lengthy cross-examination.

I turn now to the final submissions, which, though slightly truncated (as indicated by the insertion of bracketed ellipses), sets out the key factual and legal arguments. As is normal in asylum appeals, the HOPO began first.

HOPO [addressing the IJ]: I rely on the Refusal Letter and case law copied to you, which is MA 2008 and 2009, the Court of Appeal case (. . .).

There is no fear of persecution. The appellant has said his fear is of 'past persecution'. This is no longer valid; it is speculative (. . .). He was not deported; he was released from detention legally; he was asked to comply with reporting conditions; he choose not to report; it was his uncle's idea [for him] to leave (. . .). After his release from detention he realized his documents were taken, but he never attempted to replace those cards.

I would ask you to make adverse credibility findings: when he was released in 2001, he did not attempt to locate his father or brothers. There is a good chance they were not deported. It is not credible that he was detained . . . and not deported. He has provided no documentation of this.

There is no evidence that the appellant was sought by the police; no arrest warrants have been produced.

I refer you to paragraphs 9–15 of the Refusal Letter: there have been massive changes in Ethiopia since his departure. His (. . .) fear is not well founded.

See the objective evidence in the Country of Origin report on Eritrea and the 2008 Home Office OGN.

There is no objective evidence on current risk of persecution.[12]

Regarding *MA Ethiopia*, at paragraph 85, the onus is on the appellant to show risk of deprivation of nationality. At paragraph 83 it states that the appellant must take relevant steps; this appellant has not taken such steps. At paragraph 86 it states that if he is a *de jure* national, Ethiopia will accept him as a national.

There is no reason why he will not be seen by the embassy as a national (. . .).

His Article 3 rights will not be breached if he is returned.

Regarding Article 8, the appellant has spent 25 years in Ethiopia; his removal there would not be disproportionate.

Regarding his partner's evidence, they are aware of each other's status therefore there is no legitimate expectation for them to remain in the UK. His partner doesn't have a legitimate expectation of remaining in the UK beyond 2011.

The relationship is not as close as they say (. . .).

The expert report should be looked at in the round.

Regarding the psychiatrist's report, the appellant suffers from depression, but shows signs of recovery. He can obtain relevant treatment in Ethiopia.

I invite you to dismiss the appeal.

In reply to the HOPO's disjointed submissions, DY's counsel spoke in more measured tones.

F: Many legal hares have been loosed today by my friend [the HOPO] . . .

Regarding case law, the relevant issues in *EB Ethiopia* concern the appellant's 'mixed [ethnic] background'. Note that EB's account [was accepted] by the Court of Appeal. The only action was deprivation of nationality. EB left at the end of the war, see paragraph 62. The AIT had ignored the issue that the removal of her documents constituted deprivation of nationality.

I want to look at the objective evidence before the CoA in detail (. . .). *EB* shows arbitrary or unlawful deprivation of nationality, including core rights attaching, it will be persecution for a Convention Reason (. . .).

The case of *MA* (2008) is not a Country Guidance case; it . . . is not binding on the court.

My principal submission: Ethiopia won't have them [ethnic Eritreans] back. They were detained and arrested because of their ethnic background. They are no longer citizens despite the fact that they have a right to it [citizenship]. Ethiopia has consistently refused to recognize such persons as nationals. My skeleton refers to the relevant Human Rights Watch report documenting the nature of the arrests and expulsions (. . .).

Regarding the Ethiopian Directive of 2004, note that deportees and resident Eritreans were all denationalized during the war. The CoA has dealt with the 2004 Directive. Our position here is the same. All the evidence, including the Expert Report, is consistent on this issue (. . .).

Regarding the embassy visit: all required documentation was changed, even his birth certificate is of no value; the official knew his

(continued)

(continued)

documents were seized (. . .). The appellant faces a real risk of persecution by way of his Eritrean background and his past experience of deprivation of his rights; he is therefore a refugee.

Regarding Article 8, there is evidence of his family life. A proportional argument would conclude that his partner's [legal] status is significant. She came from Ethiopia, and she would not go back to Ethiopia. There is also the position of the child to consider.

IJ: Yes?
F: On my friend's plausibility issues, see the Expert Report.
IJ: You have made your points. Thank you.

The hearing concluded at 4:46 p.m. Ten days later the IJ issued his decision (PR 17), which began by summarizing the history of the appeal. He summarized DY's evidence, which he accepted in its entirety. With respect to case law, the IJ found that the Ethiopian Directive of 2004 did not apply to the appellant because he left Ethiopia before it was promulgated. The IJ also accepted the evidence of Ms S regarding the nature of their family life. Indeed, the IJ concluded that:

> It is difficult to know what further corroboration the Appellant could produce given his evidence that almost all of his family documents were taken by the authorities . . . . [T]here is in short no cogent challenge to the evidence of the Appellant and no significant inconsistency within or surrounding it.

Finally, the IJ concluded that 'There is considerable evidence that the Appellant is no longer regarded by the Ethiopian authorities as a national of Ethiopia' and that 'although a citizen of Ethiopia at birth, he has been deprived by the Ethiopian government of his nationality without any appeal or redress'. The judge set aside the original decision by the Tribunal and allowed the appeal.

Before analysing the decision, it is worth noting that interpreters do *not* provide a running translation of proceedings to appellants, nor did DY's knowledge of English allow him to understand what was said. In common with many appellants, DY was unable to participate in his appeal in any meaningful way. While he responded to the questions put to him through the interpreter, each question had to be phrased in the form of a simple proposition which could easily be translated.

While the IJ invoked PR no. 4 – to limit legal submissions to ensure that both parties have equal time to present their arguments – he was unable to prevent the HOPO from dominating the proceedings. The situation could have disadvantaged DY's counsel, but this was partly mitigated because he had submitted a detailed skeleton. Fortunately, the IJ's decision was a balanced consideration of the arguments/evidence and was well written. In terms of how HOPOs describe judges, the decision reflected the work of a 'good' judge, and his detailed decision would be difficult to overturn on appeal.

Practice Rule no. 17 allows both parties 10 'working days' to appeal against an IJ's decision. Statistics on the outcome of appeals made by appellants and the SSHD indicate that during 2000–2004 – the only period for which complete statistics are available – less than 20 per cent of appeals brought by appellants were allowed, whereas 40–60 per cent of appeals brought by the SSHD were allowed (ICAR 2009: 12–13).[13] Data regarding applications for reconsideration against a decision by the Tribunal for the period 2006–2009 only reveal that the Tribunal allowed 32–46 per cent of appeals by both parties (see Table 6.1). The huge disparity indicated by these statistics suggests that the Tribunal defers to the SSHD (though why this occurs is not clear). Given the importance of understanding the relationship between the Tribunal, the Home Office and independent counsel, the government needs to collect better statistics on this issue.

Bail hearings

Every year about 30,000 individuals are placed in immigration detention. While many detainees are asylum seekers waiting for a decision on their appeal in the DFT, there are also many migrants and foreign national prisoners awaiting deportation (BID 2009). Detainees are entitled to challenge the government's decision to detain them, and according to PR 20, an application for bail should be listed for a hearing within three days.

The courtroom for bail hearings where I followed cases had recently been redesigned due to apprehension about the risk posed by appellants. Not only were all the furnishings fixed to the floor, the courtroom had three entrances/exits: a secure passage in from the main hearing centre for HOPOs, legal counsel and sureties (guarded by two security guards); an entrance for the IJ (beside the dais); and an entrance to the facility where detainees are held. When detainees are brought into court, they are escorted by three guards and seated inside a Perspex 'box'.[14] The guards surround the appellant, and an usher sits at the public entrance to alert officers outside if there are problems. Eight bail hearings were listed to be heard on the day I attended, but only six individuals were brought to court.

Table 5.1 Bail applications, 2007–2008

Year	*Granted*	*Refused*	*Withdrawn*[1]	*Total*
2007	1,982 (22%)	4,108 (46%)	2,828 (32%)	8,926
2008	1,089 (18%)	2,860 (48%)	1,993 (33%)	5,966

Source: FOI request 55519 by Bail for Immigration Detainees to MoJ dated 6 September 2008.

Notes:

1 Applications were withdrawn because the applicant failed to attend court (was not brought there by security staff) or because they had been deported. The figures provided by the MoJ do not add up.

The bail hearing of *Algeria/K*

K entered court and sat near the box to the right of the IJ. He was not represented because he could not pay a solicitor, and there was no interpreter. His Bail Summary (see Box 5.6)[15] had been served on him, and he was asked if he had read and understood it. The HOPO confirmed that a travel document was being validated to return him to Algeria, but K did not respond. The IJ read out the Bail Summary:

IJ: You came to the UK in July 2001? Your claim was refused in 2003? You appealed, and the appeal was dismissed in April 2004? There was nothing further until you were arrested in August 2005 as an illegal immigrant. Subsequently, you had problems with your girlfriend and the police were involved?

K: When she found out I was an asylum seeker, her attitude towards me changed and she asked me to leave the house, but I had nowhere to go (. . .)

IJ: You will be going back to Algeria. Why do you want bail?

K: My family is from Lebanon. I am still an asylum seeker from problems in Palestine.

IJ: If bailed, where would you live?

K: With a friend in a shared house, I have given his address.

IJ: Is he here today?

K: No, he is in Nottingham.

IJ: What do you mean 'a shared house'?

K: Several people live in it.

HOPO: Why is your friend, the landlord of the shared house, not here today?

K: [incoherent reply]

HOPO: Will you return to your own country?

K: To Palestine.

HOPO: You are not willing to return to Algeria?

K: No, there are problems for me there (. . .). My solicitor has taken 'new evidence' but has done nothing for me.

HOPO: I rely on the Bail Summary and oral evidence. He has failed to comply with reporting conditions. He is unwilling to return to Algeria. I ask that you do not grant bail.

IJ [to K]: Do you have anything new to say?
[K begins to repeat himself, and is stopped by the IJ.]

IJ: These concern your problem with the solicitor and problems of a general nature. Anything else?

K: No.

IJ: I am required to decide bail. The appellant has exhausted his appeal rights and an ETD is ready. I refuse bail for now.

The appellant was quickly taken out, and the IJ signed the relevant papers before conferring with the usher about the next case.

Box 5.6 The Bail Application Notice

The Bail Application Notice (or Bail Summary) contains:

- a the applicant's full name, date of birth and date of arrival in the United Kingdom;
- b the address of the place where the applicant is detained;
- c whether an appeal by the applicant to the Tribunal is pending;
- d the address where the applicant will reside if their application for bail is granted, or, if they are unable to give such an address, the reason why an address is not given;
- e where the applicant is aged 18 or over, whether they will, if required, agree as a condition of bail to co-operate with electronic monitoring under s. 36 of the 2004 Act;
- f the amount of the recognizance in which they will agree to be bound;
- g the full names, addresses, occupations and dates of birth of any persons who have agreed to act as sureties for the applicant if bail is granted, and the amounts of the recognizances in which they will agree to be bound;
- h the grounds on which the application is made and, where a previous application has been refused, full details of any change in circumstances since the refusal;
- i whether an interpreter will be required at the hearing, and in respect of what language or dialect.

Source: *Tribunal Procedural Rules* (2005), Pt IV, Rule 37.

Many bail applications are made without benefit of legal counsel, which increases the likelihood that bail will be refused. This occurs because, as in the case of *Algeria/K*, IJs tend to consider whether an applicant is likely to abscond, i.e. fail to comply with conditions set for bail, and they ignore 'all other factors, such as length of detention, ill-health . . . '. In short, they 'tend to reverse the burden of proof onto the applicant, by focusing on risk of absconding', which tends to support the Secretary of State's argument for continued detention (Burnham 2003: 14). Indeed, a narrow approach to deciding bail was reflected in the HOPO's submission in K's appeal. In the HOPO's view, justice would be served by detaining him until his emergency travel document was revalidated. It is worth noting that in the experience of HOPOs, the majority of IJs refuse bail applications.[16]

The procedure for hearing bail applications is that the only person who is allowed to speak with the applicant is their counsel (and only for 10 minutes in the secure facility). If an application is refused, detainees can make a further application (if they are wrongly detained, their counsel can apply for a judicial review or they can file a *habeas corpus* petition). Available statistics indicate that during 2007–2008 only one in five bail applications succeeded.

Deportation hearings

Deportation cases are normally heard by a panel consisting of an IJ and a lay judge. This hearing took place in a court attached to a London immigration detention centre. Detainees enter via the detention centre, and can be brought into a consultation room to meet counsel prior to the hearing; they enter the courtroom via a secure rotating glass door between the detention facility and the courtroom. The layout of the courtroom mirrors that found in hearing centres. There is a raised dais for the judge which is partitioned off from everyone else. In front, and facing the judges, sit opposed legal counsel; the appellant sits to the left of counsel (one security officer sits beside the appellant; a second sits near the entrance). There is space for six visitors at the back.

The principal legislation relied upon for deporting individuals is s. 3(5)A of the Immigration Act (1971),[17] which states that:

> 3(5) A person who is not a British citizen is liable to deportation from the United Kingdom if (a) the Secretary of State deems his deportation to be conducive to the public good; or (b) another person to whose family he belongs is or has been ordered to be deported.
>
> 3(6) Without prejudice to the operation of subsection (5) above, a person who is not [a British citizen] shall also be liable to deportation from the United Kingdom if, after he has attained the age of seventeen, he is convicted of an offence for which he is punishable with imprisonment and his conviction is recommended for deportation by a court empowered by this Act to do so.

The deportation hearing of *India/S*

S's solicitor arrived early, but did not attempt to meet with S prior to the hearing. In fact, the solicitor had not taken a statement from S. Twenty minutes later, the IJ and lay judge entered court to discuss preliminary issues (PR 8). However, they decided to hear another case first, so S was returned to a holding cell. About four hours later he was escorted back into court by two guards. His wife and solicitor were present.

IJ: Good afternoon. Let's do a document check [this reveals the respondent's slim bundle, the grounds of appeal and a statement by Mrs S]. Nothing more?

COUNSEL (C): There is no statement from the appellant. This is because there was confusion caused by the previous solicitor. We were told the case was adjourned to the 25th, but I was notified two days ago by the court that the hearing date was changed. I have not had an opportunity to take a statement from the appellant [. . .]. [He then calls the appellant to confirm evidence in a statement taken two years ago.] Can you confirm your name and address?

S: Mr S.

C: What is your relationship to the surety?

S: She is my wife.

C: How long have you been in the UK?

S: 10 years.

C [to IJ]: I need to check whether the appellant understands English or he needs an interpreter. [He then speaks to S in another language.]

C: He says he can understand English, but finds it difficult to speak in English. I have only met him today, was there a request for an interpreter?

IJ: No request was made.

C: I am surprised that his previous solicitor did not arrange for this.

His solicitor established that all of his family live in the UK (a wife, two children, a sister and his father-in-law) and that he has no family in India. The solicitor took him through his immigration history, including two brief trips to India. He then called Mrs S (who was in her early 30s and not well-dressed) and took her through her statement.

C: Can you confirm your name and address [she does this]. Talk loudly and speak to the learned panel. Is this your statement? I want to ask you a few questions.

MRS S: Okay.

C: Is it true?

MRS S: Yes.

C: Can you explain what difficulties you have had since your husband's arrest?

MRS S: It's been really bad. I am working three days a week and night shift.

(continued)

(continued)

C: Where are you working?
MRS S: At a grocery store.
C: How long have you been doing this?
MRS S: For 1½ years since his arrest; it's been hard. The children are at my parents', but Mom's got arthritis.
C: Are your family here?
MRS S: All my family are here. My brother, sister. I born here and the children born here. He has no parents [in] India.
C: What did he do?
MRS S: A building contractor.
C: Were you working?
MRS S: It was easy then. I worked the day shift and we had time for the children.
C: When you went to India, what was it like?
MRS S: We stayed a couple of weeks, the kids and I were [*sic*] ill. We had to go home (. . .)
C: Could you live in India?
MRS S: No, I can't live there.
IJ: Can you live without your husband?
MRS S: We've got everything here.
C: Who else lives at your address?
MRS S: Me and the children.
C: Do you own the property?
MRS S: We own it; a mortgage for nearly 10 years.
C: No further questions.

The HOPO cross-examined Mrs S about family visits to India and established that she knew that her husband only had discretionary leave to remain in the UK. He then made his final submissions to the court.

HOPO: I rely on the Refusal Letter (. . .). The SSHD seeks to deport him on the basis of his criminal conviction. The judge in the criminal trial noted of his role in the affair that if he wasn't the ring leader, he was certainly a leader.[18]
Concerning the appellant's claim: (a) there are no health issues barring his return; (b) he is self-employed, he can do the same work back in India; (c) his wife's evidence is that they own a house which can be sold and used to purchase a house in India; (d) there is nothing in the claim as to why he cannot return; there are relatives there (. . .); (e) his wife says she can't return, but she married him without knowing his immigration status (. . .); finally (f) the SSHD has made the right decision, there is nothing to show that they cannot enjoy family life in India.

C:	It would be cruel to deport him. The facts are before you. Think of the emotional strain on the wife from being separated for two years. If he is deported, he will not be able to return for at least three years. The children are of school age, and she is working unusual hours.
IJ:	That is the result of a prior sentence.
C:	Indeed (. . .). Both she and the children are raised in this country. Their previous experience there was very unhappy. It would be unduly harsh to return him, given her family here. To deport him would mean to pay the price twice. There is very little else I can add.

The appeal was concluded in 40 minutes, and the IJ reserved his decision. The poor quality of S's legal 'representation' should be evident. First, the solicitor failed to take instructions from his client. Second, he failed to confirm whether the hearing was to make a deportation order or to appeal against a deportation order. Third, he failed to make clear the amount of the bond which the appellant's wife was to provide. His failures ensured that the IJ did not consider 'bail in principle' (the first stage of a bail hearing). Finally, the solicitor failed to submit a skeleton outlining his arguments and relevant case law. As the HOPO made clear to me, there was a very strong probability that S's appeal would be dismissed and that he would be deported.

I observed a number of deportation hearings, all of which followed a standard pattern: they are of short duration, many appellants are not legally represented, and appellants tend to have been detained for fairly lengthy periods. Many individuals will have had their asylum appeal determined while in detention (IJs are reluctant to examine the history of the appeal). Indeed, it was common to hear IJs ask appellants whether they 'told the truth' at a previous hearing. It should also be recalled that most appellants do not speak English, and thus find it difficult to follow the proceedings.

The limited research on deportation hearings makes it clear that legal representation is critical to success, and that the majority of detainees are held for lengthy periods[19] (following which, some individuals are deported, though many are eventually released – see Chapter 8; see also BID 2010; London Detainee Support Group 2010; Silverman and Hajela 2012). Gibney (2008: 17) has argued that 'The government's increasing ability to detain thus appears to rest on its dubious practice of truncating and telescoping refugee determination procedures' to facilitate quick decisions and an efficient use of a growing detention estate. He notes that the number of deportations from the UK increased from 1,820 in 1993 to 16,630 in 2006 (Gibney 2008: 4). However, official data on the number of successful appeals against deportation and whether (and when) unsuccessful appellants were deported is unreliable (The Migration Observatory 2014). The data for 2010 indicate that there were 850 appeals against deportation, and that approximately 27 per cent were successful.[20]

Conclusion

The Tribunal's Procedural Rules and Practice Directions provide IJs – many of whom have limited knowledge of asylum and immigration law – with considerable power to speedily decide appeals. Efficiency is sought by regulating independent legal counsel and experts. By drawing upon the Tribunal's legal architecture, IJs define whose speech and what forms of speech are legally salient, and what weight to attach to written and oral evidence. 'Good' IJs draw out a full record of the evidence and consider all the material 'in the round' and against the background of country conditions; skeptical IJs use the Procedural Rules and Practice Directions to truncate oral evidence, enabling them to speedily refuse an appeal. Many IJs are not particularly good – a fact that is clearly indicated by the overwhelming tendency to refuse large numbers of claims on the basis that a claim lacks credibility. As the case of *Ethiopia/TG* suggests, an attack on the credibility of an applicant is an unfair way of deciding a case because such decisions are impossible to challenge.

The data on the outcome of appeals suggest that the Tribunal plays an important role in scrutinizing and overturning poor decision-making by front-line HOPOs. The evidence also indicates, however, that without good legal representation it is virtually impossible to get status, obtain bail or fight against deportation.

Two conclusions emerge from this chapter. First, and contrary to the conclusions of Meili (2013), the quality of legal counsel involved in asylum litigation varies widely: thus the barristers representing *Ethiopia/TG* and *Ethiopia/DY* both sought to invoke international law to win their clients' appeals (but only one provided sufficient objective evidence to support his arguments), while the solicitor who represented *India/DS* was incompetent. Second, the evidence suggests that with regard to bail applications and appeals against deportation, IJs unduly defer to the Home Office.

The spatial architecture of the Tribunal buttresses the power of the IJ and facilitates the 'efficiency' of appeals by segregating and controlling what parties say. Unfortunately, recruitment practices, coupled with a lack of training and the absence of guidelines on issues such as credibility, contribute to an unwarranted professional hubris which results in a relatively large number of unsustainable decisions, as evidenced by the number of appeals overturned in the CoA (see Chapter 6).

Notes

1 The quote is from the Ministry of Justice website, which sets out the nature and work of Tribunals in the UK, at: http://www.justice.gov.uk/about/hmcts (accessed 10 November 2015). As of April 2011 the various Tribunals in the UK were hearing 800,000 cases annually.

2 In late 2008 there was a rush to recruit extra judges to handle a growing backlog of appeals due in part to the Asylum and Immigration (Treatment of Claimants) Act (2004), which replaced the existing two-tier Tribunal with a single-tier system. In

effect, all appeals by asylum claimants went automatically to the High Court, which was overwhelmed by applications for judicial review; see F. Gibb, 'Extra judges drafted in to hear immigration appeals', *The Times*, 15 December 2008, available at: http://www.thetimes.co.uk/tto/law/article2214070.ece (accessed 8 August 2016).

3 Source: recent advertisements by the Judicial Appointments Commission for IJs.

4 The IJs I interviewed emphasized that their first task in hearing an asylum appeal was to ascertain the facts, then to apply the law to those facts (cf. Hickinbottom 2010).

5 'Jane Coker – Deputy Judge of the Upper Tribunal, Immigration and Asylum Chamber', at: http://jac.judiciary.gov.uk/1397.htm (accessed 24 June 2011).

6 E.g. deciding Country Guidance cases. In 2011 a small number of Upper Tribunal judges began to hear applications for judicial review against the decisions made by IJs (see Mullan 2012).

7 See Gherson Immigration, 'A step in the right direction for UKBA but further regulation required', *Gherson*, 18 January 2013, available at: http://www.gherson.com/blog/a-step-in-the-right-direction-for-ukba-but-further-regulation-required/ (accessed 8 August 2016).

8 The judges I interviewed said that they attempted to read a case file prior to the hearing to avoid any surprises and to familiarize themselves with the relevant law and submissions.

9 The Ethiopian Orthodox calendar is based on the Gregorian system and is 267 years out of sync with the European calendar; see 'Ethiopian calendar', *Selamta*, available at: http://www.selamta.net/Ethiopian%20Calendar.htm (accessed 8 August 2016).

10 A second RFL suggests that a HOPO believed the original decision was not sustainable.

11 Both witnesses took an oath on the Bible. On the witness table/stand a Holy Bible, the Koran and the Bhagavad Gita are available for swearing in witnesses.

12 The HOPO was relying on s. 3.8, 'Persons of mixed Ethiopian/Eritrean origin', in the 2008 Home Office OGN on Ethiopia (UK 2008a). However, the OGN provided an incomplete assessment of the evidence, and thus an incorrect view of the risk facing 'Ethiopians of Eritrean parentage'.

13 Attempts to obtain more recent data using the Freedom of Information Act reveal that neither the MoJ nor the Home Office consistently recorded this data after 2005.

14 At the time of the hearing the box was judged to be too low to prevent the appellant from vaulting over it and attacking the IJ or self-harming. Prior to each hearing the usher was informed about the appellant's state of mind, and warned the IJ accordingly. At the first sign of trouble IJs were instructed to leave quickly via their exit, though most male IJs tended to sit through the 'rant'.

15 A Bail Summary is produced for each applicant based on data from government databases. The form is divided into three parts: (i) the individual's immigration history; (ii) a summary of why bail should be refused; and (iii) a check on the appellant's sureties. Only a copy of the Bail Refusal Summary is provided to appellants.

16 I was present at one appeal where the applicant was released into the custody of his well-off brother who brought a criminal solicitor to attest to the sureties standing in the community. Recently, many bail applications are heard using Skype, with applicants appealing from prison to an IJ sitting in a remote hearing centre.

17 See 'Immigration Act 1971', c. 77, Pt I, s. 3, available at: http://www.legislation.gov.uk/ukpga/1971/77/section/3 (accessed 8 August 2016).

18 There was a family dispute during which an individual was kidnapped and beaten before being released. The appellant was convicted of kidnap and aggravated assault.

19 In 2011, following lengthy litigation, the UK Supreme Court found that the Home Office had, since 2006, been operating a 'secret' and unlawful policy of detaining

foreign nationals. See A. Wagner, 'Secret foreign nationals detention policy was "serious abuse of power"', *UK Human Rights Blog*, 23 March 2011, available at: http://ukhumanrightsblog.com/2011/03/23/secret-foreign-nationals-detention-policy-was-serious-abuse-of-power/ (accessed 8 August 2016).

20 See the figures provided by the Human Rights Futures Project, 'Deportation and the right to respect for private and family life under Article 8 HRA', July 2011 (London: Human Rights Futures Project, London School of Economics), available at: http://image.guardian.co.uk/sys-files/Guardian/documents/2011/10/04/KlugDeportation.pdf (accessed 8 August 2016).

6 The politics of 'permission' and the Court of Appeal

A limited right of appeal against a decision by the SSHD was established in the Immigration Act (1971) and was substantially broadened in the Asylum and Immigration Appeals Act (1993). Subsequently, the HO has argued for, and Parliament has adopted, legislation and policies which have substantially reduced the right of appeal. This chapter examines the appeal process as it operated between 2007 and 2009. In particular, I examine the basis on which appeals were made and how the Tribunal and the Court of Appeal decided asylum appeals.

In this chapter I only examine in-country asylum appeals.[1] As will be discussed below, the government sought to limit the number of asylum (and immigration) appeals reaching the Administrative Court by reducing the right of appeal and by reorganizing the appeal system. I begin by reviewing government policy for the period 2002–2007, which, in the words of Richard Rawlings (2005: 378), witnessed an attempt by the government to introduce 'a revenge package' of measures 'designed to pre-empt or drastically reduce a whole activity of formal legal challenge' to asylum law and policy. In the second section I examine how AIT decisions were reviewed by the Tribunal, which 'filtered' and limited appeals to the CoA. The third section examines how counsel for appellants challenged the Tribunal's refusal to reconsider an appeal by making an application on 'the papers' to the CoA, and if that failed, by making an 'oral application' to a Lord Justice for permission to appeal. I look at three 'oral' applications and one statutory appeal which illustrate how the CoA reviews and decides appeals. I conclude by noting the fundamental role played by the CoA in its oversight of the Tribunal.

The government and the asylum process: review, revenge, retreat . . . legislate

In an effort to prevent the appeal system from being 'abused' by asylum seekers, four major pieces of legislation were introduced prior to 2007 to reduce the appeal rights of asylum seekers.[2] First, the Asylum and Immigration Act (1996) extended the fast-track appeals process to include individuals who were deemed to have come from 'safe countries'. The Immigration and Asylum Act (1999) introduced a general right of appeal based on the Human Rights Act (1998), but it also allowed certain claims to be certified as 'manifestly unfounded' (with a restricted right of appeal). The Nationality, Immigration and Asylum Act (2002) prohibited an in-country right of appeal for individuals whose claims were certified as 'clearly unfounded' and for individuals coming from an larger number of 'safe countries', and it ended the possibility of appealing against an IJ's assessment of the facts of a case. Overall, if an asylum application was not certified, the individual was able to access their appeal rights.

The Tribunal was also subject to continuous reforms, including the appointment of a High Court judge as its president, the creation of Country Guidance cases and 'starred' decisions to provide greater consistency in decision-making, the creation of Designated Immigration Judges to oversee the training and management of IJs, and the re-categorization of adjudicators to differentiate between Senior Immigration Judges and Immigration Judges (the former are expected to provide judicial management and leadership; Thomas 2005: 489f.).

In 2003 the government announced the Asylum and Immigration (Treatment of Claimants etc.) Act, but before it was scheduled for parliamentary scrutiny, a massive debate arose over the Bill. As Rawlings (2005) argued, the 2004 Act represented a broad-based attack against the asylum system. First, it attempted to sharply reduce the legal aid budget, and thus the supply of legal services. Second, it sought to abolish the Immigration Appeal Tribunal – the second tier which heard appeals – and to sharply reduce rights of appeal. Finally, it would have eliminated oversight of the Tribunal by the appellate courts by introducing an ouster clause preventing judicial review and appeals to the CoA. The politics surrounding the initial draft of this Bill were discussed in Chapter 2. It is worth noting, however, that while the government initially backed away from an all-encompassing Bill, it adopted a more tactical approach by subsequently reintroducing each contentious issue in separate legislative Acts which came into effect after 2009.

The 2004 Act, as adopted, introduced a single-tier appeals process and new Procedural Rules for hearing appeals,[3] but it did *not* eliminate the right of applicants to appeal to the CoA. The new procedures created a 'notice of decision' that required both parties to lodge an appeal with the Tribunal within five working days. The completed form should set out the legal reason(s) why the appeal should be granted (ICAR 2007a). There were three broad grounds on which an appeal could be made: (1) if removal of the applicant breached the UK's obligations under the Refugee Convention, the European Convention on Human Rights or the UK Human Rights Act (1998); (2) on the basis of racial discrimination;[4] and (3) on the basis of a serious error of law.

The government decoupled the issue of legal aid from the 2004 Bill, but pursued two different measures towards the same end. In 2004 the government introduced a consultation on 'proposed changes to publicly funded immigration and asylum work' (UK 2004a). Following the 'consultation' – which most of those who commented on the proposal clearly did *not* support – a 'new financial threshold' was introduced of a maximum of five hours of legal aid to pay a caseworker to take and file the initial asylum claim; no additional funding was allowed without prior authorization by the LSC. The government also announced that formal accreditation[5] would be required for all asylum caseworkers and that there would be a move to recognize 'a smaller number of suppliers' of legal services through a system of tendering for legal service contracts. In short, the government introduced a market for legal services. In 2004 the effect of the cuts on the fees earned by immigration barristers was offset by the introduction of a special 'risk premium' which mitigated the risk of taking on clients whose cases might not be particularly strong (UK 2004b). The government introduced a 35 per cent 'uplift' payment to barristers/advocates if they successfully argued such appeals (though payment was subject to long delays).

In 2005 the Department for Constitutional Affairs, citing the rapid growth of expenditure on legal aid and a 'growing legal practitioner market', reformed legal aid (UK 2005a; see Chapter 8 in this volume). Those opposed to the proposals argued, with what proved to be considerable prescience: (a) that the proposals would undermine access to justice by the most vulnerable; (b) that many law firms would be forced out of business; and (c) that practitioners would quit legal aid work. During the next four years legal practitioners, led by the Law Society, unsuccessfully attempted to rally support against cuts to the legal aid budget and associated 'market' reforms.[6] Unsurprisingly, between 2005 and 2009 growing numbers of immigration law firms closed, with the result that in many areas of England, Wales and Scotland to which asylum applicants were compulsorily 'dispersed', law firms were not available to assist asylum applicants to file and litigate their asylum claims (see Table 4.2).[7]

The elimination of a two-tier Tribunal and its replacement by a single-tier one was intended to counter the high number of applications for 'leave to appeal' against Tribunal decisions. In fact, even though the onward right of appeal to the CoA was not eliminated, the abolition of the second tier slowed the Tribunal's ability to hear appeals and added to the backlog of appeals caused, in part, by the failure of the Judicial Appointments Committee to recruit IJs (ICAR 2007a: 13).[8] Thus during 2001–2003 only 43 per cent of appeals were determined by the Tribunal within 17 weeks (against a target of 65 per cent; ICAR 2009). In 2004/2005 the Tribunal met its revised target by processing 67 per cent of substantial appeals (the target was 60 per cent), and in subsequent years the Tribunal met its revised target by deciding 40 per cent of appeals within six months. (in 2007 IJs were expected to hear three cases per day and issue determinations on the following day; ICAR 2007a: 11). The backlog of appeals continued to build up until 2008, when the MoJ took the extraordinary step of 'drafting in extra High Court Judges, senior barristers and circuit judges' to clear the backlog of asylum appeals.[9]

Delays in processing cases were also attributable to HO caseworkers, who took a long time to decide initial asylum applications and to respond to fresh asylum applications (Thomas 2005: 482; Campbell 2013b: chap. 6). Caseworkers decided 61 per cent of claims in 2006/2007, but only 35 per cent of claims in 2007/2008 (the target was 60 per cent of claims within two months of receipt; ICAR 2009). Unsurprisingly a huge backlog of cases requiring decisions developed

Regardless of problems in the Tribunal and in the UKBA, ministers pressed ahead with plans to block appeals by failed asylum applicants (many of which had been successful) even though the volume of asylum applications was declining.[10] One important legislative change was s. 101(1) of the 2002 Act, which came into force in April 2005. Section 101(1) restricted appeals against Tribunal decisions to 'points of law'. Prior to the Act, many appeals had successfully overturned Tribunal decisions that had erred in the analysis of the facts of the case, i.e. facts provided by oral testimony or in expert evidence (Sweeny 2007). In the words of LJ Sedley in *Karanakaran* v *SSHD* [2000] EWCA Civ 11:

> The issues for a decision-maker under the Convention (whether the decision-maker is a Home Office official, a special adjudicator or the Immigration Appeal Tribunal) are questions not of hard fact but of evaluation: does the applicant have a well-founded fear of persecution for a Convention reason? Is that why he is here? If so, is he nevertheless able to find safety elsewhere in his home country? Into all of these, of course, a mass of factual questions enters.
>
> (para. 15)

In addition, s. 101 of the 2002 Act:

> imposed an obligation on decision-makers (including IND (HO) officials and the tribunal system) to have regard to any behaviour on the part of a claimant which they believe is likely to mislead or conceal information or obstruct or delay the taking of a decision when assessing the individual's credibility.
>
> (Thomas 2005: 474)

Counsel for appellants now had to clearly differentiate between matters of fact and matters of law in appealing against a decision, because once the Act came into force it would be impossible to challenge many Tribunal decisions (e.g. on credibility issues; see 'The case of *Ethiopia/TG*' in Chapter 5).

The wording of the Act led the CoA in *R (Iran) and Others* v *SSHD* [2005] Civ 982 to provide 29 pages of detailed guidance about how to interpret s. 101 because, as the CoA found, the government had not issued a 'White Paper, Parliamentary Statement or other document' to show what parliament 'intended' (para. 74). In short, the government's rush to adopt legislation gave rise to litigation that could have been avoided.

The role of the AIT in 'filtering' applications for reconsideration

The impact of legislative and policy reforms on litigation is difficult to assess because legislative Acts come into force several years after their passage into law and because some reforms were only partially realized. While one objective of the

2004 Act was to prevent cases from being appealed to the CoA by reorganizing the Tribunal, this was not achieved.

However, in 2005 market reforms began to radically restructure access to legal representation because law firms closed or withdrew from legally aided asylum and immigration work. Cuts in legal aid and growing controls by the LSC over the disbursement of legal aid partially reduced appeals against Tribunal decisions. This was offset, however, because the remaining law firms and barristers' chambers appear to have stepped in to meet the demand for legal services created when firms closed.

What was the onward appeal process between 2007 and 2009? Following an IJ's decision, an applicant and the HO had five working days to file an 'application for reconsideration'.[11] The appeal could only succeed if the IJ made a serious error in law and/or if conditions in the applicant's country of origin had changed significantly such that there was now a risk that if they were returned there their human rights would be violated. This application was assessed in a review of the papers by an SIJ (a process referred to as the AIT 'filter'). If the application was approved, the case would be re-heard in part or in whole (*de novo*), depending on the errors identified in the IJ's decision.

Unfortunately, official data do not provide a very clear picture regarding how the Tribunal decided these applications because the government changed the way statistics on this issue were collected and compiled. Prior to 2006 the MoJ and the HO collected and recorded data on the total number of applications for reconsideration made to the Tribunal which differentiated between the number of applications made by appellants (and the outcomes) and the number of applications made (and the outcomes) by the respondent (the Home Office). ICAR (2007b: 12–13) reported that during this period approximately 18 per cent of applications brought by appellants were allowed by the Tribunal, whereas 45–60 per cent of applications made by the SSHD were allowed.

However, after 2006 official statistics *only* record the total number of applications for reconsideration made to the Tribunal (by percentage won, lost or withdrawn), without indicating which party brought and won the appeal (see Table 6.1). It is therefore impossible to assess the outcome of applications made during 2006–2009.[12] What is clear, however, is that the high level of applications granted between 1998 and 2006 – i.e. between 22 and 46 percent of applications – indicates the poor quality of IJ decision-making. Finally, and for reasons which remain obscure, the Tribunal granted far more applications made by the SSHD.

There are three possible explanations why a higher percentage of applications for reconsideration were granted. First, it may reflect, as the CoA observed, the fact that the Tribunal interfered 'too readily with adjudicator's determinations and . . . [were] not confining themselves to its proper reviewing role' (quoted in Thomas 2005: 487). Second, it may be that the Tribunal was deciding cases that raised new and complex legal issues, which resulted in unsustainable decisions.[13] Finally, to the extent that SIJs only examined the paper application for review and did not see the entire case file, it may be that they erred on the side of safety by granting reconsideration.

Table 6.1 Number and percentage of applications for reconsideration decided by the Tribunal by year and outcome, 2006–2009

Year	*No. of disposals*	*% granted*	*% refused*	*% withdrawn/abandoned*
2006	7,418	32	60	7
2007	10,320	42	51	7
2008	8,820	46	47	7
2009	6,514	44	45	11

Source: FOI Request 83081, annex C, to MoJ dated 20 June 2013.

Following a decision by the Tribunal to reconsider a case, it is listed for a hearing and reconsidered (a new decision generates a further right of appeal by both parties). The Tribunal's decision to reconsider a case is seen by independent counsel as positive, and by the government as an indication of vexatious litigation (official statistics fail to differentiate between first decisions and reconsiderations). If the AIT refused to grant an application for reconsideration, an applicant's legal counsel could appeal to the CoA.

The Court of Appeal

In Chapter 5 I argued that due process in the Tribunal has been eroded by continuous reforms and because IJs rely on legal and spatial enclosures to rapidly process asylum claims. In this section I examine due process in the CoA. It will be recalled that Spaulding (2012) has argued that Procedural Rules and practice reflect a movement away from the careful consideration of individual cases to a situation characterized by the mass-processing of demands for justice which contributes to the erosion of due process.

Appeals against the Tribunal's refusal to reconsider an asylum appeal are heard in the Civil Division of the Court of Appeal,[14] where the Master of the Rolls presides over 37 Lord Justices who hear appeals. LJs invariably begin their career as barristers and at some point are elevated to sit as judges in the High Court,[15] from where a few are eventually selected to join the CoA. The age of LJs ranges from 62 to 67; there are 7 women and 30 men. LJs are overwhelmingly white. When presiding over civil cases, LJs wear the 'civil robe' with gold tabs on the neck of a black gown. No wig is worn. However, counsel who appear before LJs to plead a case are wigged and gowned.

Every LJ keeps one day a week free to read case files or to write a judgment. On days when they sit in court, cases are listed for hearing between 10.30 a.m. and 4.15 p.m. with a break for lunch. Time is required for additional preparation and judgment writing, and to deal with other work commitments. The 'legal term' is divided into slots of three weeks. Over a 12-week period an LJ who covers the full range of work might expect to have two slots in the Civil Division, one in the Criminal Division and one in the Divisional Court. In addition to judging cases, most LJs have responsibilities in the wider court system or on other bodies related to the justice system.[16]

In the nineteenth century court architecture, which borrowed heavily from the design of English town halls and churches, began to exhibit a common style. Court design reflected the aspirations of a growing legal elite for monumental, gothic-style legal temples with functional interiors that segregated different court users – judges, lawyers, officials, criminals and members of the public – from one another (Mulcahy 2011). Court design accelerated the adoption of highly segmented courtrooms used to stage adversarial trials where the power of the judiciary and the oratorical skills of lawyers could be seen and heard.

The architectural design of courts reached its apogee in the late nineteenth century, when in 1873 Parliament commissioned George Street to design and oversee the construction of the Royal Courts of Justice in London where the CoA sits (Brownlee 1983). The court was completed in 1882 and opened by Queen Victoria to considerable fanfare. Its exterior was designed in Monastic gothic style replete with multiple turrets capped by statuary. Statues – of Moses, Christ, King Alfred the Great and the like – adorn the exterior walls where the coats of arms of eminent jurists are emblazoned to emphasize 'the essentially flexible, Christian, and English qualities of British jurisprudence' (Brownlee 1983: 328).[17] Along the ground level there are parallel arcades or arches, including a massive arched front entrance which leads directly into a large, magnificent arched public hall which members of the public were initially excluded from (they entered via separate doors and moved about the court along separate corridors). Exits out of the central hall lead to the West and Central Blocks, which parallel each other and which contain courtrooms. Each courtroom was designed to be unique, and each was furnished with specially designed woodwork and furnishings. Various extensions to the original block have since been built to provide dedicated space for other courts. Today the Royal Courts of Justice contains 1,100 rooms and has 3½ miles of corridors, many of which are accessible only to court staff, judges or the police (police cells are located below the East Block). Today, in common with other nineteenth-century courts, many courtrooms are not in use (Roberts 2009).

While all British courtrooms are partitioned or segmented, a considerable difference exists between criminal courts and the Tribunal and CoA. In criminal courts space is sharply segmented by walls, barriers, partitions, the position of tables, and benches; even the raised dais for the judge focuses attention on the dock from where oral evidence is given in a trial. However, courtrooms in the Tribunal and the CoA are – with the exception of the much richer woodwork and furnishings in the Royal Courts – similar. A further important difference is that asylum applicants and the public do not attend appeals in the CoA, which means that the spatial dynamic which reinforces judicial control over the proceedings is seldom witnessed. Indeed, the nature of the proceedings, the language used by LJs who focus on 'the law' and the abruptness with which LJs control hearings make it clear who is in charge and what submissions will or will not be allowed.

In addition to relying upon spatial dynamics to enforce their authority, LJs draw upon their judicial experience and the authority invested in them by the CoA's Procedural Rules and Practice Directions (see Boxes 6.1 and 6.2). The Rules and Directions require all parties to comply with the court to expedite the hearing of a case. Failure to comply ensures that the appeal will be dismissed. In the cases discussed below, I indicate (in brackets) in the text when a specific rule/direction is engaged.

Box 6.1 Court of Appeal legal architecture: Procedural Rules

General rules about appeals (scope and interpretation)

Rule 52.1 Parties to comply with Practice Directions 52A to 52E
Rule 52.2 Permission
Rule 52.3 Appellant's notice
Rule 52.4 Respondent's notice
Rule 52.5 Variation of time
Rule 52.6 Stay
Rule 52.7 Amendment of appeal notice
Rule 52.8 Striking out appeal notices and setting aside or imposing conditions on permission to appeal
Rule 52.9 Appeal Court's powers

1 affirm, set aside or vary any order or judgment made or given by the lower court;
2 refer any claim or issue for determination by the lower court;
3 order a new trial or hearing.

Rule 52.10 Hearing of appeals

1 Every appeal will be limited to a review of the decision of the lower court unless
   a) a practice direction makes different provision for a particular category of appeal; or
   b) the court considers that in the circumstances of an individual appeal it would be in the interests of justice to hold a re-hearing.
2 Unless it orders otherwise, the appeal court will not receive
   a) oral evidence; or
   b) evidence which was not before the lower court.
3 The appeal court will allow an appeal where the decision of the lower court was: (a) wrong; (b) unjust because of a serious procedural or other irregularity in the proceedings in the lower court.

4 The appeal court may draw any inference of fact which it considers justified on the evidence.
5 At the hearing of the appeal a party may not rely on a matter not contained in his appeal notice unless the appeal court gives permission.

Rule 52.11 Non-disclosure of Part 36 offers and payments
Rule 52.12 Statutory appeals – court's power to hear any person
Rule 52.12 AII Special provisions applying to the Court of Appeal (second appeals to the court)
Rule 52.13 Assignment of appeals to the Court of Appeal

Source: UK (2015c).

Box 6.2 Court of Appeal legal architecture: Practice Directions

Section I: introduction and interpretation

Section II: starting an appeal to the Court of Appeal, grounds of appeal and skeleton arguments

1 Grounds of appeal

5 (1) The grounds of appeal must identify as concisely as possible the respects in which the judgment of the court below is: (a) wrong; or (b) unjust because of a serious procedural or other irregularity, as required by Rule 52.11(3).
(2) The reasons why the decision under appeal is wrong or unjust must not be included in the grounds of appeal and must be confined to the skeleton argument.

Section III: respondent's notice, respondent's skeleton argument, time limits

Section IV: procedure where permission to appeal is sought from the Court of Appeal

1 documents for use on an application for permission;
2 determination of applications for permission to appeal;
3 permission hearing;

(continued)

(continued)

4 appellant in receipt of services funded by the Legal Services Commission applying for permission to appeal;
5 limited permission: Rule 52.3:

(1) If, under Rule 52.3(7), the court grants permission to appeal on some issues only, it will –
(2) refuse permission on any remaining issues; or (b) adjourn the application in respect of those issues to the hearing of the appeal.

6 Respondent need not take any action when served with an appellant's notice.

Section V: timetable

Section VI: management of the appeal

1 listing and hear-by dates;
2 Appeal Questionnaire;
3 time estimates;
4 multiple appeals;
5 expedition.

Section VII: bundles, amendment and supplementary skeleton arguments

1 bundles;
2 appeals from the Upper Tribunal Immigration and Asylum Chamber;
3 bundle of authorities;
4 amendment of appeal notice: Rule 52.8;
5 skeleton argument;
6 supplementary skeleton arguments.

Source: http://www.justice.gov.uk/courts/procedure-rules/civil/rules/part52/practice-direction-52c-appeals-to-the-court-of-appeal.

There are important differences between the rules and procedures operating in the Tribunal and those in the CoA, where the Home Office is *not* expected to attend permission applications unless the court directs it to do so (PD 52C, 16). Importantly, in the period prior to an appeal a barrister instructed by TSol will have attempted to 'knock out' the appeal by filing sufficiently robust counter-arguments (see Chapter 2). The exception is when an appeal is 'politically sensitive'.

Permission applications

Applications for reconsideration which are refused by the Tribunal can be appealed to the CoA. Once again an appeal form, outlining the case and setting out errors of law by the Tribunal, is submitted to a Lord Justice who reviews the 'paper application' and decides whether the case merits reconsideration. This decision is not final unless the LJ decides that the case is 'totally without merit' (PD 52.3(4A)).

Table 6.2 provides official statistics on the number of 'applications on the papers' seeking permission to appeal. As with all asylum-related statistics, they must be read with caution because official statistics do not distinguish between paper and oral applications or between applications and statutory appeals. Tables 6.2 to 6.4 are based on data provided by the MoJ because they ***appear*** to be more comprehensive.[18] Because official statistics do not differentiate between asylum and immigration applications and appeals heard in the CoA, caution is needed in generalizing from the statistics and the cases examined here.

The data in Table 6.2 show that the vast majority of applications are from appellants (not the HO), and that on average one in three applications were successful. If the figures from column 5, 'allowed with consent' – which means that prior to or during the hearing both parties agreed that the case should be reconsidered by the Tribunal – are included, the success rate creeps up to 40 per cent. A successful application at this stage means that the Tribunal must reconsider the appeal. This is a damming indictment on the Tribunal's review of applications for reconsideration.

Some barristers brave a refusal 'on the papers' and make an oral application to a single LJ in the CoA. The statistics on the outcome of oral applications (see Table 6.3) suggest that 98 per cent of oral applications are made by applicants, and that on average 38 per cent are successful.

I will examine three oral applications to illustrate how the process works and the significance which attaches to a decision by a panel of LJs to refuse, stay or allow an appeal. I begin with a fairly straightforward case where an asylum applicant appeared before an LJ as a 'litigant in person' to plead his own case.

Table 6.2 Number of asylum and immigration 'applications on the papers' to the Court of Appeal by year and outcome, 2006–2009

Year	*From Home Office*	*From appellant*	*Allowed*	*Allowed with consent*	*Refused*	*Dismissed with consent*	*Other*[1]
2006	7	583	234 (39%)	28 (5%)	282 (48%)	27	19
2007	3	605	256 (42%)	17 (3%)	276 (45%)	25	34
2008	21	775	280 (35%)	20 (2%)	358 (45%)	50	88
2009	16	574	230 (39%)	20 (3%)	212 (36%)	63	65
Total	47 (0.5%)	2,537 (99.5%)	1,000 (36.7%)	85 (3.2%)	1,128 (43.6%)	165 (6.3%)	206 (7.9%)

Source: FOI Request 89021 to MoJ dated 27 March 2014.

Note: The category 'other' refers to cases which were withdrawn before the case was listed to be heard. It could be that the parties came to an agreement, or that the barrister running the case got cold feet and withdrew the case.

Table 6.3 'Oral applications' for permission to appeal to the Court of Appeal on asylum and immigration claims by year and outcome, 2006–2009

Year	*From Home Office*	*From appellant*	*Allowed*	*Allowed with consent*	*Refused*	*Dismissed with consent*	*Other*
2006	2	252 (99%)	88 (35%)	4	160 (63%)	1	1
2007	2	217 (99%)	89 (40%)	0	127 (58%)	1	2
2008	11	271 (94%)	103 (36%)	0	178 (63%)	1	0
2009	6	198 (92%)	86 (42%)	0	116 (57%)	1	1
Total	21	938 (98%)	366 (38%)	4	581 (60%)	4	4

Source: FOI Request 89021 to MoJ dated 27 March 2014.

The case of *Gambia/LK*

On 11 November 2008 LK arrived at 9:45 a.m. in courtroom 16, a relatively small room located in the West Block. For reasons which were not clear, he was not represented by counsel. Unusually, however, the Home Office was represented by a barrister who was accompanied by his instructing solicitor from TSol (PD 52(C), s. III). Apparently, the CoA had directed the HO to attend because TSol had failed to submit its grounds of resistance in time and perhaps because the appellant was unrepresented. At 10 a.m. the usher announced the case – *LK (Gambia)* v *SSHD* – and the LJ entered and commenced the hearing. Because LK was unrepresented, the LJ directed his questions to counsel for the HO, with whom he spoke for 20–25 minutes to clarify the issues that arose from 'a short judgment' by the IJ who had decided the claim. When the LJ was satisfied that all the submissions had been made, he turned to K (dialogue reproduced from field notes).

LJ: You have heard what has been said? Have you had an opportunity to read the skeleton [submitted by the SSHD]?
K: It was only sent yesterday.
LJ: I haven't said anything about it, but the SSHD has a lot of responsibility for the failure to do so [i.e. serve the skeleton in advance of the case]. What would you like to say? . . . Do you accept that this document shows, that though she [your mother] was victimized, that she was cleared by the court [in Gambia]?
K: Yes, but . . .
LJ: Anything else?

In typical fashion, the LJ immediately began summarizing the key issues. He reviewed the key submissions, and noted that while 'it was not clear what the IJ made of the evidence by the appellant regarding the incident, which was an error of law, nevertheless that error was not material and did not impact on the decision'. The LJ then refused permission for the appeal to be heard.

There are no statistics on the number of oral applications for permission made by litigants in person to the CoA, which makes it difficult to know whether the outcome of LK's appeal is indicative of the general position of individuals with little or no knowledge of asylum and immigration law. Litigants in person are at a significant disadvantage in court – a situation that leaves the judge with two choices (Moorhead 2006). The judge either 'descends into the arena' to ensure fairness to the litigant, or relies on the litigant's opponent to 'make the running' in the case (as occurred here), which could undermine the litigant's case. In this case LK clearly did not understand the legal arguments, and he left court feeling that the system was unjust.

The case of *Zimbabwe/HS*

A very different situation occurred on 2 July 2008, when an oral application for permission to appeal was made before three LJs in the case of *HS (Zimbabwe)* v *SSHD* in courtroom 68. Very unusually, the court was packed. In attendance were five journalists, a press officer for the Refugee Council and an individual from Bail for Immigration Detainees. All these individuals sat in a designated area for the press to the left of the raised dais. The two legal teams sat on wooden benches facing the dais: the appellant's team sat on the left, and the HO team on the right. For the HO there were five members from its Legal Adviser's Branch, an instructing solicitor from TSol and a QC. HS was represented by a QC, a junior barrister (who had run the case) and two caseworkers from the Refugee Legal Centre.

When counsel for the appellant had appealed 'on the papers' to the CoA, the LJ concluded that the appeal grounds were 'factual points dressed up in law', and he refused permission for it to be heard. Subsequently, however, there was a further development: a case raising related issues had been decided by the Special Immigration Appeals Commission (SIAC) and had been appealed to the House of Lords. When the oral permission hearing for *HS (Zimbabwe)* was called to order, counsel for the appellant stood to present his case, but was immediately interrupted by the presiding LJ:

(continued)

(continued)

> We have read all the papers and have satisfied ourselves about the case, but we want to raise a point with Mr T [counsel for the HO, who also represented the HO in the SIAC case]. We want to know the implications of this case for permission to appeal *MT (Algeria)* for HS. It is difficult to see otherwise . . . that [case] puts us in doubt about what we hold in this case.

For the better part of an hour the three LJs questioned Mr T about *MT (Algeria)* v *SSHD* [2008] – which had subsequently been linked with two related cases and renamed *MT, RB and U* v *SSHD* [2007] EWCA Civ 808 – which was listed for a hearing in three months' time in the HoL.[19] The LJs were not willing to decide *HS* because *MT (Algeria)*, a terrorist/Control Order case, raised the same issues of fact-finding and law. The issue, as the LJs saw it, was that the Tribunal's fact-finding exercise in relation to returning an individual to Zimbabwe was potentially flawed because it had not given sufficient weight to certain witnesses and had failed to approach the evidence 'in a fair and balanced manner'. In addition, there was the possibility that returning an individual to Zimbabwe might breach Art. 3 of the ECHR ('No one shall be subjected to torture or to inhuman or degrading treatment or punishment').

The LJs questioned Mr T regarding the legal argument/position in both cases, about how the appeal to the HoL had been drafted and whether the HoL's case had any implications for *HS (Zimbabwe)*. On each issue Mr T refused to accept that the case before the HoL affected *HS*, and argued instead that the CoA should proceed with the case. However, the LJs' dilemma was articulated by the presiding LJ in the following terms: if we go ahead with this case and *MT* succeeds, our decision will be attacked and subsequent litigation will 'clog up the courts'. In addition, *HS* was a Tribunal Country Guidance decision decided in 2007, and it is not appropriate for us to review the facts because the Tribunal is better placed to make such decisions. Furthermore, a decision to stay the case would probably mean that the Tribunal would list a new case to give guidance on safety of return which looked at the current situation in Zimbabwe.

After nearly 50 minutes of discussion, counsel for the appellant stood and formally asked the court to stay the case behind *MT (Algeria)*. The presiding LJ immediately summarized the key arguments and issues in the case, and announced that the case was stayed; the other two LJs agreed. Mr T then asked to have to have the case relisted for permission as quickly as possible after *MT (Algeria)* was decided.

The LJs left the courtroom through one exit, and the two QCs left via the public entrance; the Refugee Legal Centre caseworkers handed out prepared (but slightly amended) press releases and answered questions from the media. Channel 4 News then staged a press announcement by filming its reporter, Simon Israel, walking out of the entrance of the Royal Courts to announce the decision and spell out its implications.[20] A stay in *HS (Zimbabwe)* meant that the Home Office was unable to return HS *and* approximately 11,500 other 'failed' Zimbabwean asylum applicants and their dependants. Nine days after *HS (Zimbabwe)* was stayed, the government announced that 'there would not be any forced removals to Zimbabwe during the current situation', a policy that continued until October 2010 (even though *MT Algeria* was refused by the House of Lords in October 2008).

When an oral application is granted, the case is usually referred back to the Tribunal to be reconsidered. However, for various reasons – e.g. there are a number of similar appeals or because the cases raises important questions of law (PD 52(11)) – the CoA can list a case for a panel of LJs to hear. This is what occurred when an oral application for permission was granted in the case of *GM (Eritrea)* v *SSHD.*

The case of *Eritrea/GM*

The asylum appeal of GM was heard and refused by the Tribunal in August 2006, but on appeal an error was found and it was reconsidered in August 2007, when once again it was refused. The barrister appealed against the Tribunal's decision on the basis of an error of law; however, the Tribunal refused to reconsider it.[21] In December 2007 the barrister appealed 'on the papers' to the CoA, where an LJ refused permission to appeal. In early February 2008 she appeared before a panel of LJs to make an oral application. As soon as she began to present her case she was interrupted by the first of a series of abrupt and hostile questions.

LJ: We have looked at the papers. Where does *MA (Draft Evaders – Illegal Departures – Risk) Eritrea CG* [2007] UKAIT 00059 take us on this case?

BARRISTER (B): The appellant in *MA* was a military deserter. *MA* considered the issue of exit visas and made a number of positive findings.

LJ: As a deserter, he couldn't have gotten an exit visa.

B: Eritrean national service is an indefinite obligation, it is unending. No demobilization has taken place. Individuals in national service cannot obtain an exit visa [to leave the country] . . .

(continued)

(continued)

LJ:	GM left illegally?
B:	The IJ's finding was not based on an examination of the objective evidence, but the SSHD accepted that he had entered into military service in 1998 . . . . Once you are in national service it continued until after the [Eritrea–Ethiopia] war, and has been extended to everyone aged 18 to 50. He was in national service . . . [no one was demobilized].
LJ:	We've got that point. Are you saying that anyone who can get out of Eritrea is entitled to asylum?
B:	We have to have reference to specific findings that he participated in national service.
LJ:	Then *MA (Eritrea)* applies?
B:	Yes.
LJ:	There are quite a few categories of exemption?
B:	Yes. But not all the categories apply. Individuals in national service cannot apply for an exit visa. There are also draconian steps taken by the Eritreans to prevent exit from the country . . .
LJ:	Were you counsel in *MA (Eritrea)*? Do you have other applications before this court?

The barrister informed the LJs that she was counsel in *MA*, and that at least four other cases were listed for permission hearings. She argued that in her case the Tribunal had assessed the facts without carefully considering the objective evidence. Once again an LJ sought to clarify her argument: 'You are saying that someone who was called up for national service and who claimed asylum in the UK should be considered a deserter?' 'No,' she answered, 'a finding needs to be made about an individual against the objective evidence.'

The two LJs retreated into the hall, where an animated discussion could be heard. On returning, the presiding LJ immediately summed up the case by noting that the IJ had failed to make a finding regarding GM's national service, and the evidence in relation to illegal exit from Eritrea needed to be reconsidered. They expressed their doubts that the IJ had in fact erred in law, nevertheless they granted permission on one point of law (PD 52.6): did GM leave Eritrea unlawfully?

Table 6.3 indicates that substantially fewer oral applications are made than applications 'on the paper'. Unsurprisingly, 98 per cent of all oral applications are made by appellants; however, 35–42 per cent of oral applications were granted. While the ability of the HO to 'knock cases out' at this stage is very high, statistics indicate the important role played by the CoA in overseeing the work of the Tribunal.

Statutory appeals

The case of *GM (Eritrea)* v *SSHD* was listed for a hearing in May 2008, and two other cases (*YT* and *MY*) were joined to it which raised the same issue: illegal exit from Eritrea. The junior barristers who ran the appeals agreed on the appointment of the Queen's Counsel to plead their case. However, even though they disagreed on the strategy that should be pursued in the CoA, they were compelled by PD 52(C), s. VI(4) to agree a common approach and file a single appeal bundle. The junior barristers were agreed that the findings in *MA (Eritrea)* should be preserved, as far as was possible, from a possible narrowing of interpretation by the CoA.

The case of *GM, YT and MY v SSHD*

The case was heard on 7 May in courtroom 75 before a panel of three LJs.[22] A fairly large legal team assembled, and their spatial/seating position in court reflected the structure of the appeal and the status of each individual. Thus on the left side of the court, in the first of three benches facing the raised dais where the LJs presided, sat the QC who was to plead the case for the appellants; directly behind him, on the second bench, sat two junior barristers whose cases were being heard, and directly behind them, on the third bench, sat instructing solicitors from the firms who had filed the asylum appeals. The SSHD was represented by a barrister, not a QC, who sat on the second bench on the right of the court; his instructing solicitor from TSol sat directly behind him, on the third bench. Seats for the public and the press were unoccupied. During the hearing all communication was initiated by the leading counsel, who spoke to their juniors/ instructing solicitors; the latter did not initiate any discussion with counsel, nor did they speak to the other legal team.

At 10:48 a.m. three LJs entered and sat behind the raised dais; the usher opened the proceedings by reading out the name of the appeal. The QC stood up and introduced all the parties to the court. Immediately, an LJ grumpily made his feelings about the case known: 'We have read the material, though personally I have not read every paragraph of *MA (Eritrea)*. The material has been summarized several times for us. Do you want to add additional grounds?' [PD 52 (C)].[23] After a few preliminary comments by another LJ, the following arguments were made.

QC: Our position on *YT* and *GM* and *MY* is that: (a) much of the evidence was disbelieved by the Tribunal; (b) their nationality was accepted as Eritrean; (c) their ages are not in dispute; (d) given their age, they have been called up for national service; (e) the various

(continued)

(continued)

parts [of their claims] fall together with indefinite national service to the age of 50, the absence of general demobilization. The Tribunal should have concluded that they were not demobilized.

LJ: 'Desertion' is a wide phrase. They've completed military service, and not civilian occupations. What do you mean by 'deserter'? From military service?

QC: In Eritrean terms . . .

LJ: It must follow that they left illegally or from military service.

QC: It is necessary to keep the two aspects discrete.

LJ: We don't know that.

QC: This is the ineluctable conclusion that the Tribunal had to reach.

LJ: I don't understand why it must be the case that they are deserters and they left illegally.

QC: I will come to illegal exit . . . . There has not been any demobilization for this, and they must be considered deserters.

A little later, the QC's arguments became clearer.

QC: The submission is that debate about illegal exit falls away. It leaves the authorities to conclude that a person is a draft evader and the Tribunal should have been driven to this conclusion.

LJ: Wait a minute. Exit arguments [are proved] by the fact that they are in the UK?

QC: The Eritrean authorities will regard these persons as having left Eritrea illegally. They infer that they are draft evaders or deserters . . .

LJ: Anybody who is in this country whose claim has not been accepted would be at risk? How does this fit with Tribunal arguments that [some] failed asylum seekers are not at risk?

The arguments moved on to named categories of persons who are given exit visas. At this point, counsel for the SSHD objected that the reasoning relied upon by the appellants was circular. Discussion then moved to the fact that none of the applicants had given any evidence regarding illegal exit. Barring such evidence, as one LJ remarked to the QC, 'You say we simply don't know. There must be an alternative answer, but at the present stage there is no evidence of departure. My colleague argues that there are no facts, but you argue that we can succeed'. Indeed, the LJ's comments became quite pointed, namely that the claimants had not provided evidence that their fear was well founded in accord with the *Sivakumaran* standard of proof.[24]

Argument focused on the nature of the evidence considered in *MA (Eritrea)*, which was partly in the form of statements made by country experts and statistical data on Eritrean exit visas submitted by the Foreign and Commonwealth Office. The LJs were unhappy with the suggestion that they should rely on 'generic or statistical evidence'.

QC: Put that way, I accept what you are saying, but I do not rely on the facts specific to the case.
LJ: The facts that they . . . with a specific group, but not in relation to their departure from Eritrea.
QC: Setting aside the first submission, our case is that when individuals leave illegally, [in a situation] when categories of those who can leave are very narrow, there needs to be some evidential burden on the SSHD that a person falls within a specific category.

Even though counsel attempted to differentiate between the evidential and legal burden in the case, his argument was not accepted because the burden of proof lay on the appellant, not on the SSHD. Discussion returned to evidential submissions in *MA*, where one LJ noted that at para. 363, 'it cannot simply be assumed that an Eritrean claimant who has left Eritrea has done so illegally'.

QC: Our second additional ground of appeal is that . . . the Tribunal adopted the wrong approach when it asked itself in each case whether the applicant had in fact left Eritrea lawfully. It should instead have asked itself how they [the applicants] would appear to the Eritrean authorities on return . . .
LJ: I am not certain this adds anything.

Almost two hours later, counsel for the SSHD stood to make his argument. He took exception to how his learned friend, counsel for the appellant, had construed military desertion and the categories of persons who were allowed to exit Eritrea legally. More importantly, he argued that 'The appellants must show that they left Eritrea illegally and [they] must be believed by the adjudicator [IJ] to the lower standard of proof . . . '.

Shortly thereafter, an LJ interjected: 'Does he [the appellant] have to show that they left illegally? They are unlikely to get a visa.'

QC: They might do. Party members of family or officials [can obtain visas]. We simply don't know. [There] Is not much for the appellant to do. To do otherwise is to shift the burden of proof; this is not the SSHD's job. It falls to . . . the asylum applicant to give an account.

(continued)

(continued)

Following a break for lunch, the hearing resumed with counsel for the SSHD reiterating that it is not the SSHD's responsibility to provide evidence in asylum hearings. He also reviewed the IJ's assessment of the case of *MY*, and argued that illegal exit cannot be proved because the appellant was found to lack credibility in answering questions about how she left Eritrea.

Counsel for the appellants summed up his position regarding the evidence accepted by the Tribunal in *MA (Eritrea)*, to which an LJ replied: 'It is somewhat Delphic.'

QC: It is not fair to take that position or to argue that it is based on exaggeration.
LJ: He [the expert] says exit is inconsistent with age.
QC: It is as far as I can take it given the Delphic paragraph . . .
LJ: [It] looks like a freestanding reading.
QC: If you are satisfied, then our appeal won't succeed.

The appeal closed shortly after 2:30 p.m. The CoA promulgated its decision two months later,[25] and after addressing several preliminary issues identified in the discussion – notably the issue of credibility – concluded that because the burden of proof lies with the appellant, all three appeals were dismissed. This was the end of the line for these applicants. However, in one of the curious twists in asylum law, they were not returned to Eritrea because, as set out in *MA (Eritrea)*, there was a high risk that on return the authorities would find that they would be indefinitely detained under conditions that would breach their human rights.

Table 6.4 shows that 98 per cent of all cases heard by the CoA were appealed by counsel for asylum applicants. At this level the appellant is normally represented by a QC, who pleads the case, and the HO is normally represented by a senior barrister. Cases are listed to be heard for varying periods of time depending upon the number of cases joined to the lead case and the issues which the court has agreed to consider. Appeals last from two to three hours to two days.

Somewhere between 10 and 25 per cent of asylum and immigration appeals heard by the CoA are granted (this may include a small number of HO appeals). However, MoJ statistics indicate that, apparently, due to the pressure on both parties, a surprisingly large percentage of appeals are 'allowed with consent'. This means that either immediately prior to a hearing or during it, both parties are put under pressure to reconsider their position and to jointly agree for the appeal to be reheard by the Tribunal.

Table 6.4 Number of asylum and immigration appeals heard by the Court of Appeal by year and outcome, 2006–2009

Year	*From Home Office*	*From appellant*	*Allowed*	*Allowed with consent*	*Refused*	*Dismissed with consent*	*Other*
2006	5	323	32 (10%)	195 (59%)	48 (15%)	26 (8%)	27
2007	6	334	58 (17%)	196 (57%)	50 (15%)	31 (9%)	5
2008	5	393	61 (25%)	214 (54%)	65 (16%)	40 (10%)	18
2009	11	306	45 (14%)	169 (53%)	53 (17%)	32 (10%)	18
Total	27 (2%)	1,356 (98%)	196 (14%)	777 (56%)	216 (16%)	129 (9%)	68 (5%)

Source: FOI Request 89021 to MoJ dated 27 March 2014.

An appeal from the CoA to the House of Lords (now the Supreme Court) is made in the first instance 'on the papers' to the CoA, which, unlike the lower courts, has the power to refuse the application (though a small number of written applications are accepted by the HoL: PD 52.3). Sometimes the CoA will appeal a case directly to the HoL if it believes that a particular point of law needs clarification (see UK 2016a). For the vast majority of cases heard in the CoA, its decision is final.

The finality[26] of decisions at this level is experienced in two ways (Atkins 1990). First, a decision dispenses 'visible benefits' to the winning party (e.g. for applicants, litigation justifies the work involved in challenging the authority of the state and the reputation of the legal team is enhanced). Second, a decision can have a public benefit in the sense that a victory, in effect a reasoned 'interpretation' of the rules or law, establishes current policy. Thus victory for the HO legitimizes government policy, i.e. litigation blocks a case that might have thrown government policy into disarray. However, if the issue in the appeal is sufficiently important, the HO will appeal against the decision in the CoA to the HoL. But even if the HoL refuses to hear the case, the HO is very likely to continue to litigate against cases which raise the same issue. The HO will probably also attempt to introduce new legislation or rules to close the 'loophole' created by the appeal (see Chapter 8). A further concern relates to financial costs: unsuccessful litigants will have the cost of litigation awarded against them (for appellants, this may be met by legal aid, whereas the government pays the cost of HO litigation). The long and short of it is that appellate decisions are not merely opportunities to correct errors made in the lower courts, they are political interventions which have consequences throughout the legal/asylum system (which explains the conservative decisions taken in appellate courts).

Conclusion

In the period preceding my fieldwork in 2007, the right of appeal against Tribunal decisions was amended by legislation. By 2007 an individual could apply to the Tribunal to reconsider a case only if an IJ had made a serious error of law in deciding the claim or if conditions in the applicant's country of origin were such that their human rights would be violated if they were returned there.

Reforms to the structure of the Tribunal and delays by the UKBA created a backlog of cases which delayed decisions on first-instance appeals and on applications for reconsideration. Table 6.1 indicates that between 2006 and 2009 the Tribunal allowed 32–46 per cent of all applications for reconsideration, which indicates the flawed nature of SIJ decisions. Even more worryingly, the data in Tables 6.2 to 6.4 show that during 2006–2009 between 32 and 44 per cent of appeals heard in the CoA against Tribunal decisions were successful. Two clear conclusions emerge from this. First, judicial decisions by IJs are of poor quality. Second, government attempts to 'pre-empt'/reduce an asylum applicant's right of appeal were misguided and might well have resulted in a miscarriage of justice for many asylum applicants.

My analysis of 'applications on the papers' and oral applications in the CoA illustrate the important role of the appellate court in overseeing the work of the Tribunal. The power of LJs, which, *pace* Spaulding, is reinforced by legal and spatial enclosures, can clearly be seen in the cases examined in this chapter. Most appeals in the CoA are clearly not vexatious; they raise important issues of life and liberty which hinge on well-argued litigation against, it must be said, the mean policies pursued by the Home Office.

A final comment about the poor quality of official statistics on asylum (and immigration) appeals is in order. First, poor-quality statistics limit the ability to assess the work of the CoA. Second, the absence of reliable statistics underlines the extent to which government reforms have been pushed through in the absence of reliable data, because without good data it is not possible to assess the work of the Tribunal or the CoA, nor is it possible to assess how the courts exercise their oversight of the Home Office.

Notes

1 I do not examine out-of-country appeals or judicial reviews. For material on the importance of JRs, see Woolf (1998), Horne (2006) and Bondy and Sunkin (2009).

2 The legislation, including subsequent amendments, can be viewed at: http://www.legislation.gov.uk/

3 The new rules – which created a paper-based review that looks only at whether 'there was an arguable error of law' – established a standard of review considerably below that of judicial review (Thomas 2005: 491).

4 This type of claim is based on the Race Relations Act (2000); see 'Race Relations (Amendment) Act 2000', available at: http://www.legislation.gov.uk/ukpga/2000/34/contents (accessed 8 August 2016). Appeals were restricted to potentially discriminatory decisions taken by an official.

5 While the process was not without problems, it improved the standards of asylum and migration casework. The pity is that Home Office caseworkers are not required to undergo a similar process of accreditation.

6 See e.g. 'Legal aid', *The Law Society*, available at: http://www.lawsociety.org.uk/a-z/legal-aid/ (accessed 8 August 2016).

7 See UK (2007a) and S. Leech, 'Solicitors "deserting" legal aid', *BBC News*, 5 November 2006, available at: http://news.bbc.co.uk/1/hi/uk/6115514.stm (accessed 8 August 2016).

8 See F. Gibb, 'Blunders left 210 judges waiting for jobs', *The Times*, 13 November 2006, available at: http://www.thetimes.co.uk/tto/law/article2214070.ece (accessed 8 August 2016).

9 See F. Gibb, 'Extra judges drafted in to hear immigration appeals', *The Times*, 15 December 2008, available at: http://www.thetimes.co.uk/tto/news/politics/article2026625.ece (accessed 8 August 2016).

10 See A. Travis, 'Ministers aim to block high court appeals by failed asylum seekers', *The Guardian*, 22 August 2008, available at: http://www.theguardian.com/politics/2008/aug/22/immigrationpolicy.immigration (accessed 8 August 2016).

11 The Tribunal's calculation of time, specifically the 'five working days' within which an appeal must be made, was the subject of litigation between 2005 and 2009. Because the issue was so important to appellants, and because the AIT consistently refused to consider applications made 'out of time', it took a decision by the High Court to compel the AIT to reconsider the issue and clarify the meaning of 'time'. See '[2009] EWHC 335(Admin)', available at: http://www.refworld.org/docid/49affb602.html (accessed 8 August 2016).

12 In February 2010 yet another system of data collection was instituted which disaggregated data by appellants and respondents; this data is also problematic because the categories used differ from those used previously; source: FOI Request 83081 to MoJ dated 20 June 2013.

13 See [2007] EWCA Civ 801, *England and Wales Court of Appeal (Civil Division) Decisions*, available at: http://www.bailii.org/ew/cases/EWCA/Civ/2007/801.html (accessed 8 August 2016).

14 The divisions of the CoA which are not examined include the High Court (Chancery, Queen's Bench and Family Division) and the Criminal Division, which hears appeals from the Crown Courts. Judicial reviews and some statutory reviews from the Tribunal were heard by the Administrative Court until 2013.

15 In the past a decision to elevate an individual to become a judge was taken by senior judges; recently, individuals are encouraged to apply to the Judicial Appointments Commission when vacancies arise.

16 This paragraph is adapted from 'Court of Appeal judge', *Courts and Tribunals Judiciary*, available at: http://www.judiciary.gov.uk/about-the-judiciary/who-are-the-judiciary/a-day-in-the-life/court-of-appeal-judge/ (accessed 8 August 2016).

17 Spaulding notes that the 'facades of justice' on the exterior and interior of court houses should not be seen as unequivocal symbols of justice, but rather as polysemic, which is to say that 'they draw together, without necessarily resolving, radically different expectations and didactic objectives for the rule of law' (Spaulding 2011–2012: 1077).

18 Data from TSol concerning its work in the CoA was provided by FOI Request RM/18/12 to TSol dated 20 March 2012; its statistics differed substantially from the information provided by the MoJ. My attempt to clarify discrepancies in the statistics provided by both institutions only provided conflicting data and different explanations.

19 I attended the permission hearing and took notes which differ substantially from the reported decision on the case; see [2008] EWCA Civ 915, *England and Wales Court of Appeal (Civil Division) Decisions*, available at: http://www.bailii.org/ew/cases/EWCA/Civ/2008/915.html (accessed 8 August 2016). The decisions in most

permission hearings are not published; in cases where decisions are published, the record can vary considerably from the legal arguments, submissions and questions raised during the actual hearing.

20 In 2002, following litigation, a public campaign was launched to bring pressure on the HO to suspend returns to Zimbabwe. For press coverage of this case, and the resumption of removing individuals to Zimbabwe, see O. Bowcott, 'Asylum seekers: Pressure grows to free detained Zimbabwean asylum seekers', *The Guardian*, 3 July 2008, available at: https://www.theguardian.com/uk/2008/jul/03/immigration.immigrationpolicy (accessed 8 August 2016); B. Russell and N. Morris, 'Labour retreats on deportation threat to Zimbabweans', *The Independent*, 13 July 2008, available at: http://www.independent.co.uk/news/uk/politics/labour-retreats-on-deportation-threat-to-zimbabweans-865060.html (accessed 8 August 2016); and A. Travis, 'Home Office to lift ban on deporting failed asylum seekers to Zimbabwe', *The Guardian*, 14 October 2010, available at: http://www.theguardian.com/uk/2010/oct/14/asylum-seekers-home-office-lifts-zimbabwe-deportation-ban (accessed 8 August 2016).

21 Source: interviews with the barrister running the case (8 May and 16 September 2008). I was also given copies of her submissions.

22 The account of the arrangement of the court and the proceedings is from my field notes; see also the final judgment, [2008] EWCA Civ 833, *England and Wales Court of Appeal (Civil Division) Decisions*, available at: http://www.bailii.org/ew/cases/EWCA/Civ/2008/833.html (accessed 8 August 2016).

23 PD 52 (C), s. IV (5) states that neither party is allowed to raise grounds not previously agreed by the court. However, PDs 52.9 and 52.11 allow the court to strike out, impose or vary the conditions of its order.

24 See 'R v Secretary of State for the Home Department, Ex Parte Sivakumaran and Conjoined Appeals (UN High Commissioner for Refugees Intervening)', available at: http://www.refworld.org/docid/3ae6b67f40.html (accessed 8 August 2016).

25 See [2008] EWCA Civ 833, *England and Wales Court of Appeal (Civil Division) Decisions*, available at: http://www.bailii.org/cgi-bin/markup.cgi?doc=/ew/cases/EWCA/Civ/2008/833.html&query=GM+and+(Eritrean)&method=boolean (accessed 8 August 2016).

26 'Finality' refers to a legal decision which sets a precedent on a point or points of law about which no further litigation is possible. However, the finality of asylum claims decided by the Tribunal between 2000 and 2003 was overturned in 2004 by the CoA, which found that the Tribunal had followed 'conflicting approaches' in its approach to 'the facts' and its willingness to admit new evidence, see [2004] EWCA Civ 49, *England and Wales Court of Appeal (Civil Division) Decisions*, available at: http://www.bailii.org/ew/cases/EWCA/Civ/2004/49.html (accessed 8 August 2016).

7 The Kafkaesque experience of seeking asylum in the UK

In this chapter I seek to understand how individuals experience the process of seeking asylum in the UK, an issue that raises questions about the quality of justice at play in the asylum system. In this regard, Rawls' notion of 'justice as fairness' seems applicable. For Rawls, justice comes into play where 'each person has an equal right to a fully adequate scheme of equal basic rights and liberties' (1985: 227). He was concerned to set out a possible system of justice for *citizens* living in a modern democracy, whereas I am concerned with the system of justice that a democracy extends to *foreigners*. A different way of stating the problem would be to say that before the law, everyone is accorded the same rights, that legal decisions are based on 'due reflection' on a case, and that legal procedures are fair and transparent (i.e. the emphasis is on 'procedural justice'; Fabienne 2009).

From the point of view of asylum seekers, an alternative reading of justice might be found in Carlen's (1976) study of British magistrates' courts. She argues that the effect of the court's formal rules, its legal rituals and its spatial architecture is to control proceedings such that a defendant's experience is one of coercion and absurdity. The experience of justice is absurd, she argues, when persons finds themselves in situations where they lack knowledge of the appropriate rules and/or where the rules they are made aware of are unpredictably enforced, rendering them unable to participate in the proceedings.

A fictional example is found in Franz Kafka's *The Trial* (1925 [1994]: 4–5), where the author sets out a dystopic view of modernity in which an Austrian citizen, 'K', wakes up to find two strangers in his bedroom who refuse to identify themselves. When he queries them, one states:

> 'You are not allowed to go from here. You are under house arrest.' 'So it would seem,' said K. 'And for what reason?' he then asked. 'It's not our job to tell you that. Go into your room and wait. The proceedings have now been started and you will learn everything in good time. I am exceeding my instructions by talking to you in such a friendly manner.'

The two men seize his personal property, eat his breakfast and disregard his identity papers. When asked whether they had made a mistake in arresting him, one replies:

> 'There is no room for mistake. Our authorities, as far as I know them, and I know only the lowest grades, do not go in search of guilt in the population but are, as it says in the law, drawn to guilt and must send us warders out. That is the law. Where could there be a mistake in that?' 'This law is unknown to me,' said K. 'All the worse for you,' said the warder.

K was released from house arrest, but was accused of an unstated crime. Subsequently, neither K nor his lawyer were allowed to submit evidence in his defence, and strangers provided him with contradictory 'legal' advice. He was tried *in absentia*, found guilty and executed.

I draw upon the work of Rawls and Carlen to understand how individuals experience seeking asylum in the UK. I begin by assessing Home Office statements and media reports that asylum seekers represent a threat to the UK and that policy measures to prevent them from obtaining asylum are justifiable. In the second section I briefly outline ideas and arguments drawn from the 'market' which inform asylum law, policy and practice. The third section explores the bureaucratic and socio-temporal impacts of asylum policy on asylum seekers. Finally, I conclude that there are many reasons why individuals seeking asylum experience the process as essentially unknowable, absurd and unjust.

What do asylum seekers know about the UK prior to their arrival?

The British media have amplified statements by politicians and the Home Office that a large – indeed, disproportionate – number of asylum seekers come to the UK. Three assumptions appear to lay behind this claim: that most asylum seekers are really economic migrants, that asylum seekers have a detailed knowledge about the UK prior to their arrival, and that they chose to come to the UK. The argument is that they come 'because of the generosity of the welfare state and the ease of finding work in the growing informal labour market, because the UK has no identity cards and because of a fairly poor record on sending home unsuccessful asylum applicants' (Gilbert and Khoser 2006: 1209). In recent years the political elite and the media have transformed asylum seekers and migrants into a 'social problem' and a 'foil' against which an 'illiberal political economy' has created a society in which access to welfare and justice is predicated on the exclusion of asylum seekers, migrants and 'foreigners' (Holmes 2016).

Over the past two decades asylum policy in the UK and Europe has: (a) restricted access to state territory by asylum seekers/migrants; (b) severely restricted the right to work and access to welfare benefits; (c) substituted forms of temporary protection for permanent asylum (Schuster 2000); and (d) created a massive 'prison industrial complex' to incarcerate and deport non-citizen residents (Bosworth 2012; Global Detention Project 2011).

Against this backdrop, the Home Office (UK 2005b) has argued that there is a clear relationship between the adoption of restrictive policies and a decline in the number of asylum applications. Is there evidence to support this claim? First, it is not the case that the UK receives a disproportionate number of refugees. When applications are adjusted for population size, statistics for the period 1999–2013 indicate that the UK received on average the ninth highest number of refugees out of the 13 countries in the EU (Fiddick 1999: 7–8).[1] Furthermore, and apart from 'pre-entry' measures which block entry into the UK/EU by individuals without visas, Crawley has argued that there is a 'weak correlation between asylum applications and policy-related deterrence measures' (2010a: 15).

Second, it is not the case that the UK provides generous benefits: over the past decade legislation has made it illegal for asylum seekers to work and receive benefits other than weekly food vouchers and basic accommodation on a 'no choice' basis while they wait for a decision on their claim (Campbell 2013b: chap. 6). If an asylum application is refused, all support is withdrawn; the individual becomes destitute, and is subject to arrest and deportation.

Nor has research has found evidence that the UK is a major destination of asylum seekers (Gilbert and Khoser 2006; Robinson and Segrott 2002; Crawley 2010a). Indeed, the majority of individuals fleeing persecution leave their country of origin hurriedly and have little control over where they arrive. The majority of refugees do not choose a specific country, rather their objective is to reach a safe place. Because of restrictive policies, asylum applicants are unable to legally enter Europe and are increasingly reliant on smugglers/'agents' to bring them in. The overwhelming finding of research is that many asylum seekers did not choose a specific destination when they decided to leave their country of origin, and many did not specifically want to come to the UK (Crawley 2010a). In the majority of cases the decision regarding where an individual was taken was made by their agent.[2] Furthermore, and in line with previous studies:

> whilst many respondents reported the presence of family or friends in the UK, only a minority of people had direct or close contact prior to leaving their country of origin and even fewer received any information that might have directly informed the decision making process.
>
> (Crawley 2010a: 29)

In short, most asylum seekers possess limited knowledge about the UK (though most assumed that they would have to work to support themselves and their families). Of particular interest is the fact that individuals seeking asylum have increasingly relied on 'agents'/smugglers to get into the UK/Europe (Crawley 2010a: 32). A review of quantitative and qualitative research by James and Mayblin (2016: 2) found that 'violent conflict was the single biggest predictor of refugee migration'. They argued that asylum seeking decisions about where to go were not dictated by economic gain, nor were they influenced by policies that restrict the economic rights of asylum seekers.

However, 'a belief that a destination respects human rights and the rule of law in general' was an important consideration (James and Mayblin 2016: 6).

Asylum law and policy: chopping and changing, reorganizing and refusing

As discussed in Chapters 2 and 3, the Home Office/UKBA is a powerful but largely dysfunctional bureaucracy which is tasked with implementing poorly conceived policies. The HO has increasingly attempted to micro-manage front-line staff to secure compliance with policy, but this has led to poor decision-making and spiralling legal challenges.

In the 1990s the government's response to the arrival of migrants/asylum seekers was to introduce a succession of legislative Acts aimed at regulating entry into the UK and restricting access to asylum. Thus, between 1971 and today eight primary pieces of legislation have been adopted. As a Home Office minister commented when introducing the 1998 government White Paper *Fairer, Faster and Firmer – a Modern Approach to Immigration and Asylum*, the rationale for new legislation was that:

> Piece-meal and ill-considered changes over the last 20 years have left our immigration control struggling to meet . . . expectations. Despite the dedication and professionalism of immigration staff at all levels, the system has become too complex and too slow and huge backlogs have developed.
>
> (quoted in Fiddick 1999: 28)

In 1999, when the White Paper became law, government imported ideas of 'efficiency' and 'speed' from the private sector into politics, notably the idea of creating streamlined and 'cost-effective' asylum procedures to rapidly process claims. Legislation also limited an individual's right of appeal against decisions, and 'fast-tracked' individuals with 'unfounded' claims into a newly created detention estate where asylum claims were supposed to be decided in 21 days (UK 2013c).[3]

In reality, neither legislation nor the SSHD's policies have produced the desired result. First, when the number of asylum applicants has dropped, thereby reducing pressure on officials, poor initial decisions continue to be made, e.g. at least one in four decisions by HO caseworkers are overturned on appeal. Furthermore, applicants have been dispersed across the UK, where they are forced to live in destitution and without adequate support. The net effect of the categorization, criminalization and ill treatment of asylum seekers has been to create a complex, powerful but dysfunctional bureaucracy whose operation creates a fundamental clash 'between the lived temporalities of refugees and the institutional mechanisms that characterize the time politics of asylum' (Cwerner 2004: 80). In short, for asylum seekers the asylum field, which possesses its own rhythms and temporalities, is unknowable and unpredictable.

The government has prioritized 'speed' at the expense of justice and efficiency at the expense of democracy, which requires time to pause, consider and reflect on policies and their social and legal impact (Chesneaux 2000). By accelerating official decision-making, the ethics of the market have replaced a system ostensibly based on notions of justice and 'fairness' with one in which officials are not held to account for their decisions. In effect, legislation and policy have criminalized asylum seeking. Furthermore, by constantly shifting asylum applicants between localities, in and out of detention and between different legal statuses, officials conceal the myriad problems and inadequacies inherent in government policies, and blame the problems which arise on 'devious' asylum seekers.

Bureaucratic indifference and the experience of claiming asylum

Individuals arriving at a port of entry are interviewed by IOs who have the authority to place them in the DFT. The detention estate is used by the Home Office to warehouse approximately 30,000 people each year for immigration-related offences (BID 2009). DFT procedures are supposed to expedite an asylum hearing and conclude all appeals within 21 days (UK 2012b; ILPA 2008: 13). A detainee is supposed to be provided access to a legal representative shortly after arriving at the detention centre; they are interviewed by the HO on day two, and the HO decision is served on them the following day. The detainee has two days to appeal against the decision, and a further three days to lodge their 'bundle' with the Tribunal before an appeal hearing on the ninth day; the Tribunal has two days to make a decision, and the applicant a further two days to appeal against it. By the twenty-first day a detainee should be 'documented' and capable of being returned to their country of origin. This is not, of course, what happens.

Immigration detention centres hold a mix of individuals. In addition to individuals detained as they seek to enter the UK, there are also individuals who were initially allowed to enter the UK to make an asylum claim that was subsequently refused, individuals who illegally entered the UK (and were later arrested), individuals who overstayed their visas, and foreign nationals convicted of a criminal offence. The following cases – many of which were decided in a Tribunal hearing centre located inside a detention centre – provides a sense of how the system operates and the frustrations and misunderstandings experienced by detainees.

The spatial and legal architecture which governs tribunals applies with even greater force in detention centres, where proceedings take place in a hearing room where all entrances/exits are locked. If appellants are able to speak to their lawyer before the hearing, it is through a glass window; they are escorted into the hearing room by security staff and compelled to sit in a designated place (sometimes this is a Perspex box). All furniture is fixed to the floor; judges enter via a separate, secure entrance. Interaction and legal argument are regulated by Procedural Rules and Directions which define the issues to be decided and limit the right of the appellant to speak. Many appellants are not legally represented, which means that appeals are short. At the end of the hearing appellants are escorted back into the detention facility: IJs only announce a decision at the end of a bail application (in all other appeals the individual is returned to detention without knowing the outcome of the hearing).

In Chapter 2 I discussed the case of *Eritrea/TM*, who was detained for seven months, only to be released and given Indefinite Leave to Remain because a human rights activist took his case to the European Court of Human Rights in Strasbourg. Most of those in the DFT experience a different outcome.

The case of *Albania/KJ*

In May 2008 a young Albanian male arrived at Heathrow airport and was discovered to be in possession of a Polish passport. He was arrested and placed in the DFT, where, assisted by a lawyer, his asylum application was refused.[4] At his appeal four weeks later he was unable to secure a lawyer to represent him. Very unusually, the IJ allowed the detainee scope to set out his asylum claim, which emanated from having been caught in the embrace of another man by family members in a very conservative Muslim area of northern Albania. The young man was beaten by family members, threatened with death, and was pursued to Italy, from where he fled to the UK on a false passport. In what follows I focus on the difficulties he experienced in the DFT rather than his detailed and credible account of persecution at the hands of family and relatives.

Though there was no record of his interview by an IO at Heathrow, it was clear that he co-operated with the officer. He showed the IO the documents he had travelled on, including a valid Italian ID. He was then detained and questioned. Shortly after being taken to Harmondsworth Detention Centre he was interviewed by a HO case owner and was quickly issued an RFL, which he could not read and which was not translated for him.

At his asylum appeal the HOPO argued that: (1) 'there are strong reasons' for suspecting the applicant's credibility; (2) there were inconsistencies in his account; (3) he was an 'economic migrant'; and (4) under s. 8 of the Immigration and Asylum Act (2004) he submitted a passport that was not his own in an attempt to enter the UK by deception. The HOPO argued that the appeal should be refused and KJ should be returned to Albania.

The appellant's response to the HOPO, via an interpreter, was eloquent and to the point.

KJ: It is quite unfair and unjust. Despite my sincerity still they [the HO] maintain I am not credible and that I've lied. I can't remember every point, if I can be taken [through them] one by one?

IJ: I am not going to repeat them. He [the HOPO] gave us excerpts from the RFL which you have read . . .

KJ: Yes. I was unable to read . . . understand due to language difficulties. If I could ask more about my credibility? He said something about 1995?
HOPO: I am happy to explain.
IJ: Do.
HOPO: I was referring to the 'OGN'.
KJ: What is OGN?
HOPO: The Home Office Operational Guidance Note at paragraph 3.11.2 states that before 1995 homosexuality was illegal under the penal code; after that date, 20 January 1995, it was decriminalized. It's the background specific to you, if homosexuality is not illegal . . .
KJ: Yes, laws may be. But a lot are not implemented or they do not offer security. In relation to myself . . . Muslim feeling . . . about that, they could do about my behaviour. The hatred they feel, you can't ignore that . . . . I have relatives all over Albania. I had thought of going elsewhere in Albania, but it's impossible. Can someone explain, when 72 per cent of the population are Muslim, that I would be able to live by myself or with another man? My life would be in danger . . . . You mentioned about the authorities. Had I gone to complain about my ill-treatment, despite the law, I am certain I would have been abused by the police.

After two hours the IJ adjourned the hearing and the applicant was returned to the detention facility;[5] it was not clear whether his case was sufficiently compelling to be granted. However, bearing in mind existing case law on this issue – specifically *IM (Risk – Objective Evidence –Homosexuals) Albania* CG [2003] UKIAT 00067, it was very likely that he would be refused status and returned to Albania.

The case of *Afghanistan/AH*

In August 2008 an Afghan male in his early twenties was caught by police after illegally entering the UK. He was held in police cells for four days, where he was interviewed before being transferred to Harmondsworth Detention Centre. In short order he was interviewed by a case owner, who quickly issued an RFL. He then attended, with a lawyer, his appeal, which the Tribunal refused. The discussion below is based on the proceedings of his reconsideration hearing, which was concluded, without a lawyer but with the assistance of an interpreter, in 1 hour and 3 minutes.

(continued)

(continued)

The applicant could not read or speak English, and thus could not read the RFL or the Tribunal's decision refusing his appeal. Furthermore, no one had translated or explained these documents to him. The IJ swiftly dealt with this procedural difficulty by asking him 'Did you tell the truth?' to the police who interviewed him in police custody, in his HO interview, at the asylum appeal and to his solicitor (who had submitted documents to the court).

The crux of the HO case against AH was that he had illegally entered the UK. However, as a result of questions asked by the IJ and the HOPO, a narrative of persecution and flight gradually emerged. He had fled his home in Khost, Afghanistan and gone to Pakistan rather than join the Taliban. In 2007 he returned briefly to Afghanistan to take his mother and siblings to safety in Pakistan. During the visit he and his girlfriend secretly had sex; subsequently, her family found that she was pregnant and were searching for him.

The HOPO focused on the issue of illegal entry, but via his questions it emerged that the young man had been trafficked from Pakistan to the UK. The HOPO perfunctorily dismissed AH's evidence by arguing that: (1) the appellant could return to Afghanistan despite his alleged fear of the Taliban; (2) he resumed a relationship with the girl openly, which was not approved by their families; (3) if he was in genuine fear of the Taliban, he would not have had a sexual relation, but would have taken his family away; (4) if there was a relevant fear of return, (internal) relocation would not be unduly harsh. The HOPO concluded by asking the IJ to dismiss the appeal.

At the end of the hearing, AH was returned to the detention centre. The IJ almost certainly decided that he should be returned to Afghanistan because this was the prevailing policy at the time.

A third categories of person held in detention are individuals who were granted asylum but who were subsequently convicted of a serious criminal offence which led the judge to recommend that they be deported.

The case of *Burundi/K*

K's case was unusually complex because it revolved around his disputed nationality. He was a young black man who appeared for a bail application at a London Tribunal after having been detained for nearly two years. K's 'Catch-22' predicament, which he was completely unable to resolve, emerged at the hearing.

IJ:	He has been detained for a lengthy period of time. The HO don't seem to be able to deport him anywhere, but the HO maintain it's his fault.
HOPO:	Yes, in January 2006 he was interviewed to obtain his bio-data – 21 months ago. Within two months of his entry into immigration detention. A large part of the delay is due to the appellant haven given partial or incomplete evidence. The Liaison Officer at the Burundian embassy suggests that he be tested for his knowledge of Burundi. Efforts are being made at the shipping agent[6] as of 30 September. I would remind the court that the delay is due to the contradictory information in his asylum claim.
IJ:	Yes, in his own bundle. What information is at odds? It is difficult for me to identify.
HOPO:	In his asylum claim he claimed fear of persecution from the Tutsis. He left in 1995. He left the country at six months of age, but was many times in and out of Burundi. He has been all over Rwanda, Brazzaville, DRC [Democratic Republic of the Congo], Zimbabwe, Botswana and the Republic of South Africa. He says his claim is about homosexuality . . . that he is not a Burundian, but from elsewhere. He is using his claim to frustrate return. Regard his horrible criminal history . . .
COUNSEL (C):	There is no excuse to detain for such a long time. It is established in law that there is a time when detention becomes unlawful. What does it mean, he was unhelpful? He was granted refugee status and . . . the High Court did not decide his application until August 2008. He was in the right not to co-operate given his original case. He has complied with documentation procedures and has had a phone interview with the Burundian officials. Since April 2008 it is not his fault that he was not interviewed until July.
IJ:	I accept there is a catalogue.
C:	It was found by the AIT that he was Burundian and he was granted refugee status. The HO did not appeal that decision. The court accepted his nationality . . .

A little later in the hearing the appellant stated that the result of his telephone interview with a Burundi official was negative: 'They said I had no close ties. They asked if I had a family there. I said no. I left at six months. They said I can't help you.' Eventually, the IJ stated that he was not prepared to grant bail. He told the applicant: 'help the Burundian authorities to accept you'. K was taken back into detention despite the inability of the HO to progress his deportation.

A fourth category of persons held in immigration detention includes individuals who were allowed into the country to make an asylum claim and who were subsequently arrested – either at their residence (see Box 7.1) or at a government office where they are required to 'sign in' to register their compliance with the law – and detained. Many of these individuals are repeatedly arrested, detained and subsequently released without explanation. However, many individuals are also deported (see Chapter 8).

Box 7.1 Dawn raid on 'failed' asylum seeker

Mary, an asylum seeker from Uganda, explained how she and her children had twice experienced dawn raids in Glasgow. She explained that they were woken up and forced to dress in front of the immigration officers. They were then transported from Scotland to the Yarl's Wood Removal Centre in Bedfordshire in a cage in the back of a van, given no substantial food and little water:

> Mary said: 'My children and I were treated like animals in that cage. We were hungry and had to watch while the guards ate at a petrol station. But the detention centre was even worse – we felt like criminals.' Mary broke down as she recounted her experience of the second dawn raid after her family was released from Yarl's Wood. The terrified family hid in a neighbour's flat and heard the immigration officers banging on the door of their home.

Source: Independent Asylum Commission (2007).

In addition to the experience of being detained and the frustration of grappling with unintelligible legal procedures, detainees must also cope with the socio-temporal effects of asylum policy which speed up and slow down the assessment of their claim. Individuals are imprisoned and released, sometimes repeatedly, without explanation.

To explore this issue, I will look at cases of individuals who were allowed to enter the UK to make an asylum claim and who had to file their claim within five days. This means that they had to quickly find out how to make a claim. Officials do not provide advice to asylum seekers, and applicants are further disadvantaged because on arrival they are disoriented, have limited formal education and do not speak English. In this situation asylum seekers tend to rely on unofficial 'gatekeepers', i.e. fellow nationals residing in the UK who claim to be interpreters or lawyers.

The case of *Ethiopia/HT*

HT, an Ethiopian woman, and her two sons arrived in the UK from Ethiopia in December 2004 and claimed asylum. Her case provides insight into the role of 'gatekeepers' and the socio-temporal effect of repeated detention. Shortly after arriving in the UK, another asylum seeker put her in touch with an Ethiopian 'lawyer' who interviewed her and 'coached' her into giving a (false) claim which he filed with the HO. The family was put into a 'hotel' in London, and in January 2005 they were dispersed to Gateshead. Her appeal was heard and refused in May 2005 because the judge decided that her claim lacked credibility. An appeal against his decision was unsuccessful.

In mid-2005 UKBA officials arrested and detained her. They sought to 'document' her for deportation – which involved taking her to be interviewed at the Ethiopian embassy – and eventually put her on a plane to Ethiopia. However, she disrupted the flight, and the pilot refused to carry her. She was taken back to the detention centre, and was released a short time later. Repeated attempts to contact her Ethiopian lawyer failed. In December 2006 officials came to her accommodation, checked her ID, and without explanation arrested and detained her. During approximately 10 months in detention the UKBA once again attempted to remove her.

In June 2006 a new lawyer filed a fresh asylum application on her behalf. For reasons which are unclear, she was released from detention in October 2006. However, in January 2007 she was again detained. In March 2007 her new lawyer filed a judicial review against the HO for failing to decide her fresh asylum application; two months later she was released. Several months after her release she and her sons were given ILR. She had no idea why she was repeatedly detained, nor for that matter why she was eventually released and given status.

The London Detainee Support Group has summarized the general experience of detainees like HT:

> The apparent arbitrariness of the system was a major theme. Interviewees felt themselves confronted by a system of implacable hostility and disinterest. Interviewees described attempting to connect their own and other detainees' situations and actions with what happened to them, but [were] unable to discover any link. Minor with serious offenders; the quietly well-behaved with perceived trouble-makers; those who wanted to return with those who didn't; all stay detained regardless. Except when they didn't; and interviewees could discern no logic in the pattern of who was released. The result was an impression of absolute disenfranchisement: nothing they could do seemed to have any impact on the overwhelming fact of their detention, so better to do nothing and wait on inscrutable fate and the Home Office.
>
> (London Detainee Support Group 2009: 18)

In fact, detainees share one key attribute: as foreigners, they can be incarcerated indefinitely and summarily deported (Bosworth 2012). Indeed, how long they spend in detention depends entirely on how quickly the HO processes their case. The task of processing a claim does not, despite the rhetoric of the 'fast' track, move smoothly or in accord with normal temporal processes. Instead, a case speeds up or slows down in parallel with unseen bureaucratic action/inaction which defines how a detainee experiences time – whether understood existentially, biologically or biographically – behind bars (Vitus 2010).

Detention cuts individuals off from normality; it severs family and social relations, and it prevents effective legal representation. Detained asylum seekers have much higher rates of self-harm and suicide than convicted criminals, and for many years after their release they struggle to cope with the social and medical/psychiatric problems caused by detention (Cohen 2008; Coffrey et al. 2010). Time seems to stand still. Indeed, time may regress backwards. Just as importantly, the problems which caused individuals to flee their country of origin count for nothing in the DFT.

The case of *Eritrea/BH*

The situations confronting asylum applicants who are allowed into the UK to make a claim are only slightly less Kafkaesque than those of individuals detained at the border. Take the case of one young refugee who was smuggled into the UK by an agent in 2001 and abandoned in a café in south London. When he realized that the agent was not going to return, he walked the streets until dark and slept in a subway. He was 15 years old. Fortunately, an Ethiopian couple found him and took him to a law firm. They then took him home over the weekend. The following Monday they escorted him to the Home Office, where he waited in a queue from 11 a.m. to 8 p.m. before his claim was registered. However, rather than taking him to a hostel, officials merely gave him a map. He walked around Croydon for some time, but could not find the hostel. By chance, he ran into one of the Ethiopians who had befriended him, and was taken to their home. The next day they took him to the hostel, but it was closed; the guard told them to leave him at the police station. Once again they brought him home for the night then escorted him back to the HO, where, after an eight-hour wait, he was allocated to another hostel. However, when the official rang the hostel, the warden said it was full. His benefactors insisted that he be given a place to stay, and he was finally put into a third hostel (some time later, he was placed with a foster family).

This case illustrates the role of a different kind of 'gatekeeper'. The Ethiopian couple who befriended him had almost certainly been refugees, and they knew the importance of contacting a lawyer. The law firm, however, merely directed him to the HO, where standard procedures and long queues led to a perfunctory acknowledgment of his claim before he was sent on a fruitless search for a hostel.

The case of *Ethiopia/MT*

A sense of dislocation and official indifference was also experienced by another Ethiopian woman, MT. She travelled to the UK in 2002 with an agent who took her through Heathrow airport before abandoning her in a London café. A stranger took her to an immigration law firm, where she was given a map and a bus ticket to the Home Office to register her claim. However, when she got off the bus she could not find her way. Because she spoke no English, she went up to strangers and touched them to get their attention and showed them a paper on which was written 'Home Office'. No one helped her. Eventually, she found the building, but had a panic attack and quickly left: 'I go in, and I come back out again. Cause I can't [go] in because the police stop me or something bad [will happen].' She eventually returned and waited in a queue before speaking to an interpreter who helped to register her claim and who gave her directions to a hostel where she stayed for three weeks before she was dispersed to Wolverhampton. For three weeks she refused to speak to anyone because she heard voices which caused a panic attack: ''cause when I hearing somebody speak Amharic: Oh my god, somebody is coming to get me now. When I hear somebody speak Tigrinya, all these peoples will kill me.'

Her confused state of mind should have been apparent from her behaviour – she was subsequently diagnosed as suffering from post-traumatic stress disorder. Unfortunately, her paranoia worsened each time officials found her story of imprisonment and rape lacking in credibility. Furthermore, repeated refusals to accept her claim compelled her to move in and out of government accommodation, onto the street and into a church to live, until a fifth 'fresh application' for asylum was successful eight years after her arrival.[7]

The case of *Eritrea/MA*

Another young Eritrean, MA, arrived in the UK in the back of lorry in early 2005; he was caught by police and detained for two days before being registered as an asylum seeker. He was placed in designated accommodation for six months before the HO interviewed him, at which time they gave him a list (in English) of law firms to contact for legal advice. By chance, he met another Eritrean asylum seeker who gave him the phone number of an Eritrean interpreter who helped file his asylum claim. After staying three months in Kent, he was suddenly

(continued)

(continued)

dispersed to Newcastle. Within six months of filing his claim (about 12 months after entering the UK) he was wrongly told by his lawyer that the HO had refused his claim and that 'his case was weak' (i.e. the firm would no longer represent him). At this time government support ceased, and he was made homeless. He said of this period: 'It was terrible, the worst thing was thinking about what's going to be my case [what is going to happen to me]? Where am I going to end up mentally?' He contacted a law firm known to assist Eritreans, and they filed an appeal on his behalf. For a month he lived with Eritrean friends who fed, sheltered and supported him until he was allocated government housing and given £35 a week for food and clothing.

It is notable that UKBA officials failed to take his claim for six months. Officials appear to have assumed that their duty of care towards an asylum seeker is fulfilled by handing them a piece of paper on which is written contact details for law firms. This assumption is ludicrous because most asylum seekers cannot read or speak English.

An important element in MA's account concerns how he linked up with resident nationals. There were many stories circulating about 'interpreters' touting for business at the hostels where asylum seekers stayed. These 'interpreters' capitalize on their culture/language and tenuous links to immigration firms to make money by bringing a client to a firm where they are paid to interpret the applicant's claim. Some of these 'entrepreneurs' are deceitful and do little to advance an individual's claim, which, when it is refused, transforms individuals into deportable 'failed' asylum seekers.

Unaccompanied asylum-seeking children are faced with additional difficulties, in part because they do not know whom to trust (see Box 7.2). Earning the trust of these children takes considerable time and effort, a task which is undermined by cultural and linguistic differences, the indifference of officials, and barriers created by the asylum system. Children are likely to be shunted from carer to carer, and they often live at some distance from social services and their lawyer. For this reason, children are often 'silent' when they are interviewed by the HO. The following case illustrates the problems which such children face.

Box 7.2 Home Office interviews of unaccompanied asylum-seeking children

1 Children over the age of 12 are routinely interviewed by HO officials.
2 Inconsistencies in interview procedure and practice undermine the ability of an individual to present their account.

3 The attitude of officials towards these children is negative and disbelieving.
4 Separated asylum-seeking children have only a partial knowledge of the circumstances of their flight.
5 When interviewed shortly after arrival, they are often confused and disoriented.
6 Many of these children have been exposed to high levels of violence.
7 Many are confused and upset by the interview and the failure of the official to respond appropriately.
8 There are many reasons why children provide a restricted view of their life before arriving in the UK.

Sources: Crawley (2010b); Kohli (2005); Jones (2001).

The case of *Eritrea/SK*

SK arrived in London from Ethiopia after he walked across the Eritrean border in 1998. He was 13 years old when he arrived in the UK, and was brought by an 'agent' who introduced him to an Eritrean lawyer. The law firm sent him to the HO with an interpreter to attend the screening and substantive interview before filing his initial claim, which the HO refused. There was a long delay until his appeal was scheduled in 2007.

Because SK was 'introduced' by an agent to an Eritrean immigration caseworker who spoke his language, the caseworker built up a significant level of trust and was able to explain to the boy a great deal about how his case would be handled. Prior to his appeal, seven years after an RFL had been issued to him, he told us:

> I had a mixed feeling. First I thought that I would have been successful had I followed what I wanted and said, but he [the barrister] was weak . . . I only met him there [in court]. The barrister presented my case on religious ground although my request was political. My barrister was weak . . . . The interpreter [from the law firm] who was with me was so surprised by his incompetence that he said he had never seen such an inexperienced lawyer before.

SK gave oral testimony, which he thought had gone well: 'I told them everything myself. There is no more to say.' While he thought the firm's interpreter was of considerable help in following the appeal, nevertheless

(continued)

(continued)

he said: 'I understood only half of it. Listening to them and the interpreter clashed and was not easy [to follow]. I also thought that the [court] interpreter was not passing all the information [to the judge].'

While he was granted asylum, his experience of seeking asylum were negative: 'It is very bad. I can't work or get educated. I'm caught in a limbo . . . I have somehow managed to cope, but there are others who have become insane, and even suicidal.

Two issues stand out in relation to SK's case. First, and regardless of extensive contact with his legal team mediated by interpreters and a caseworker who spoke his native language, he never understood the legal process. For instance, he constantly confused interpreters for lawyers, he was sure that the court-appointed interpreter did not truthfully interpret his evidence at his appeal, and he consistently misunderstood legal argument. At what turned out to be his final appeal in 2007 he had to be persuaded by his counsel not to introduce a new element in his claim (which would have resulted in his appeal being refused). His confusion stemmed in part from having only a primary school education, his inability to speak English, and a mistrust of 'officials' – Home Office officials, but also lawyers and judges – who, as far as he could see, had repeatedly refused to believe his evidence. SK's perception about the way his claim was handled is shared by many asylum seekers.

The case of *Ethiopia/DS*

The problems confronting asylum applicants is demonstrated by DS, who fled his country in 2000 and arrived in Heathrow only to be abandoned by an agent. He was able to file his claim quickly, but equally quickly, his claim was refused due to a case of mistaken identity with another Ethiopian who had the same name. He heard nothing about his claim for two years until he asked the local MP to write to the HO, but this intervention merely triggered a demand that he attend another interview. The case of mistaken identity was only resolved by chance in 2003 when he met the other Ethiopian and was able to satisfy the HO that they had misidentified him.[8]

He lost his initial appeal in 2004 and two reconsiderations in 2005 and 2006. However, all three decisions were overturned because the judge erred in deciding his case. The effect of successively losing appeals compelled him to move in and out of government accommodation and from London to Liverpool and back to London, where he was allocated a small shared bedroom in a dirty house with seven other asylum applicants where he stayed for nearly three years. Complaints about housing were met with indifference; officials told him, 'if you don't like it, you can leave' (Hocking 2006; Hynes 2011). In 2005 another Ethiopian and fellow Jehovah's Witness invited him to stay rent-free in his flat in London, an arrangement that lasted three years.

Shortly after his first appeal was refused the law firm representing him closed. Coincidentally, he was volunteering as an interpreter when he met a barrister who was handling a case similar to his own. The barrister referred him to another law firm,[9] and represented him in successive appeals until he obtained status in 2008.

Unlike the cases discussed above, DS spoke English reasonably well. Even so, his story was at odds with his case file. However, unlike many others he maintained faith in the system, probably because of his strong religious beliefs and the support of other Jehovah's Witnesses.

The case of *Ethiopia/MB*

Another Ethiopian male, MB, arrived in 1999 on a student visa, but within one month he applied for asylum and was interviewed by the HO. Six months later an advice worker referred him to an immigration lawyer; he was given a £35 a week food voucher and allocated government-approved accommodation. For nearly four years he heard nothing about his case. In 2004, and in violation of the Immigration Rules, he was allowed to work.

During this time other asylum seekers offered him advice. He said:

> I spoke to people who have been here, other asylum seekers, refugees, totally told me a different story . . . . They told me how the Home Office worked, and that was a big shock to me because they said you have to, you should have said you are Somalia? You should have said you are Eritrea. [And that] I should have changed my name, you know! How can I? I'm educated. How can I change my identity? . . . I found everything bizarre and strange actually, how they work in the Home Office.

When the HO refused his application and his appeal was refused, he was shocked because he had provided oral testimony. As he said, 'I gave them

(continued)

(continued)

all the facts, all the documents. . . . I thought, you know, why is that? You know if you have the facts [of my case], you have all the details, if you have all the facts why can't you check them to find out about those facts?' At his 2007 appeal he confronted a further inexplicable problem: his barrister did not let him give evidence:

> I was told I wouldn't be able to speak . . . . It's just sitting there; actually I didn't say a thing. I was just listening . . . that surprised me because if they dispute about me, why didn't they ask me? . . . As [my barrister later explained] 'it is all about the law, they discussed more about the law' for two-and-a-half hours.

Two months later he found out that he had won his appeal. During the eight years it took him to get status his mother had died, his younger sister was adopted by strangers and his education was put on hold. He told me: 'I'm okay. I'm studying. Actually, I started this course because I was fed up. I couldn't sleep. I have been taking sleeping pills for years.'

Confusion among asylum seekers regarding how or why their claim was granted or refused is widespread, and the reasons for this state of affairs are not difficult to ascertain. First, most asylum applicants receive a Refusal Letter from the HO which states that their claim is not recognized and that they should return to their country of origin. While this refusal triggers an automatic right of appeal, the process is difficult to fathom, for many reasons. First, the organization of legal practice means that the law firm which take an individual's initial asylum claim is not involved in the appeal – because they instruct a barrister to litigate the case (and there is very little communication between barristers and appellants). Second, cuts to legal aid led to the closure of many law firms, leaving many individuals without legal representation. Furthermore, IJs frequently err in deciding asylum claims, which means that the claim needs to be reheard. Indeed, the average time for the claims cited in this chapter to be concluded was six years. Small wonder, then, that most applicants do not understand why their asylum claim was refused or granted.

A state of confusion?

I began by referring to Rawls' notion of 'justice as fairness', with its emphasis on 'procedural justice', and to Carlen's and Kafka's depiction of law – from the defendant/asylum applicant's point of view – as unpredictable, lacking in transparency and impossible to participate in. Do the cases discussed in this book support this view? How should we understand the experience of individuals seeking asylum in the UK? What kind of justice do they receive?

While asylum policy *per se* – as opposed to the UK's 'opt-out' of European Union asylum and migration policy (discussed in the 'Conclusion and postscript') – does not deter asylum seekers from entering the UK, British policies do compel individuals to turn to 'agents' to enter the country and to make an asylum claim. Asylum seekers also turn to other refugees – ethnic 'entrepreneurs', translators and 'lawyers' – for assistance, which can undermine their claim and which reinforces discourses that stigmatize them as illegal migrants. The cases analysed in this book demonstrate fundamental problems with the system. Throughout their time in the 'asylum field' asylum seekers experience bureaucratic indifference bordering on racism. Their experience of Home Office policies and procedures, which notionally reflect market-based conceptions of efficiency and cost-effectiveness, renders policy unintelligible – a situation reinforced by the failure of officials to explain to applicants what they need to do. Asylum applicants and detainees experience a system that prioritizes speed over justice (except when decisions are not made in a timely manner or when they are not informed about decisions) and administrative efficiency over fairness (except for detainees who are left to languish indefinitely).

Government officials are not held to account for poor/unlawful actions. Clear examples of Home Office failures include: failure to take a decision in a timely manner; failure to communicate an official decision; communicating to applicants in English, a language which most individuals can't understand; procedural rules which curtail the evidence an individual is allowed to provide; judicial decisions which are not explained to appellants; 'Catch-22' bureaucratic procedures which keep individuals in detention (without explanation); and enforced movement around the country, and in and out of detention.

The work of Home Office officials, immigration lawyers and judges is tied to 'work targets' which prioritize time and procedure over the careful consideration of a case – a situation which dehumanizes the process, leads to a growing indifference to asylum applicants and results in poorly considered decisions on individual claims. Thus, *pace* Das (2004), even though Home Office and judicial decisions emerge from an apparently rational bureaucratic process, written decisions exhibit a 'magical' quality in the sense of being incomprehensible while having a decisive effect on their lives. The high cost of falling afoul of officials, together with the cultural misunderstandings created by the spatial and legal architecture of the courts, renders asylum law and policy unintelligible and unknowable to most asylum applicants; officials are to be avoided and feared, rather than respected.

For the reasons discussed above, we should not be surprised to learn that at the end of a very lengthy process most asylum seekers are left in a 'state of confusion' about the law and their legal status (Ordonez 2008). To put the matter differently, asylum applicants do not possess the linguistic or cultural competence to understand how the 'asylum field' is structured and how it operates. Furthermore, because of the complex nature of law and the speed with which officials decide their claims, individuals experience the process of seeking asylum as unfair and mystifying. In short, for most applicants the 'asylum field' constitutes a theatre of the absurd.

From the point of view of 'the law', it doesn't matter if the asylum applicants do or do not understand the law as long as their claim is fairly decided. We have seen, however, that there are factors at work which produce much unfairness. A different way of viewing the situation is to note that a significant percentage of individuals who confront the problems identified in this chapter eventually secure some form of status and go on to secure ILR and British citizenship. It should be evident that, grateful though they may be for eventually being granted refuge, their experiences do not encourage them to embrace British cultural and political values. If anything, as 'Black' Britons they remain apart from, and are not integrated into, British society.

Notes

1 For EU statistics, see 'Statistics explained: Asylum statistics', *Eurostat*, available at: http://epp.eurostat.ec.europa.eu/statistics_explained/index.php/Asylum_statistics (accessed 8 August 2016).
2 While the route a refugee/migrant takes from their country of origin partly reflects the haste with which they leave, it also reflects the relative cost – whether in financial terms or the danger involved – of specific routes. Smuggling is expensive and hazardous: the number of people who drown crossing the Mediterranean or the Strait of Hormuz runs into the tens of thousands.
3 Between 2 and 5 per cent of asylum claims heard in the DFT system are granted (as compared to 20 per cent of first appeals heard by the Tribunal; BID 2009).
4 At the time, Albania was designated by the HO as a 'safe country of origin' (Clayton 2012: 416–418), which should have meant that his asylum claim was certified as 'clearly unfounded'.
5 In a meeting after the hearing the IJ confirmed that the appellant had proved to be a good advocate for his case and that his testimony was consistent and credible.
6 Presumably he entered the UK as an illegal stowaway.
7 The fifth application was supported by extensive psychiatric documentation from the Helen Bamber Foundation, which had assisted her for many years.
8 Curiously, the issue of mistaken identity which he felt had obstructed the progress of his case was not indicated in his case file.
9 When the second law firm closed, the barrister helped him get representation in a third firm.

8 Interest groups, asylum policy and Home Office intransigence

This study has identified extensive problems with the British asylum system, many of which stem from government policy and policy implementation. Have NGOs and other institutions in the asylum field identified similar problems, and if so, have they been able to influence government asylum policy?[1]

I begin by reviewing the literature on political lobbying on asylum policy, following which I set out my approach to this question. The second section looks at the work of three very different organizations that have draw attention to fundamental problems with asylum policy and practice and which pursued different strategies to influence the government: the Immigration Law Practitioners' Association (a UK professional organization), UNHCR London (a specialized agency of the United Nations) and the Independent Chief Inspector of Borders and Immigration (a government organization created to monitor the HO/UKBA). I conclude by noting that the government has responded to political lobbying by taking steps to insulate the HO/UKBA from criticism.

Elite versus the 'organized public'? Problems in analysing political lobbying

There is surprisingly little research which examines links between asylum and immigration policy and political lobbying in the UK. Research on this issue has been dominated by political scientists, who have focused either on the role of the state, the role played by specific bureaucracies/institutions or the role played by 'interest groups' in shaping immigration policy (cf. Freeman 2011).

Research on interest groups involved in political lobbying provides some insight into asylum politics. Ellis (2004) describes an NGO campaign in 1999–2000 in which Oxfam UK and the Refugee Council (at that time a government-funded organization) publicly campaigned against subsistence vouchers issued to asylum applicants (a policy that came into effect with the 1999 Asylum and Immigration Act).[2] Ellis, who was involved in the campaign, describes how the campaign was organized, how Oxfam involved the Transport and General Workers' Union, and how together they generated media attention to lobby the governing Labour Party to scrap the voucher system in early 2002.

Hailed as an important example of effective NGO lobbying on asylum issues, it is important to note how subsequent events have undermined the campaign's achievements. First, there was significant public support at the time for policy reform (this soon changed; see Page 2009; UK 2011b). Second, the unions, which provided substantial funding to the Labour Party, and Labour were enjoying a relatively good political relationship, which meant that initiatives adopted by the unions were viewed positively by the party (this too was to change). Finally, in 2006 Labour made a policy U-turn and reintroduced vouchers for individuals whose claims had been refused under s. 4 of the 2002 Act.[3] This decision gave rise to extensive, but ultimately unsuccessful, NGO campaigns which argued that government policy was responsible for the enforced destitution of asylum seekers.

Ellis's paper illustrates a number of problems encountered in analysing political lobbying (Statham 2003; Brazier, Kalitowski and Rosenblatt 2007; Parvin 2007; Bernhagen 2012). The difficulties are empirical (gathering sufficient data on a large and differentiated range of institutions/political actors) and analytical/theoretical (e.g. differentiating between the statements of organizations about lobbying and assessing their actions and the actual impact of lobbying). Additional problems relate to analysing the link between lobbying on a specific issue and wider political debates on asylum and immigration, assessing the link between lobbying and how policies are actually formulated, drafted and implemented, and the need to assess the influence of the European Union and transnational institutions on British policy. In what follows I draw on published work on political lobbying on asylum and immigration in the UK to outline my approach to this issue.

Statham (2003) examined public debates and public understandings about asylum and immigration between 1990 and 2002 and attempted to understand how they influenced government policy. His principal data was derived from an analysis of reports in the national media which indicated 714 'claims-making acts' (which allowed him to identify seven types of civil society actors involved in lobbying) and from fieldwork in south London and Bradford (in northern England) which examined local discourses about asylum.

Statham concluded that in a context in which asylum was increasingly being depicted in the press and by politicians in negative terms, national public debate was dominated by the state and NGOs/civil society actors, which made relatively few 'claims', which tended to be from the left of the political spectrum, e.g. human rights and welfare organizations and pro-migrant NGOs. Furthermore, local-level discourse on asylum was highly normative in nature (depicting outsiders/asylum applicants in openly racist terms) and was strongly influenced by statements from politicians which were carried in the media. Significantly, local discourse reflected discontent with local conditions which were not related to asylum.

Statham extended his initial research to analyse 'organized public collective action' by interest groups involved in 'immigration politics' (Statham and Geddes 2006). This research found that the 'main cleavage over immigration in Britain is enacted between a dominant restrictionist government and a pro-migrant NGO sector that is relatively isolated in civil society' (Statham and Geddes 2006: 257).

The authors argued that the political environment was strongly shaped by the state, which meant that the political field was skewed strongly against NGOs – which tended to lack the symbolic and financial resources to mobilize effectively[4] – that supported migrants and asylum seekers. In short, they found that immigration policy was largely insulated from potential challenges by civil society organizations, churches, the judiciary[5] and political party opponents.

Based on interviews with 29 organizations in the asylum field, Statham and Geddes (2006) mapped 'networks of influence', i.e. the organizations which others sought to influence, networks of disagreement and networks of co-operation. They found that over a five-year period:

1 The party in government, and the state, were the major focus of lobbying by other organizations.
2 Organizations which were state-supported (e.g. the Refugee Council) or which were 'intermediary interest groups' (churches, state bodies for racial equality, trade unions and the ILPA) exercised some power to affect state policy.
3 The majority of civil society actors were ineffective.
4 Disagreements were directed against the state – especially the HO and the National Asylum Support Service – state actors and political parties.
5 Networks of co-operation were much denser than networks of disagreement, and civil society organizations were central in influencing others, especially organizations that were supported by the state and intermediate interest groups.

Statham and Geddes concluded that:

> immigration policy is determined 'top-down' in a relatively autonomous way by political elites. Of course elites gauge potential challenges over immigration issues, especially from party political opponents, and to a less extent pressure from lobby groups. In addition, possible policy responses from other institutional actors, national and transnational, such as courts, and imperatives deriving from EU involvements, will play some role in decisions . . . . The relative importance of such factors and the direction they shift immigration policy will vary, over time, across different issues within immigration, and across countries, according to political context.
>
> (Statham and Geddes 2006: 266)

Their findings are broadly supported by Menz's (2009) analysis of lobbying on immigration/migration issues in the UK, and by research on the negative role played by politicians in setting the policy agenda and on the role of the media in exacerbating the 'public trust deficit'/credibility gap between the public and politicians (Page 2009; Somerville 2009; UK 2011b). It is important to note that Page's analysis of opinion survey data found that 'the public agrees that genuine refugees need protection and that immigration makes the country more open to new cultures' (2009: 144). It is also worth noting, however, that the distinction between 'genuine' refugees and 'bogus' asylum seekers is poorly drawn by politicians and the media.

The picture of immigration politics and lobbying which emerges from this research is that politicians – the 'elite' – increasingly pursue policies which attempt to restrict the admission of foreigners into the UK (whether these be asylum seekers or immigrants). At the same time, the negative characterization by the elite of migrants/asylum seekers as a 'problem', which is not supported by accurate information on asylum and migration,[6] directly contributes to public perceptions that politicians are unable to control the border. In this context it becomes more difficult for civil society actors to lobby or influence the government or politicians to reform existing policies, much less adopt less restrictive policies. Indeed, research (Menz 2009) and personal observation suggest that public policy consultations convened by the government have increasingly become a cosmetic exercise which leaves the government insulated from criticism and lobbying by civil society organizations. Even if this were not the case, however, data and methodological issues present insurmountable problems in proving the effectiveness of political lobbying.

If it is not possible to prove the effectiveness of political lobbying by NGOs, it *is* possible to build on the research undertaken by Statham and Geddes (2006) by providing a more in-depth analysis of three very different organizations which have attempted to influence British asylum policy. I look first at ILPA, which was identified by Statham and Geddes as a relatively successful 'intermediary interest group': ILPA is a professional association of immigration lawyers. The second organization I examine is UNHCR London, a specialized agency of the United Nations. The third organization I examine is the Independent Chief Inspector of the UK Border Agency, which didn't exist at the time when Statham and Geddes did their research. It is a state agency with a remit to monitor and inspect HO and UKBA policy and practice. Each organization was very differently positioned in the asylum field. I examine selected aspects of each organization's work which sought to influence asylum policy and practice between 2005 and 2010.

Who influences asylum and immigration policy?[7]

ILPA, a membership-based association of immigration and nationality lawyers in London, was founded in 1984. Its objectives are to improve the quality of legal advice, disseminate information on law and practice, co-ordinate the activities and interests of law practitioners and 'secure a non-racist, non-sexist, just and equitable system of immigration and nationality law practice'. From 300 members in 1988, ILPA's membership expanded to over 1,000 by 2005. ILPA's activities include:

- liaising with government, NGOs and other institutions;
- co-ordinating and distributing submissions to parliamentary committees, the government and European institutions;

- improving and expanding legal training;
- updating members on immigration and nationality law and practice.

Here I focus on ILPA's policy-related work, though it is important to note that ILPA has significantly upped the ante by providing training to lawyers to better equip them to challenge HO/UKBA asylum and immigration decisions. Between 2005 and 2009 ILPA members sat on, and sought to lobby, a large number of organizations. Its members:

- attended HO consultations;
- attended court user groups;
- attended meetings with international organizations, government departments and NGOs;[8] co-ordinated and submitted responses to UK and EU proposals and consultations.[9]

In 2005 ILPA used its reserves to create the post of a Legal Officer – which was subsequently funded by the Joseph Rowntree Charitable Trust – who was tasked with facilitating ILPA's lobbying efforts and providing legal advice to other organizations. This post greatly enhanced ILPA's ability to network with and assist growing numbers of organizations in the asylum field. It was the work of the Legal Officer, alongside ILPA's executive and ordinary members, which helped it to become an effective 'intermediary interest group'.

What were ILPA's concerns during this period, and how were they reflected in its work? In 2005 its key concern was the tendency of the HO 'to make administrative changes with little or no notice, and without proper or any transitional provisions'. This tendency was exacerbated by the speed with which new legislation was introduced and by the creation of the UKBA. ILPA responded to every major change in the structure and operation of the HO and the courts by providing updated legal training for members, making submissions and representations to government and by providing legal and practical advice to organizations.

ILPA's asylum-related lobbying[10] – which reflected significant research and litigation – focused on five issues which can only be briefly discussed here.[11] In 2005 ILPA and others became concerned that individuals held in the Detained Fast Track were unable to access legal advice, and that key aspects of the process were unfair to detainees. Meetings with, and submissions to, the HO and the LSC secured an agreement that the LSC would: (a) fund training for lawyers representing individuals in the DFT; (b) fund publication of a 'best practice guide' by ILPA for lawyers representing individuals in the DFT; (c) write to all legal representatives involved in the DFT setting out their responsibilities to clients; and (d) extend a pilot scheme for representing individuals in the DFT to other detention centres.

In 2006, following the SSHD's statement that the HO was 'not fit for purpose', the government gave a public commitment that the Immigration and Nationality Directorate (which would soon become the UKBA) would adopt and follow 'a clear and simplified legal framework'. There followed three years of consultations, in which ILPA played an important role, which focused on: (a) consolidating (and in some cases, changing) primary immigration legislation, by way of a new Immigration Bill; (b) rewriting the guidance to officials and Immigration Rules that underpin primary legislation;[12] and (c) overhauling the technology and administrative processes used by the UK Border Agency to process applications (Gower 2010: 1). In 2008 a draft consolidation Bill was published for consultation which partly addressed the objectives set out by the SSHD. This was followed, however, by another new Act which became the Borders, Citizenship and Immigration Act (2009). The government subsequently promised that a consolidation Act would be pursued. At this point parliament consulted widely on a draft Bill. In 2009 a second draft of the consolidation Bill was published for further consultation. However, the Bill was not allocated parliamentary time for scrutiny. In 2010 the newly elected Coalition Government dropped the consolidation Bill from its legislative agenda (ILPA 2008/2009), and successive governments have failed to take this Bill forward.

ILPA was also concerned that the HO frequently refused to accept court decisions and to update its policies to reflect case law. These failures became the focus of its lobbying and of further litigation. One longstanding concern, which began in 2000, concerned the HO's creation of a 'special immigration status' for nine Afghanis who were prosecuted and acquitted for hijacking an aircraft which landed at Stansted airport – their Leave to Remain was not extended (Symonds 2008).[13] Another example concerns HO Operational Guidance Notes, which are intended to guide HO case owners in their assessment of asylum applications. Because some OGNs do not include correct information on case law, the decisions based on them are wrong and result in unlawful deportations even where the Tribunal had decided that it is unsafe to return individuals (IAS 2009a and 2009b). Other examples include a refusal by the HO to produce new policy guidance reflecting the right of third-country family members of EU nationals (arising from *Metock* v *UK* Case C-127/08) and the unlawfulness of HO rules on marriage (arising from *Baiai* [2008] UKHL 53.

In 2008 litigation revealed 'secret', i.e. unpublished, HO policies (e.g. *R (Abdi and Ors)* v *SSHD* EWHC 3166) which secured the right of individuals who had made fresh asylum claims to work (see *ZO (Somalia)* EWCA Civ 442). In both cases the HO took action to restrict the impact of these court decisions. In 2009 several judicial reviews – e.g. *Muuse* [2010] EWCA Civ 453 and *MA (Nigeria)* v *SSHD* [2009] EWCA Civ 1229 – revealed the extent to which the HO relied on unlawfully detaining individuals, and its consistent failure to assess initial applications in a timely manner. While litigation obtained compensation for the individuals affected,[14] it did not change HO policy or practice.

Following submissions on government proposals to change legal aid which were first mooted in 2004, ILPA became increasingly involved – alongside the Law Society – in an attempt to lobby the LSC and government about the negative impact such cuts would have on the availability of legal aid to asylum seekers, immigrants and British citizens. In one of its earliest submissions ILPA argued that it was:

> disappointed that the LSC has seen fit to give the appearance of pre-empting the Department of Constitutional Affairs' consultation process by rushing to publish implementation plans before the conclusion of that process, and thus before the final version of what is to be implemented is known.
>
> (ILPA 2005/2006: 1)

ILPA also argued that:

> The Legal Services Commission must be acutely aware of the difficulties faced by conscientious immigration practitioners facing the blizzard of recent funding changes and restrictions. Exacerbating those difficulties is no way to raise standards, or to enable the Commission to fulfil its function of providing effective legal services in this highly contentious area of law.

ILPA also argued that:

> In the past year some highly regarded firms have given up the unequal struggle and abandoned publicly funded immigration work altogether. Others are reluctantly reducing the size of their departments . . . . As a result we anticipate an increasing dearth of competent immigration practitioners in future – the very opposite of the result to which the LSC has previously asserted that it aspires.
>
> (ILPA 2005/2006: 4)

ILPA was still fighting this battle in 2009 when, in yet another letter to the LSC about the civil fees scheme, it argued that:

> suppliers and the Counsel they instruct ought always to be paid for the actual number of hours they spend working on a case, subject to the work carried out being necessary in the client's best interests and justified in terms of the funding Code Criteria.
>
> (ILPA 2009/2010: 7)

Having provided evidence that the proposed cuts created false economies, in 2010 ILPA argued that:

> If the Government really wants to save money then rather than looking to the legal aid budget it should look to the departments making the decisions. If a department wants to pass lots of laws (in immigration there have been Acts of Parliament in 1993, 1996, 1999, 2002, 2005, 2006, 2007, 2008 and 2009, plus many more regulations and rule changes) or change procedures, it should meet the costs of these for the legal aid budget and the court system. If it passes laws in haste, or implements new procedures, without thinking them through, it should meet the costs generated for legal aid and for the courts by those bad laws. If its poor decision-making and delay leads to challenges, it should meet the costs to the legal aid system and to the courts of those challenges. If its conduct of any litigation arising out of a case causes costs, it should meet those costs.
>
> (ILPA 2010)

ILPA and the Law Society lost this battle, with the result that cuts were progressively implemented which reduced fees to refugee lawyers and reduced the number of lawyers working in this field.

Litigation sometimes proved to be a significant factor in compelling the HO to reconsider its policies and practice. Thus litigation successfully challenged the HO's ability to remove 'failed' asylum seekers to Zimbabwe (*AA (Zimbabwe)* v *SSHD*), Ethiopia (*HB (Ethiopia)* v *SSHD*), Sierra Leone (*JL (Sierra Leone)* v *SSHD*), etc. Lengthy litigation on the issue of returning 'failed' asylum seekers to Sudan reached the Supreme Court in 2007 (*SSHD* v *AH (Sudan) and Others* [2007] UKHL 49), which decided that the HO had the right to send individuals back. Litigation before the ECHR (*NA* v *UK* (Application 25904/07)) prevented the expulsion of a Tamil to Sri Lanka. However, in 2008 the ECHR upheld British detention policy; see *Saadi* v *UK* (Application 13229/03).

I turn now to consider the UNHCR's role in the UK's asylum field.[15] Its principal role arises from its mandate given by the UN General Assembly[16] to protect and assist refugees and find solutions to their problems. In the UK its role is reinforced by the UK's accession to the Refugee Convention (1951), which means that under Art. 35 of the Convention (see Box 8.1) the UNHCR has a 'supervisory' role in relation to the implementation of the 1951 Convention. The UNHCR's work in the UK is exercised in four ways: (a) it publicly advises/lobbies governments about whether their policies provide 'fair and efficient asylum procedures'; (b) it engages in diplomatic discussions with governments about their policies; (c) it may bring diplomatic pressure to bear on the UK to bring its policies into line with its international legal obligations; and (d) it may engage in litigation to 'safeguard the rights and well being of refugees'.

Box 8.1 The supervisory role of the UNHCR

1 The Contracting States undertake to co-operate with the Office of the United Nations High Commissioner for Refugees, or any other agency of the United Nations which may succeed it, in the exercise of its functions, and shall in particular facilitate its duty of supervising the application of the provisions of this Convention.

2 In order to enable the Office of the High Commissioner or any other agency of the United Nations which may succeed it, to make reports to the competent organs of the United Nations, the Contracting States undertake to provide them in the appropriate form with information and statistical data requested concerning:

a) the condition of refugees;
b) the implementation of this Convention; and
c) laws, regulations and decrees which are, or may hereafter be, in force relating to refugees.

Here I look at two strands of its work in the United Kingdom, namely policy advocacy and litigation.[17] This work is undertaken by a small number of staff in the London office in consultation with the regional and Europe UNHCR offices and with the UNHCR's Division of International Protection.

An example of diplomatic discussion occurred following a series of public statements in 2001 that the UK government would 'rewrite Britain's commitment to the 1951 Geneva convention on refugees in an attempt to reduce the number of unfounded asylum seekers reaching Britain'.[18] In response to such statements, the UN High Commissioner for Refugees, Ruud Lubbers, sought an urgent meeting with the British Prime Minister and Home Secretary in 2003. At this meeting he reminded ministers that the government's obligations under the Refugee Convention were non-negotiable and that the UNHCR was concerned that British asylum policy was not 'fair and efficient'. Shortly afterwards the government issued a statement saying that it would honour its commitment to the Refugee Convention[19] and that it would allow the UNHCR to monitor how the HO processed and decided asylum claims (creating the Quality Initiative, or QI).

The QI consisted of a small team of UNHCR staff who monitored/audited the work of Home Office case owners. Their reports[20] were forwarded to the Home Secretary for discussion with the objective of agreeing acceptable standards and procedures which Home Office case owners were expected to meet. In the period up to 2009 UNHCR staff observed: first-instance decision-making by caseworkers; HO interviews of asylum applicants; substantive interviews by the Asylum Case Work Directorate; decisions by New Asylum Model case owners; first-instance decisions taken in the DFT; and asylum decisions taken in the Solihull Pilot Project. The following problems were identified by the QI, and have remained largely unchanged:

1. problematic assessment of, and decisions on, initial asylum applications;
2. the misapplication of the law – especially the Refugee Convention – in deciding claims;
3. a failure to read/understand country of origin information;
4. a failure to consider the European Convention on Human Rights or the UK's Human Rights Act when deciding claims;
5. case owners placed unreasonable expectations on asylum applicants to produce 'evidence' to support their claim;
6. case owners failed to apply the benefit of the doubt where this was appropriate in assessing a claim;
7. there were consistent problems with the manner in which case owners assessed the 'credibility' of applicants to establish the facts of a claim;
8. many of the above problems were also observed in the DFT and were compounded by the way case owners decided to detain and/or remove individuals from the DFT, by the problematic way they assessed medical evidence, and by the expedited nature of decision-making.

The failure of the HO to implement many of the agreed standards and procedures is understood by the UNHCR to arise from a number of factors. First, there was/is an apparent lack of engagement by government ministers with the issues identified by the QI which require the Home Office to rethink its policies and processes rather than merely adopt a decision or specific recommendation. Second, problems were compounded by the managerial culture of senior officials who did not appear to understand the complex nature of asylum and migration policy.

A second focus of the UNHCR's work involves litigation. The UNHCR's first intervention in British courts was in 1987, but litigation was sporadic until 2003, at which point the number of cases it pursued stabilized at four to six per year,[21] which reflects its limited capacity to monitor and engage in asylum-related litigation. The UNHCR litigates in an attempt to pursue an important policy issue in the hope that a case will create a legal precedent in the UK and, by implication, in the British Commonwealth, in common law countries and elsewhere.[22]

Here I look at one issue in which the UNHCR has repeatedly intervened, and at the HO response (see Campbell 2016). The UNHCR has over the years raised concerns about the UK's failure to honour Art. 31(1) of the Refugee Convention (see Box 8.2).

Box 8.2 Refugee Convention, Art. 31: refugees unlawfully in the country of refuge

1 The Contracting States shall not impose penalties, on account of their illegal entry or presence, on refugees who, coming directly from a territory where their life or freedom was threatened in the sense of article 1, enter or are present in their territory without authorization, provided they present themselves without delay to the authorities and show good cause for their illegal entry or presence.

2 The Contracting States shall not apply to the movements of such refugees restrictions other than those which are necessary and such restrictions shall only be applied until their status in the country is regularized or they obtain admission into another country. The Contracting States shall allow such refugees a reasonable period and all the necessary facilities to obtain admission into another country.

Illegal entry into the UK, Europe and North America became an issue in the early 1990s when national legislation introduced 'carrier sanctions' on transport operators who brought passengers lacking a valid visa into a country where a visa was required. Between 1993 and 1996 approximately 555 individuals were prosecuted in the UK for illegal entry; many of those convicted were attempting to flee persecution and did not possess a national passport or an entry visa (Dunstan 1998). These individuals, including persons who were subsequently granted asylum, were convicted and sentenced to varying periods of imprisonment.

The case of *R* v *Uxbridge Magistrates Court and Another, Ex Parte Adimi* [1999] EWHC Admin 765

This was the first appeal against conviction to reach the appellate courts. The UNHCR intervened in this case to argue that, as a signatory to the Refugee Convention, the British Government was required to comply with Art. 31. The UNHCR also argued that the HO and the Crown Prosecution Service had failed to meet this requirement.[23] The court allowed all three appeals against the SSHD. The Lord Justices noted the inequities of existing administrative arrangements, and stated:

> both of us express a strong preference for what may be called the Secretary of State solution, we should expect the Respondents [the Secretary of State for the Home Department and the Crown Prosecution Service] to give careful consideration as to how they propose now to give effect to Article 31.
>
> (para. 104)

In an effort to bring government policy into line with *Adimi*, ILPA together with Lord Avebury lobbied the government to create an 'Article 31 defence' (which they wrote), a version of which was subsequently incorporated into s. 31 of the Immigration and Asylum Act (1999). This defence was supposed to ensure that the UK would not breach its obligations under the Refugee Convention. However, the HO and the Crown Prosecution Service has continued to prosecute and convict individuals fleeing persecution who illegally enter the UK.

The case of *R* v *Asfaw*

R v *Asfaw* [2008] UKHL 31 concerned an Ethiopian national who had been imprisoned, tortured and raped on account of her alleged political opinions. With the help of an agent, she fled Ethiopia by air and arrived in the UK in an effort to transit to the US, where she intended to claim asylum. In transit at Heathrow airport, her false passport was detected; she was arrested, charged with two criminal counts, found guilty, and sentenced to

(continued)

(continued)

nine months' imprisonment even though shortly after her trial the Home Secretary recognized her as a refugee. She appealed against the court's decision on one point of law, namely:

> If a defendant is charged with an offence not specified in sec. 31 (1) of the Immigration and Asylum Act 1999, to what extent is he entitled to rely on the protections afforded by article 31 of the 1951 United Nations Convention Relating to the Status of Refugees?[24]

The UNHCR intervened in this case to argue that, despite the Art. 31 defence in the 1999 Immigration and Asylum Act, the UK government had not taken 'concrete steps' to ensure that 'refugees and asylum seekers within its terms are not subject to penalties'.[25] The House of Lords held that s. 31:

> should not be read as limited to offences attributable to a refugee's illegal entry into or presence in this country, but should provide immunity, if the other conditions are fulfilled, from the imposition of criminal penalties for offences attributable to the attempt of a refugee to leave the country in the continuing course of a flight from persecution even after a short stopover in transit.[26]

The decision should have changed the way that the British authorities processed claims by refugees entering the UK on false identity papers. However, the Home Office continues to arrest individuals arriving with false papers, and the Crown Prosecution Service has continued to prosecute and convict these individuals. Between 2009 and 2012 there have been 19,160 convictions of an estimated 11,000 individuals for illegal entry into the UK, though it is not clear how many of those convicted were refugees/asylum seekers.[27]

The case of *Eritrea/SH*

In early 2014 SH was deported from Saudi Arabia as an illegal migrant – a country where she was born and where she had resided for 30 years – to Eritrea. She fled Eritrea to Sudan, from where she was taken to Libya and to Europe, where an agent assisted her to get to Denmark. In Denmark she acquired a false Italian identity card which she used to travel by air to the UK, but immigration officers at the airport arrested her for entering on false documents. At this point she claimed asylum. She was imprisoned for two weeks before being released into the custody of a relative.

The CPS indicted her for 'possession of an identity document with improper intention contrary to sec. 4(1) and (2) of the Identity Documents Act 2010'; she was tried in Crown Court in May 2014. At her trial her counsel wrongly advised her to plead guilty, which she did.[28] After a two-day jury trial, she was found guilty and was given an 18-month sentence despite the fact that she had clearly intended to apply for asylum (her asylum claim was not submitted to the SSHD until after her conviction).

It should be clear that the decision in *R* v *Asfaw* has not set a binding legal precedent, and that the Home Office and the Crown Prosecution Service do not use the Art. 31 defence. Instead, they prosecute and convict large numbers of refugees entering the UK on false identity papers. While other interventions by the UNHCR have changed UK asylum policy, there are clear limitations on the UNHCR's ability to change asylum policy and practice by intervening in British courts, particularly when the government repeatedly violates national and international law.

The final organization to be examined is the Independent Chief Inspector of the UKBA, which was created in 2008 'to assess the efficiency and effectiveness of the UK's border and immigration functions. He reports annually to the Home Secretary and his reports are placed before Parliament.'[29] The ICI has no remit to examine UKBA policy, but he does examine:

1 the UKBA's overall performance;
2 practice and procedure in making decisions;
3 the treatment of claimants and applicants;
4 consistency of approach;
5 discrimination in the exercise of functions;
6 enforcement powers;
7 the handling of complaints;
8 country of origin information.

The ICI is assisted by a team of inspectors and by four stakeholder groups which he convenes. The groups are: the Refugee and Asylum Forum (established 2009), the Seaports Stakeholder Forum (established 2011), the Aviation Stakeholder Forum (established 2011) and the Independent Advisory Group on Country Information (established 2009). Each group is composed of representatives from organizations working in that specific field; the groups advise the office of the ICI about its work, and they raise issues for his inspection team to investigate.

The Refugee and Asylum Forum (RAF)[30] – composed of 16 organizations, including ILPA[31] and UNHCR, with an interest in asylum and migration – did not meet until April 2009. An examination of the RAF's minutes indicates that the group actively identified and discussed its concerns about HO policy and practice.

RAF forum discussions show that:

1 Membership on RAF effectively linked the ICI to members' organizations and to national consultations and committees in the wider field of asylum.
2 The ICI reported that:

   a) the UKBA concentrated its resources on achieving its management targets during 'specific milestone months' when it knew that its work would be reviewed, and that targets were not achieved at other times;[32]
   b) the UKBA was unable to show that the detention of individuals, in line with a promise made by the SSHD, was pursued as a last resort;[33]
   c) the 'dawn raids' to arrest individuals and families prior to their removal from the UK were not the result of a 'case by case' decision, as the SSHD had declared, but a policy decision;[34]
   d) in some cases the UKBA had not provided sufficient information to allow the ICI to assess its work;[35]
   e) reliance by the HO on management targets created strong disincentives for staff to release individuals from the DFT;[36]
   f) the UKBA's Public Sector Agreement, which required the agency 'to conclude 60% of applications by the end of December 2008, 75% of applications within six months by the end of 2009, and 90% of applications within six months by the end of 2011', appeared to have been set 'with little consultation of UKBA staff'.[37]

I turn now to the inspections carried out by the ICI between 2008 and 2010 which primarily addressed asylum policy and practice. In 2008–2009 the ICI inspected visa offices at Rome and Abuja (Nigeria), and made an 'unannounced' inspection of the Liverpool Asylum Screening Unit. The inspection of the Liverpool Asylum Screening Unit, one of several units where asylum applicants must register their claim and undergo a screening interview, found that the appointments system was of 'limited benefit to customers', who waited four to five hours to complete the process.

In 2009–2010 the office of the ICI expanded its work and issued 18 reports about the UKBA's work.[38] Here are the asylum-related inspections which were completed and the principal problem(s) identified:

1 *Border controls at Manchester airport*, where passengers and freight are screened for entry into the UK: the UKBA team had 'indicative' rather than specific targets to measure their contribution, but they were not held accountable for meeting them. In addition, the screening area was not secure; passengers could pass through without being screened.
2 *Local Immigration Teams (LITs) in northwest England*: LITs had recently been created by the UKBA to 'undertake as many functions as practicable at a local level in a defined area within a region' and were being rolled out across the UK to improve service delivery and liaison with local agencies. However, there were no specific performance measures which allowed the

UKBA to assess how LITs were to meet management targets. Staff lacked an understanding of the actual role of a LIT, where they fitted in and how they were contributing to new policy objectives.

3 *Loughborough Reporting Centre*: the UKBA requires people who are liable to be detained, such as those with outstanding asylum claims or whose claims were refused, to report to Loughborough to confirm their identity and their current circumstances. In addition, people receiving asylum support have their fingerprints taken there. However, interpreters were not available at the centre, which gave rise to misunderstandings and led UKBA staff to use other asylum applicants to translate potentially sensitive and private information.
4 *Family removals*: the UKBA has responsibility for identifying and removing those who have no right to be in the UK. However, there was limited evidence that individual action plans existed for each family that took account of the family's welfare needs and arrangements for them to return home. In addition, there were inconsistent standards for promoting voluntary return.
5 *UKBA operations in Wales and southwest England*: there was a lack of communication and engagement with regional stakeholders, and a lack of adequate tools and technology for staff to perform their roles in securing the border. There was also evidence of understaffing and of poor relationships between management and staff.
6 *The New Asylum Model and arrangements for processing 400,000-plus 'legacy' asylum and migration claims (UK 2010a)*: first, the UKBA was unable to meet the 'performance milestones' contained in its Public Service Agreement, and on the basis of current staffing levels and the complexity and volume of cases, its target of concluding 90 per cent of cases within six months was unachievable. Second, 30,000 cases under the NAM had not been concluded within a six-month period. Finally, there was no systematic analysis of the reasons why appeals against its decisions were being allowed by the Tribunal.

In 2012 the Home Affairs Select Committee (UK 2012e) discovered that, contrary to what the UKBA had been telling parliament since 2006, the agency had not carried out key aspects of its mandate and that it had regularly supplied wrong information to the ICI which that organization needed to review Home Office operations. The Select Committee stated that:

> We are astonished that the Agency provided this Committee, and its predecessors, with information that turned out to be patently wrong on so many occasions over the last six years. If it was not attempting to mislead the Committee then it must be a sign that senior officials had no idea as to what was actually going on in their organisation. We find it very hard to believe that no one within the Agency had any idea that checks were not being carried out as they should have been and we expect the Agency to share the findings of its disciplinary investigation with us as soon as it is completed.
>
> (UK 2012e: 39, para. 3)

The ICI's findings indicate the cynical manner in which the UKBA operated and its inability to meet the public commitments made by the SSHD to parliament. ICI reports also make clear the UKBA's complete lack of regard for its 'customers' (asylum seekers, migrants and citizens) and for its front-line staff.

Conclusion

There is some evidence that in the period prior to my fieldwork, lobbying by Oxfam and the ILPA was partially successful. Indeed, the work of ILPA's Legal Officer and the litigation engaged in by its members were important in galvanizing the sector, shining a bright light on HO policy and practice and securing status for asylum applicants. However, efforts to lobby for the passage of a consolidation Act and against the reduction of legal aid – without doubt the two most important issues with an impact on the entire asylum field – proved ineffective.[39] With regard to the effect of litigation, it seems that the HO is not bound by the rule of law in the same way that citizens are.

While the UN High Commissioner for Refugees was able to stop the UK Government from publicly questioning the relevance of the Refugee Convention, the UNHCR's 10-year 'partnership' with the HO to assess and revise HO assessment of asylum applications has proved to be difficult, though the UNHCR believes that its interventions have led to improvements in protecting a growing number of applicants.

Significantly, the ability of the HO to ignore litigation against it, including the House of Lords decision in *R* v *Asfaw*, has meant that the UK regularly contravenes its domestic and international legal obligations. During this period the government was prepared to enter into a policy dialogue with the UNHCR which established a humanitarian admissions programme, better training for caseworkers and the introduction of an internal audit of caseworker decisions. It would appear that the UNHCR's influence is limited to improving the HO's ability to manage its staff, but that the UNHCR has not changed government asylum policy.

Several observations are in order with respect to the work of the ICI. First, when pieced together, the ICI's work provides a comprehensive picture of the problematic nature of HO/UKBA policy and practice. However, even though the SSHD formally accepted nearly all of the ICI's recommendations, there is scant evidence to indicate that she has acted on them.[40] Indeed, subsequent inspection reports on the conclusion of legacy cases (UK 2012b and 2012e) clearly indicate that despite the assurances given to parliament, limited progress on this and other issues has been achieved.

It seems clear that the government and the Home Office are well insulated from political lobbying on asylum issues – a situation helped in part by negative statements from officials and negative press coverage which has minimized public support for 'liberal' policy reform. An equally significant factor, however, has been the way that HO/UKBA officials have maintained an 'arm's length' distance between themselves and their (highly critical and vociferous) 'stakeholders'.

This applies not only to discussions with and representations by ILPA, UNHCR and ICI, but indeed across the entire asylum field. Political insulation from lobbying can be seen, for instance, not only in HO/UKBA resistance to reforms, but also in terms of the sharp contrast between HO discussions with the National Asylum Stakeholder Forum[41] (which extensively criticized its policy and practices) and the *ad hoc*, anodyne reporting by the HO on these discussions to its staff.[42] It is also important to note that, following the May 2010 elections, the HO and UKBA stakeholder consultation groups were terminated.[43] While this shift in policy has not ended political lobbying, it ended meaningful consultation, and it has made it much easier for officials to deflect, downgrade and/or ignore criticism.

Notes

1 There is insufficient space here to examine public appeals against the deportation of specific individuals and litigation initiated by organizations such as the Public Law Project, Bail for Immigration Detainees, etc.

2 Vouchers were issued to registered asylum seekers at a value of 70 per cent of the income support which unemployed British nationals are entitled to receive, and were redeemable at select stores. They expired within four weeks of issue.

3 See A. Travis, 'Asylum seekers forced to return to using supermarket vouchers', *The Guardian*, 20 March 2006, available at: http://www.theguardian.com/politics/2006/mar/20/immigrationandpublicservices.immigration (accessed 10 August 2016).

4 Some organizations and inter-agency partnerships do not lobby the government, either because their mandate does not permit it or because they are contracted to the HO to deliver services to asylum applicants. Even so, they make submissions to parliament and they gather information for use by other organizations to campaign and lobby the government (sources: interviews with Renae Mann, Co-ordinator, Interagency Partnership on NAM, on 2 April 2007, and with Nev Jeffries, British Red Cross, on 2 March 2007). These organizations meet with HO officials to put across their views.

5 As discussed elsewhere (Campbell 2013b: chap. 6), the scope for the judiciary to curb the restrictionist nature of executive decisions was brought to an end by legislation in the late 1990s.

6 Data published by the All Party Parliamentary Group (UK 2011b) and the government (UK 2008a) make clear the huge disjuncture between public opinion which perceives that asylum seekers/migrants are a problem and the actual flow of such people into the UK.

7 Unless otherwise indicated, this section is based on an analysis of ILPA's Annual Reports; see 'Timeline', *Immigration Law Practitioners' Association*, available at: http://www.ilpa.org.uk/pages/ilpa-timeline.html (accessed 10 August 2016).

8 In 2005 the ILPA met with seven NGOs, and in 2009 it met with more than 40.

9 ILPA made 35 submissions in 2005, and 68 in 2009.

10 ILPA successfully lobbied the HO regarding a statement laid before parliament in 2008 which set out new 'grounds for refusal' (Toal 2008).

11 ILPA regards political lobbying and litigation as separate but integral strands of its efforts to change government policy and practice. In this sense, it is very different from other civil society organizations.

12 In early 2015 no 'new-style' rules had been promulgated. However, a draft of the new-style visitor rules had been circulated for comment (but were not yet law). A small amount of modernized guidance has also been circulated and agreed.

13 This situation was not resolved until publication of the Criminal Justice and Immigration Act (2008).

14 The high level of and regularity with which compensation has been awarded to asylum applicants by the Home Office for false imprisonment/detention, injury during detention, etc. underlines the poor quality of decisions made by officials. Following litigation in 2009–2010, approximately £12 million was awarded in compensation, and in 2010–2011 £14.2 million; Daily Mail Reporter, 'Anger as more than £12m paid out in legal costs and compensation to immigrants and asylum seekers in just a year', *Daily Mail*, 15 August 2011, available at: http://www.dailymail.co.uk/news/article-2026206/UKBA-paid-12m-compensation-legal-costs-migrants-year.html (accessed 10 August 2016).

15 This information derives in part from interviews with Mr Roland Schilling, the UNHCR representative in London, and Mr Peter Grady, Legal Protection Officer, on 2 July and 17 July 2014 respectively.

16 This mandate was given in its statute by UN General Assembly Resolution 428(V) of 14 December 1950.

17 The UNHCR is only allowed to intervene in asylum-related litigation in the European Court of Human Rights if it has first intervened in the case in the UK or Republic of Ireland.

18 See A. Travis, 'Home office to rewrite Geneva refugee agreement', *The Guardian*, 5 October 2002, available at: http://www.theguardian.com/uk/2002/oct/05/immigration.immigrationandpublicservices (accessed 10 August 2016).

19 See P. Wintour, 'Quitting UN agreement on refugees "not feasible"', *The Guardian*, 26 January 2005, available at: http://www.theguardian.com/society/2005/jan/26/asylum.immigrationasylumandrefugees (accessed 10 August 2016).

20 QI reports can be found at: http://www.unhcr.org/uk/search?query=Quality%20Initiative%20reports (accessed 11 August 2016).

21 Data on this issue come from cases filed on *Refworld*; see http://www.refworld.org/.

22 The emphasis is to clearly state 'the correct legal position' rather than to support a specific asylum claimant; thus securing a precedent in a case may not necessarily mean that the asylum claim is successful.

23 For the judgment on this case, including the UNHCR's submissions, see 'R v Uxbridge Magistrates Court and Another, Ex Parte Adimi', available at: http://www.refworld.org/docid/3ae6b6b41c.html (accessed 10 August 2016).

24 'R v Asfaw', para. 1, available at: http://www.refworld.org/docid/4835401f2.html (accessed 10 August 2016).

25 See 'UNHCR Intervention before the House of Lords in the Case of Regina (Respondent) and Fregenet Asfaw (Appellant)', available at: http://www.refworld.org/docid/483d12222.html (accessed 10 August 2016).

26 'R v Asfaw', para. 1.

27 Source: FOI Request 09/013 to UK Crown Prosecution Service; question: 'What is the number of people prosecuted for entering the UK using a false passport between 2009 and 2012?'

28 It is common practice for criminal solicitors, who lack training in immigration law, to instruct their clients to plead guilty to a criminal charge of illegal entry. Such instructions are, however, an 'abuse of the law', and result in wrongful convictions for their clients (see Holiday 2012). It is possible for individuals such as SH to have their conviction set aside by the Criminal Cases Review Commission, but very few solicitors or convicted asylum applicants know this.

29 See 'About us', *Independent Chief Inspector of Borders and Immigration*, available at: http://icinspector.independent.gov.uk/about/ (accessed 10 August 2016).

30 Information about the RAF and its minutes can be found at: 'Refugee and Asylum Forum', *Independent Chief Inspector of Borders and Immigration*, http://icinspector.independent.gov.uk/stakeholder-engagement/refugee-and-asylum-forum/ (accessed 10 August 2016).

31 The ILPA, and presumably other civil society organizations, also met with the ICI in bilateral meetings which were felt to be more useful.

32 Source: RAF Minutes, 20 April 2010, point 2.10.
33 In the House of Commons in October 2009; *Hansard*, 12 October 2009, col. 534W. See also RAF Minutes, 14 September 2010, point 3.
34 Source: RAF Minutes, 14 September 2010, point 3.
35 Source: RAF Minutes, 19 January 2010, point 2.6.
36 Source: RAF Minutes, 14 September 2010, point 4.
37 Source: RAF Minutes, 20 April 2010, point 2.11.
38 See 'Inspection reports', *Independent Chief Inspector of Borders and Immigration*, available at: http://icinspector.independent.gov.uk/inspections/inspection-reports/ (accessed 10 August 2016).
39 ILPA have told me that their discussions with the HO about the problems that would arise if legal aid for asylum work were cut were generally accepted; however, the Ministry of Justice, which oversees legal aid, was not convinced.
40 For instance, in the 2012 Review of the UKBA's performance by the Parliamentary Home Affairs Committee (UK 2012e), the UKBA failed to meet 10 of its 11 performance targets, including reducing the backlog of immigration claims, deciding new asylum claims within six months and processing in-country migration cases. Indeed, the agency was still detaining children, etc.
41 The minutes of this group can be found at 'Minutes of previous meetings', *Home Office UK Border Agency*, *The National Archives*, available at: http://webarchive.nationalarchives.gov.uk/20140110181512/http:/www.bia.homeoffice.gov.uk/sitecontent/documents/aboutus/workingwithus/stakeholders/209086/nas-fminutes/ (accessed 10 August 2016).
42 Very basic information on the consultations was included, together with important operational information, in the UKBA's regular publication, *Update on Key Migration and Border Issues*. A few copies of these are available on the internet; however all publications are now archived at 'Search resources', *Immigration Law Practitioners' Association*, available at: http://www.ilpa.org.uk/resources2.php?action=search&advanced=&&page=387 (accessed 11 August 2016).
43 See 'Publications: All consultations', available at: https://www.gov.uk/government/publications?publication_filter_option=consultations&topics%5B%5D=borders-and-immigration (accessed 10 August 2016). However, the asylum 'stakeholder' group re-emerged quickly, and dealt with all asylum and related matters, detention, children asylum seekers, etc.

Conclusion and postscript

I have followed appeals made on behalf of asylum applicants to see what litigation reveals about individual claims and about the wider socio-political system in which they are argued and decided. Fieldwork has revealed that a focus on 'law' obscures rather than illuminates the complex processes which link together a number of institutions/organizations and which sometimes result in compliance with 'the law', but which may also contest and resist legal orders. This situation prevails because of the complex relationships between the institutions that compose the field and the type of 'connections' within and between institutions, which, depending on the issue, give rise to tension, conflict and contrariety. In short, British asylum law and practice can be understood using Falk Moore's concept of law as a 'semi-autonomous social field' (1973).

In the asylum field, institutions generate their own rules, customs and symbols, but are at the same time partially constrained by rules, decisions and forces emanating from the wider socio-political context. An in-depth analysis of asylum litigation demonstrates the importance of differentiating between how 'law' is pronounced and how it is implemented and acquires legitimacy via a process of negotiation, contestation and conflict within and outside parliament and the courts. *The asylum field is a political arena where different institutions confront each other in an effort to influence the outcome of individual asylum claims and, ultimately, government asylum policy.*

Two points are worth noting. First, the notion that contemporary asylum procedures in the UK or elsewhere can be wholly understood as an adequate or a just means of assessing the truth claims of asylum seekers is clearly without foundation. As Fassin (2013) has argued, the demographic and political logic arising out of the globalization of asylum has given rise to a bifurcated system of protection: as long as 'refugees' remain in the global South, their claims of persecution are accepted even though they are provided with dwindling levels of assistance and 'protection'. However, as growing numbers of refugees reach the developed world, they confront a complex bureaucratic form of triage intended to limit the number of successful claims. National asylum policies and procedures invert the focus away from the perpetrators of injustice and onto the victims, in effect rationalizing access to asylum in such a way that only a minority are recognized as 'refugees'.

The second point to note is that the 'asylum field' is fluid and dynamic, in large part because of changes arising from the wider political context – increasingly restrictive asylum policy, cuts to legal aid, limitations on the right to appeal against Tribunal decisions, etc. – in which it operates. In short, there are tensions within and between key institutions, and over time these tensions reflect an expansion in the power of the Home Office and a diminution in the role played by other institutions.

The most powerful institutional actor in this field is the British state, which exercises its power by creating and amending legislation in parliament. However, the Home Office/Border Agency (advised by TSol/the Government Legal Department) plays a decisive role through its influence on national legislation, the SSHD's ability to create 'law' via the establishment of policy and executive decision-making, and its ability to implement asylum law and policy by litigating to force asylum applicants to comply with the particular interpretation or rubric it wants to enforce. The power exercised by the SSHD is contested in the Tribunal and in the Court of Appeal, where judges exercise their prerogative to review and interpret HO decisions and policy raised by refugee lawyers. Other institutions which are not involved in litigation – NGOs, state-based and intergovernmental organizations – operate on the margins of the asylum field and are much less effective in challenging and influencing asylum policy. Each institution commands differing levels and types of resources, has a distinct agenda and exercises its authority in an attempt to influence decisions on asylum claims.

Finally, there are asylum applicants who, because of the way in which their claims are processed and argued, struggle to understand how their claims are decided and what their legal status in the UK is. While the asylum field exists solely because of the UK's obligations under the Refugee Convention, the different institutions in the field relate to refugees in radically different ways: officials treat asylum applicants with contempt and indifference, whereas refugee lawyers work long hours (much of which are unpaid and/or undertaken *pro bono*) to prepare and argue their cases.

Each institution pursues it interests by using strategies that may include: (a) redefining the rules of the game by changing the law or reducing access to resources for other institutions; (b) contesting litigation; (c) using the media/press to secure public support; (d) lobbying/networking to influence policy, e.g. by briefing parties on key issues such as access to legal aid, changes in the appeals system etc.; and (e) engaging in policy advocacy. These strategies may be pursued singly or together, and they may or may not influence litigation and government policy. Rather than summarizing the arguments made in earlier chapters, I propose instead to explain how key changes which have occurred in the asylum field *after* my fieldwork ended in 2009 can be understood by seeing asylum law and practice as a semi-autonomous social field.

The 2010 national elections saw a Labour Government replaced by a Coalition – Conservative and Liberal Democrat – Government, which was replaced by a Conservative Government in 2015. The legislative agendas of both governments sought to introduce greater sovereign 'control' over the UK's borders by 'opting out' of key elements of European Union policy, particularly with regard to migration and asylum policy, and by adopting increasingly restrictive domestic policies.

The UK's *à la carte* approach towards the European Union has been widely discussed, particularly its refusal to accept a quota of the 1.3 million-plus 'migrants' currently in Europe (e.g. Briggs 2015). The net effect of the UK's position, which has been followed by other member states, has been to undermine agreement on a common approach to the current refugee 'crisis' which is manifested in the absence of adequate reception arrangements and chaotic procedural arrangements for assessing asylum applications (Moreno-Lax 2015).

One consequence of the British opt-out has been to ensure that asylum applicants/migrants are unable to cross the English Channel, which means that other EU member states have had to absorb those already in Europe.[1] Despite this obstacle, an estimated 38,370 asylum seekers managed to enter the UK in 2015 and apply for asylum; the largest group originated in Eritrea (see below). The government's response to asylum seekers has been to adopt policies and procedures which block individuals from entering Europe/the UK (Council of Europe 2016) and which prevent them from securing status in the UK.

Restrictive policies came into effect in early 2010 when the Tribunals, Courts and Enforcement Act (2007) came into effect. This Bill, which was pushed by the Home Office, reorganized the Tribunal by creating a 'dedicated' first tier (with responsibility to hear initial appeals) and an Upper Tribunal (to hear 'onward' appeals). In 2010 asylum applicants who appealed against a decision of the first-tier Tribunal now had to obtain permission from it or apply directly to the Upper Tribunal. In 2013 the Lord Chief Justice issued a Direction which substantially curtailed judicial review of decisions of the Tribunal refusing permission to appeal:[2] henceforth, all judicial reviews directed against such Tribunal decisions were restricted to judicially reviewing the decisions on the basis that the Tribunal had failed to act, or had made a decision that was irrational, perverse or unlawful. If an appeal on a point of law to the Upper Tribunal, brought with the permission of one of the Tribunals, is refused, then it is possible to make an application 'on the papers' to the Court of Appeal and a renewed oral application (though continued access to such applications is now in question; see UK 2016b). In relation to appeals against a refusal to judicially review applications by the Tribunal, the right to make an oral application to the Court of Appeal no longer exists.

The only legislation enacted by parliament between 2011 and 2015 was the Immigration Act (2014) (UK 2015a). The Act replaced appeal rights for many immigration categories (with more limited provisions for 'administrative review' of decisions), limited the grounds of appeal against refusal of an asylum or human rights application, and where a power of certification was exercised by the Secretary of State, it eliminated the right of individuals being deported from the UK to appeal *before* they were deported – i.e. deportees can only appeal from outside the UK. The 2014 Act also simplified the immigration removal process and gave greater powers to the Home Office to deport illegal immigrants. Though the Act, and cuts to legal aid, made it more difficult to secure status for asylum applicants, the volume of litigation in the Upper Tribunal grew.

Two categories of persons directly affected by the Act are individuals deemed to be illegal migrants and thousands of overseas students who have been studying in the UK. In 2014, *pro bono* litigation in the High Court and the Court of Appeal by Detention Action successfully challenged the DFT system on the basis that it possessed 'an unacceptably high risk of unfairness' due to inadequate screening by HO officials who illegally detained survivors of torture, victims of trafficking and other vulnerable people.[3] The Home Office appealed the case to the Supreme Court in late 2015, but the court refused to hear the appeal. Suspension of the Detained Fast Track resumed fairly quickly, at which point Detention Action filed a legal challenge against the legal architecture of the system, the Tribunal Rules, 'under which asylum-seekers in detention, chosen by the Home Office, would have less time to appeal against the decisions of the Home Office than if they were in the community'.[4] Following consultations between Detention Action, ILPA and the Law Society, the Tribunal Procedure Committee wrote to the Home Office and declined to create new Fast Track Rules, and it has set certain conditions for doing so which the Home Office will find difficult to meet. Nevertheless, thousands of individuals held in immigration detention remain subject to a system which seeks to deport first, and hear appeals against deportation later.

For example, in response to a 2014 BBC programme which claimed to have discovered overseas students fraudulently taking an English examination – a test that the HO requires students to take to secure a Tier 4 student visa – at one testing centre, the Home Office rapidly revoked the licences of 60 testing centres and arrested and deported tens of thousands of students. Their appeals against deportation, filed from overseas, were stayed behind a test case in the Upper Tribunal, *SM and Qadir* v *SSHD*, which was finally heard in April 2016. In this case the Upper Tribunal found that:

> In this context we highlight further the absence of any concrete evidence adduced by the Secretary of State, on whom the legal burden of proof rests. In summary, this is a paradigm illustration of the tilting at windmills which characterised much of the Secretary of State's case.[5]
>
> . . . we conclude, without hesitation, that the Secretary of State has failed to establish, on the balance of probabilities, that the Appellants' *prima facie* innocent explanations are to be rejected. The legal burden of proof falling on the Secretary of State has not been discharged. The Appellants are clear winners.[6]

The decision is hugely significant for thousands of individuals who appear to have been wrongly removed. The Upper Tribunal, which has its own procedures for reporting significant cases that have a 'persuasive value only on the facts' (UK 2015d), belatedly reported it after accusations appeared in the press that it was hiding decisions which were unfavourable to the Home Secretary.[7]

A different example of the Tribunal's autonomy can be found in the 2010 *Joint Presidential Guidance Note 2: Child, Vulnerable Adult and Sensitive Appellant Guidance* (UK 2010b). The Directive establishes 'safeguards' for hearing appeals by vulnerable appellants. Most notably, HOPOs are not allowed to conduct an 'improper or aggressive cross examination'. Unfortunately, given the varied quality of legal representation, many refugee lawyers are unaware of this guidance, and vulnerable clients continue to be subjected to inappropriate cross-examination (Campbell forthcoming).

In 2009, in the wake of the global financial crisis, the government imposed budget cuts on all government departments and to legal aid. Budget cuts in the Home Office have contributed to delays in processing and deciding initial asylum claims, and a shortage of HOPOs has delayed the appeal process. In an acknowledgement of these problems, the President of the Tribunal recently stated that 'boom and bust cycles of immigration and chamber work are causing increasing problems' for IJs.[8] In particular, the number of salaried IJs dropped from 152 in 2004 to 94 in October 2014 even as caseloads increased from 43,643 to 52,991 appeals between June 2014 and July 2015. In short, delays by the Home Office in processing asylum applications, cuts to the Tribunal's budget and rising numbers of judicial reviews filed in the Upper Tribunal are creating problems for the Tribunal.

In addition to ongoing cuts in legal aid, The Legal Aid, Sentencing and Punishment of Offenders Act (2012), which came into effect in April 2013, significantly changed access to legal aid. Applicants must now meet three criteria: (a) the case must be within scope for legal aid;[9] (b) with certain exceptions, the applicant must have a 50:50 prospect of winning; and (c) the applicant must fulfil the financial eligibility criteria. The impact of this Act has been to remove appellants' right to legal aid to pursue their rights under Art. 8 of the ECHR.[10]

As late as 2014 the MoJ continued to cut legal aid without knowing whether remaining providers of legal services could meet existing demand, whether individuals eligible for legal aid were able to access it, and despite knowing that there are many areas in the UK where no 'face-to-face' provision exists (UK 2014b). A House of Commons study (UK 2015b) indicates that cuts in legal aid have directly led to a declining number of firms providing legally aided advice and have given rise to a massive increase in the number of unrepresented litigants whose claims are clogging up the courts because they are not legally represented, whose claims may be unfairly decided. In short, a range of new 'costs' have been created because officials had not considered how reforms would affect the legal system and individual access to justice.

In a further twist, in early 2015 the Home Office suddenly issued new policy guidance on Eritrea. Whereas prior to this date most asylum applicants from Eritrea were granted some form of status, the HO now argued, contrary to existing case law, that all Eritreans could safely be returned. A blanket refusal of all initial claims caught lawyers by surprise; however, once they secured reliable expert evidence, the Tribunal overturned the vast majority of HO decisions.

Home Office asylum policy on Eritrea is a cynical attempt to prevent Eritreans – the largest group of individuals seeking asylum in the UK – from obtaining status. The policy has seen caseworkers mechanically refuse applications without assessing the evidence. The policy has also caused considerable distress and suffering for applicants who have been left destitute and subject to arrest, and it has resulted in a colossal waste of public finance (in legal aid to fund Eritrean appeals and government funds to litigate against asylum claimants). This policy, which provides a good example of the connectedness of institutions, has given rise to considerable friction and resistance across the field.

Comparative questions

As I argued at the beginning of this book, research on asylum-related issues in the UK, US (Ramji-Nogales et al. 2007; Transactional Records Access Clearinghouse 2009; Keith and Holmes 2009), Canada (Rehaag 2008; Rousseau et al. 2002) and Australia (Edwards 2003; Crock and Martin 2013; Trish 2013) has focused on judicial decision-making and, secondarily, on legislative responses to judicial decisions. Because these studies have failed to conceptualize how the judiciary and state institutions fit into a much wider asylum field, they fail to understand how the field actually works. Thus in North America judicial decision-making is portrayed as fundamentally flawed (i.e. like a lottery) and as taking place in autonomous institutions. Similarly, the legislature is seen as a powerful institution able to control asylum and immigration policy, though very little is said about how law and policy are implemented or about how policy is influenced by other institutions.

Hamlin's (2014) comparative study of Refugee Status Determination (RSD) in the US, Canada and Australia is a partial exception to the studies cited above. Her research is guided by the concept of a 'refugee status determination regime' that is composed of 'a set of institutions' responsible for conducting RSD wherein 'the relationships and power dynamics among these institutions' affects law and policy (Hamlin 2014: 9). While she calls for a holistic analysis of the entire system, in fact her research is narrowly focused on administrative law and is based on relatively brief fieldwork during which she undertook 'elite interviews' (of policy-makers, refugee advocates and legal counsel), observed a small number of legal proceedings, and collected and analysed legal cases and other documents (Hamlin 2014: 28f.).

While Hamlin's study surpasses previous research in its analysis of key institutional relationships, its strength lies primarily in the comparative questions it raises regarding how women's asylum claims, Chinese 'one child' asylum claims and grants of complementary protection are processed. Hamlin's principal conclusion is that 'in general, an RSD regime with high levels of administrative insulation results in questions about the refugee definition being more settled' (Hamlin 2014: 183). However, her understanding of how and why particular institutions may or may not possess a degree of 'insulation' from litigation or from government/legislative interference is assumed rather than demonstrated. Her conclusions reflect a reliance on 'key' legal decisions which she argues constitute a turning point in political relations between the courts and government, and unproven assumptions about why and when courts or governments intervene in certain policy areas. In short, her study suffers from serious conceptual (i.e. how to compare states with very different administrative and political processes) methodological and data problems (can limited interviews and cases provide an adequate basis for analysis?). Indeed, her analysis of Australian RSD is problematic due to the absence of due process – i.e. asylum applicants do not have a right to appeal against asylum decisions, and large numbers of asylum seekers are diverted and/or offshored.

My study of the UK's asylum field clearly shows the need to situate the courts, government and the legislature as integral parts of a much wider political field containing a range of institutional actors which attempt to influence judicial decision-making and government asylum/migration policy. This field is composed of institutions which are variously connected to one another by their focus on asylum law and practice, but which exercise very different levels of power and influence. Thus the *key* players – the Home Office, the Tribunal, the Court of Appeal and refugee lawyers – are all directly involved in litigation. Some institutions influence how the field operates, some are marginal players.

In the UK, the Home Office is the key institution because the SSHD exercises the authority to formulate and create new laws and policies which directly affect the entire field, and because it redefines policy. The SSHD also engages in litigation to secure policy objectives, changes the appeal process, restricts legal aid, appeals against Tribunal decisions, etc., which can give rise to further litigation. However, the HO/UKBA has been shown to be a dysfunctional and unmanageable institution composed of departments which consistently fail to co-operate/co-ordinate their work. Attempts by the SSHD to micro-manage officials and force them to implement poorly conceived policies have hugely complicated the tasks they are required to perform and have led to stress, poor decision-making, and litigation. In short, the accretion of power within the Home Office has not created an all-powerful institution capable of overseeing immigration and asylum and controlling challenges to its authority, rather it has resulted in growing legal challenges in an effort to overturn wrongful decisions.

Other institutions exercise important if indirect influence on the field. Thus TSol/the Government Legal Department assists the HO to litigate against challenges to policy, legal aid provides law firms with the resources to take asylum claims and prepare and argue appeals, and the Tribunal and the Court of Appeal use their legal and spatial architecture to speedily hear and decide asylum appeals (though the nature of and right to appeal against decisions by the Tribunal has been continuously eroded by legislation since 2005). Individuals in each of these institutions have been found to perform their roles with varying degrees of ability and efficiency, with all this means for arriving at just and sustainable legal decisions. Throughout the period of study the field has undergone continuous change, not least in terms of the relations between institutions (e.g. the Tribunal was restructured twice, there have been continuous cuts to legal aid, and the Court of Appeal now exercises less oversight of the Tribunal and, by implication, the Home Office).

With respect to secondary institutions in the field, ILPA, the Independent Chief Inspector of Borders and Immigration and the UNHCR exercise limited influence on Home Office policy and practice. While these organizations focus public attention on inequities/problems with asylum policy and its implementation, their impact is limited, in part because media coverage of asylum and immigration issues has been eclipsed by public debates regarding British 'sovereignty' *vis-à-vis* the European Union. In short, there is little public support to redress the problems in the asylum field that have been identified in this study.

While the asylum field is highly political in nature, the process cannot be understood as a simple turf battle between the courts and the legislature, as the 2005 showdown over proposed changes to the appeal process discussed in Chapter 6 shows. Despite the messy and uncertain outcomes of specific conflicts, it seems clear that due to the lack of public support for refugees and the growing power of the Home Office, the direction of UK asylum policy is towards ever more restrictive policies which will attempt to prevent asylum applicants from reaching the UK, and prevent individuals who do manage to file a claim from securing protection. However, unless the government eliminates legal aid and completely removes the right to appeal against Tribunal decisions – which unarguably would contravene the Refugee Convention and bring the UK into disrepute – refugee lawyers and NGOs will continue to litigate and advocate against vexatious Home Office policies and decisions which prevent individuals from securing protection.

Notes

1 For statistics on asylum seekers in Europe, see 'Asylum statistics', *Eurostat*, available at: http://ec.europa.eu/eurostat/statistics-explained/index.php/Asylum_statistics (accessed 10 August 2016).

2 See 'Judicial review and costs', *Justice*, available at: https://www.justice.gov.uk/courts/rcj-rolls-building/administrative-court/applying-for-judicial-review (accessed 10 August 2016).

3 See a summary of this litigation at 'The legal challenge', *Detention Action*, available at: http://detentionaction.org.uk/campaigns/end-the-fast-track-to-despair/legal-challenge (accessed 10 August 2016).

4 See J. Phelps, 'The fast track is dead', *openDemocracy*, 20 May 2016, available at: https://www.opendemocracy.net/5050/jerome-phelps/fast-track-is-dead (accessed 10 August 2016).

5 *SM and Qadir v Secretary of State for the Home Department (ETS – Evidence – Burden of Proof)* [2016] UKUT 229 (IAC), *Upper Tribunal (Immigration and Asylum Chamber)*, para. 84, available at: http://www.bailii.org/uk/cases/UKUT/IAC/2016/229.html (accessed 11 August 2016).

6 Ibid., para. 101.

7 See: I. Dunt, 'Secretive legal committee buries ruling against Teresa May', *Politics.co.uk*, 21 April 2016, available at: http://www.politics.co.uk/blogs/2016/04/21/secretive-legal-committee-buries-ruling-against-theresa-may (accessed 10 August 2016); J. Merrill, 'Theresa May faces Parliamentary investigation over flimsy basis for student deportations', *The Independent*, 23 March 2016, available at: http://www.independent.co.uk/news/uk/politics/theresa-may-faces-parliamentary-investigation-over-flimsy-basis-for-student-deportations-a6948796.html (accessed 10 August 2016).

8 See J. Hyde, 'Immigration judges leave in droves as caseload piles up', *The Law Gazette*, 25 February 2016, available at: http://www.lawgazette.co.uk/news/immigration-judges-leave-in-droves-as-caseload-piles-up/5053832.fullarticle (accessed 10 August 2016).

9 The Act introduced a new test whereby individuals seeking to access legal aid were to be required to legally reside in the UK for 12 months. However, in April 2016 litigation by the Public Law Project reached the Supreme Court which unanimously decided that the test was discriminatory. It would have affected members of the armed forces serving overseas, children under one year old and asylum seekers; see O. Bowcott, 'MoJ plan for legal aid residence test thrown out by Supreme Court', *The Guardian*, 18 April 2016, available at: https://www.theguardian.com/law/2016/apr/18/uk-supreme-court-throws-out-legal-aid-residence-test-justice-minister-michael-gove (accessed 10 August 2016).

10 See R (*On the Application of) Gudanaviciene and Others v The Director of Legal Aid Casework and the Lord Chancellor* [2014] EWCA Civ 1622; [2015] 1 WLR 2247.

Glossary

Acknowledgement of Service A form filed by TSol in the High Court/Court of Appeal acknowledging the lodging of an appeal against the Home Office.

AIT UK Asylum and Immigration Tribunal; see also *IAA*, *Tribunal* and *Upper Tribunal.*

ALT Appeal and Litigation Team, a unit in the Home Office which decides whether the HO should appeal against a decision by an Immigration Judge.

APIs Asylum Policy Instructions, written by the Home Office Policy Unit.

Appeal An appeal against a decision by the SSHD, which is decided by the Tribunal or the CoA.

Application for reconsideration An appeal filed either by the asylum appellant's legal counsel or the Home Office against a decision by an IJ.

Asylum case owner A junior civil servant in the HO/UKBA who assesses applications for asylum and takes the initial decision; they also decide fresh asylum applications.

Bail The 1971 Immigration Act Parts II and III, sets out the procedure for 'bail in practice' and 'bail in principle' for individuals held in immigration detention.

Bail Summary A report produced for a bail hearing prepared by a HOPO based on a search of immigration/police databases, summarizing a person's immigration history and reasons why bail should be refused, and checking the surety's criminal record.

Barrister A qualified legal practitioner, operating primarily out of a set/chamber, whose chief role is to litigate cases in the AIT and the CoA.

Border Force The UK Border Force, a department of the Home Office responsible for controlling the entry of foreigners into the UK.

Case law The judicial decisions taken by the Upper Tribunal of the AIT (in particular 'reported' and Country Guidance cases) or by the CoA.

Certificated work Under the legal aid scheme, funding for advocates/barristers to represent clients in the appellate court.

CG Country Guidance, a designated case heard in the AIT which sets a binding precedent on subsequent related asylum claims.

Chamber A barrister's office from which law is practised. These days the term refers to a shared or combined practice by a number of barristers; see also *set.*

Claimant A person appealing against a decision by the Secretary of State for the Home Department to the AIT; an asylum applicant.

CLR Controlled Legal Representation, funded by legal aid to represent an individual before a tribunal or court.

CoA Court of Appeal.

COI Country of origin information; sometimes referred to as 'objective evidence'.

COIS Country of Origin Information Service, the department within the UKBA which produces reports on the top 20 refugee sending countries to the UK. Its reports guide HO officials and others in deciding asylum claims; see also *objective evidence.*

Country experts Anthropologists, historians or regional specialists whose knowledge of a specific country qualifies them to write a report on political conditions in an asylum applicant's country of origin (where the applicant may be deported to).

CPS Crown Prosecution Service, a government department responsible for prosecuting an individual for violating criminal or civil law.

Credibility If an appellant's evidence is found to contain errors or omissions or is inconsistent, the Home Office and IJs may decide that the appeal lacks credibility and should be refused.

***De novo* hearing** A new hearing; a second, full hearing.

Department of Constitutional Affairs Prior to 2007 it was responsible for managing the courts, the Legal Services Commission, etc.; after 2007 this responsibility was transferred to the Ministry of Justice.

Deportation The forcible expulsion to their country of origin of illegal migrants, failed asylum seekers, foreign national prisoners or foreigners who have criminal convictions.

DFT Detained Fast Track, an accelerated appeal system that is supposed to quickly decide the appeals of individuals held in detention and to quickly remove the person when their appeal fails.

Document Verification Record In 2007 British embassies established offices in certain countries to undertake forgery analysis of the documents submitted by nationals applying for a visitor's visa. It is now routine for ECOs to submit a report to HOPOs which indicates when documents are forged or cannot be verified.

ECHR European Court of Human Rights in Strasbourg.

ECO Home Office entry clearance officer, stationed at a British embassy to interview and assess individuals seeking a visa to enter the UK.

Government set A barristers' chamber that specializes in government litigation; see also *set.*

Grounds of resistance Term used by TSol to refer to the skeleton outlining its response to an appeal filed against the Home Office.

Hearing centre A court in the UK run by the AIT to hear immigration and asylum appeals.

HO UK Home Office; see also *SSHD.*

HoL The UK House of Lords, which became the Supreme Court in 2009. It is the highest Court of Appeal.

HOLAB Home Office Legal Adviser's Branch, a department which provides legal advice to senior officials.

HOPO Home Office presenting officer, a junior civil servant.

IAA Immigration Appellate Authority, the first tier of the Tribunal/AIT.

IAT Immigration and Asylum Tribunal; see also *AIT*.

ICI Independent Chief Inspector of the UKBA.

IDIs Immigration Directorate Instructions, issued by the SSHD to guide case-workers in their assessment of asylum and migration claims.

IJ Immigration Judge, who sits in the AIT and decides asylum and immigration appeals.

ILPA Immigration Law Practitioners' Association.

ILR Indefinite Leave to Remain; a temporary right to reside in the UK which can be revoked by the Home Office.

Immigration detention Individuals arrested for a range of immigration offences, including when an immigration officer believes a person seeking to enter the UK has an unfounded asylum claim, are placed in a purpose-built detention centre or a prison. Their various claims for asylum, bail and deportation are fast-tracked and decided while the person remains in detention with a view to rapidly deporting them to their country of origin.

Immigration Rules Issued by the SSHD to instruct officials how to assess an asylum or migration claim.

IND UK Immigration and Nationality Department, formerly part of the Home Office, now the UKBA.

IO Immigration officer, employed by the Home Office to interview and assess individuals seeking to enter the UK.

IRs Home Office Immigration Rules.

JR Judicial review.

Justice A nebulous concept whose significance hinges upon whether one is a citizen or a foreigner.

Language analysis A Home Office policy of using private firms to assess the language of an asylum applicant to determine their country of origin.

Lawyer An individual with legal training, but who is not necessarily involved in litigation, e.g. immigration caseworkers and solicitors (including individuals employed by TSol and in other government departments).

Legal Advisory Department A department in the HO which provides legal advice to senior officials; see also *HOLAB*.

Legal aid A government means-tested fund to pay lawyers; in this context it may fund the preparation of an individual's asylum application and, if necessary, pay a barrister/advocate to represent the applicant in the AIT and CoA (the fund is also available for British citizens to appeal against various injustices).

Legal help Under the legal aid scheme, this provides funding for basic legal advice to individuals.

Litigation Legal cases, in this context, asylum appeals heard by the AIT or CoA.

LJ Lord Justice, a judge who sits in the CoA.

LSC Legal Services Commission, a semi-autonomous government department located in the Ministry of Justice which manages the legal aid budget.

Merits test Immigration caseworkers are required to assess whether the case is likely to win, i.e. does it have merit, before they take it on and before they approach the Legal Services Commission for legal aid to pay for processing the case. The test is repeated, at a higher threshold, before instructing a barrister/advocate to appeal against an IJ's decision.

MoJ Ministry of Justice. In 2007 it took over much of the work of the Department of Constitutional Affairs.

NAM The New Asylum Model, created by the Home Office in 2007, which established designated case owners for each asylum application which were placed in one of five segments to be managed and decided.

National Asylum Support Service Following the Immigration and Asylum Act (1999), the National Asylum Support Service was set up to administer the dispersal of asylum applicants across the UK.

Objective evidence A term used to describe reports containing facts verified either by the courts, by the Home Office, the Home Office Country of Origin Information Service (recently renamed Country Information and Guidance) and sometimes by country experts.

OGNs Home Office Operational Guidance Notes, country-specific summaries of COI and case law.

Onward Right of Appeal Unit The unit within the UKBA which decides whether to appeal against a decision by an Immigration Judge; see also *ALT.*

Permission hearing The hearing where a Lord Justice in the CoA considers the merits of allowing an appeal against a decision; the first stage is known as application 'on the papers', and if necessary, counsel can make an 'oral application' to the CoA.

POU Presenting Officers Unit for HOPOs; one is attached to every AIT hearing centre.

Practice Directions A body of rules setting out the courts' procedures which are used by a judge to control legal proceedings, part of the courts' legal architecture. There are specific rules for the AIT and for the CoA.

Procedural Rules A body of rules which set out the courts' power to hear and decide appeals, part of the courts' legal architecture. There are specific rules for the AIT and for the CoA.

Reconsideration When an appeal against a decision by an IJ is allowed, the case is reconsidered by another IJ.

Removal A euphemism for deportation.

Reported case An asylum appeal decided by the AIT/Tribunal, which reports it for its significance on a specific issue of law which subsequent cases are expected to follow.

RFL Home Office Reasons for Refusal Letter.

RSD Refugee Status Determination system, the administrative agencies involved in deciding claims, the courts and other institutions and organizations which seek to influence the outcome of asylum decisions and asylum policy.

Rule 35 reports The Detention Centre Rules (2001) lay out requirements for medical practitioners working in immigration detention centres to report to their manager the case of any detained person whose health is likely to be injuriously affected by continued detention. The centre and UKBA are mandated to investigate the report and take appropriate action.

Rule 39 applications Applications made to the European Court of Human Rights in Strasbourg with respect to a wrongful decision to detain and/or deport an individual for an immigration offence.

SEF Home Office Statement of Evidence Form, containing the essence of the asylum claim and completed by a Home Office case owner; a record of the substantive interview.

Set A barrister's chambers, typically combining commercial, civil and other forms of litigation and legal advice; see also *chamber*.

SI Screening interview, the first interview conducted by an immigration officer or caseworker to record basic information about the nature of the individual's claim.

SIAC Special Immigration Appeals Commission, which hears terrorist-related appeals.

SIJ Senior Immigration Judge, who sits in the Upper Tribunal and decides asylum and immigration appeals.

SPO Home Office senior presenting officer.

SSHD Secretary of State for the Home Department (the Home Secretary), who oversees the work of the Home Office, UKBA and Border Force.

Substantive interview The principal Home Office asylum interview; see also *SEF*.

Supreme Court The highest appellate court in the UK.

Surety A bond provided for an individual held in detention, usually in the form of a stipulated amount of money which is forfeited if the individual released from detention absconds; also refers to the person providing the surety.

TD Travel document, an internationally recognized document issued by an embassy which allows an individual to return to their country of origin.

Tribunal UK Asylum and Immigration Tribunal, the lower court of the Immigration and Asylum Chamber; see also *Upper Tribunal*.

TSol UK Treasury Solicitor's Office.

UKBA United Kingdom Border Agency, part of the Home Office.

UNHCR United Nations High Commission for Refugees.

Upper Tribunal The superior court of record for the Immigration and Asylum Chamber, which hears appeals against decisions made by the first-tier Tribunal; see also *Tribunal*.

Bibliography

Amnesty International. 2004. *Get It Right: How Home Office Decision-Making Fails Refugees*. London: Amnesty International.

Amnesty International. 2013. *A Question of Credibility: Why So Many Asylum Decisions Are Overturned on Appeal in the UK*. London: Amnesty International.

Anker, D. 1992. 'Determining asylum claims in the United States: An empirical case study', *NYU Journal of Law & Social Change* 19: 433.

Anon. 2005. 'Don't browbeat us, top judge tells PM', *The Express*, 12 October.

Anon. 2006. 'Immigration system unfit – Reid', *BBC News*, 23 May. Available at: http://news.bbc.co.uk/1/hi/uk_politics/5007148.stm (accessed 4 August 2016).

Anon. 2010. 'Whistleblower's claims about Cardiff asylum office', *BBC News*, 3 February, available at: http://news.bbc.co.uk/1/hi/wales/south_east/8496759.stm (accessed 4 August 2016).

Arapiles, S. 2015. 'UK Home Office Guidance on Eritrea: An instrument to refuse protection?', *Right to Remain* (26 August). Available at: http://www.righttoremain.org.uk/blog/uk-home-office-guidance-on-eritrea-an-instrument-to-refuse-protection/ (accessed 27 July 2016).

Asylum Aid. 2013. *Right First Time*. London: Asylum Aid.

Asylum and Immigration Tribunal. 2003. *Adjudicator Guidance Note: Unrepresented Appellants*, Guidance Note no. 5. Available at: https://www.judiciary.gov.uk/wp-content/uploads/2014/07/GuideNoteNo5.pdf.

Asylum Appellate Project. 2009. *Asylum Appellate Project – Second Year Report, ICAR*. Available at: http://www.icar.org.uk/11265/research-directory/asylum-appellate-project-second-year-report.html (accessed 27 July 2016).

Atkins, B. 1990. 'Interventions and power in judicial hierarchies: Appellate courts in England and the United States', *Law & Society Review* 24(1): 71–103.

Bailey, F.G. 1969. *Stratagems and Spoils: A Social Anthropology of Politics*. New York: Schocken.

Bar Council. 2016. 'Statistics: Demographic profile of the Bar', *The Bar Council*. Available at: http://www.barcouncil.org.uk/about-the-bar/facts-and-figures/statistics/ (accessed 6 August 2016).

Bar Standards Board. 2013. 'Removal of the "cab rank" rule a major threat to justice', 26 March. Available at: https://www.barstandardsboard.org.uk/media-centre/press-releases-and-news/removal-of-the-%E2%80%98cab-rank%E2%80%99-rule-a-major-threat-to-justice/ (accessed 7 August 2016).

Barnes, J. 2004. 'Expert evidence: The judicial perception in asylum and human rights appeals', *International Journal of Refugee Law* 16: 349–357.

Berends, M. 1992. 'An elusive profession? Lawyers in society', *Law & Society Review* 26: 161–189.

Bernhagen, P. 2012. 'Who gets what in British politics – and how? An analysis of media reports on lobbying around government policies, 2001–7', *Political Studies* 60: 557–577.

BID. 2006. *Working against the Clock: Inadequacy and Injustice in the Fast Track System.* London: Bail for Immigration Detainees.

BID. 2009. *Out of Sight, out of Mind: Experience of Immigration Detention in the UK.* London: Bail for Immigration Detainees.

BID. 2010. *A Nice Judge on a Good Day: Immigration Bail and the Right to Liberty.* London: Bail for Immigration Detainees.

Blacksell, M. and C. Fussell. 1994. 'Barristers and the growth of local justice in England and Wales', *Transactions of the Institute of British Geographers* 19: 482–493.

Blommaert, J. 2001. 'Investigating narrative inequality: African asylum seekers in Belgium', *Discourse & Society* 12(4): 413–449.

Bohannon, P. 1957. *Justice and Judgement among the Tiv.* Oxford: Oxford University Press.

Bohmer, C. and A. Shuman. 2008. *Rejecting Refugees: Political Asylum in the 21st Century.* Abingdon: Routledge.

Bondy, V. and M. Sunkin. 2009. *The Dynamics of Judicial Review Litigation: The Resolution of Public Law Challenges before Final Hearing.* London: The Public Law Project.

Bosniak, L. 1991. 'Human rights, state sovereignty and the protection of undocumented migrants under the International Migrant Workers Convention', *International Migration Review* 25(4): 737–770.

Bosworth, M. 2012. 'Subjectivity and identity in detention: Punishment in a global age', *Theoretical Criminology* 16(2): 123–140.

Bourdieu, P. 1987. 'The force of law: Toward a sociology of the juridical field', *The Hastings Law Journal* 38: 814–853.

Bowcott, O. 2008. 'Asylum seekers: Pressure grows to free detained Zimbabwean asylum seekers', *The Guardian*, 3 July. Available at: https://www.theguardian.com/uk/2008/jul/03/immigration.immigrationpolicy (accessed 8 August 2016).

Bowcott, O. 2011. 'Tens of thousands lose support as Immigration Advisory Services closes', *The Guardian*, 11 July. Available at: http://www.theguardian.com/law/2011/jul/11/immigration-advisory-service-closes-blames-government (accessed 6 August 2016).

Bowcott, O. 2016. 'MoJ plan for legal aid residence test thrown out by Supreme Court', *The Guardian*, 18 April. Available at: https://www.theguardian.com/law/2016/apr/18/uk-supreme-court-throws-out-legal-aid-residence-test-justice-minister-michael-gove (accessed 10 August 2016).

Brazier, A., S. Kalitowski and G. Rosenblatt. 2007. *Law in the Making: A Discussion Paper.* London: Hansard Society.

Briggs, M. 2015. 'Europe "à la carte" The whats and whys behind the UK opt-outs', *EurActiv* (7 May). Available at: http://www.euractiv.com/section/uk-europe/linksdossier/europe-a-la-carte-the-whats-and-whys-behind-uk-opt-outs/#ea-accordion-timeline (accessed 27 July 2016).

Broeders, D. 2007. 'The new digital borders of Europe: EU databases and the surveillance of irregular migrants', *International Sociology* 22(1): 71–92.

Brownlee, D. 1983. *The Law Courts: The Architecture of George Edmund Street.* Cambridge, MA: MIT Press.

Burnham, E. 2003. *Challenging Immigration Detention: A Best Practice Guide.* London: Immigration Law Practitioners' Association.

Byrne, R. 2007. 'Assessing testimonial evidence in asylum proceedings: Guiding standards from the International Criminal Tribunals', *International Journal of Refugee Law* 19(4): 609–638.

Campbell, J. 2011. 'The enduring problem of statelessness in the Horn of Africa: How nation-states and Western courts (re)define nationality', *International Journal of Refugee Law* 23(4): 656–679.

Campbell, J. 2013a. 'Language analysis in the United Kingdom's Refugee Status Determination system: Seeing through policy claims about "expert knowledge"', *Ethnic and Racial Studies* 36(4): 670–690.

Campbell, J. 2013b. *Nationalism, Law and Statelessness in the Horn of Africa*. Abingdon: Routledge.

Campbell, J. 2015. 'Expert evidence in British asylum courts: The judicial assessment of evidence on ethnic discrimination and statelessness in Ethiopia', in I. Berger, T. Redeker Heppner, B. Lawrance, J. Tague and M. Teretta, eds, *African Asylum at a Crossroads: Activism, Expert Testimony and Refugee Rights*. Athens, OH: Ohio University Press, pp. 102–120.

Campbell, J. 2016. 'Asylum v. sovereignty in the 21st century: How nation-states breach international law to block access to asylum', *International Journal of Migration and Border Studies* 2(1): 24–39.

Campbell J. forthcoming. 'Adjudicating the asylum claims of unaccompanied asylum-seeking children in the UK', in M. Crock and L. Renson, Eds. *Protecting the Migrant Child*. Cheltenham: Elgar.

Carlen, P. 1976. *Magistrates' Justice*. London: Martin Robertson.

Chesneaux, J. 2000. 'Speed and democracy: An uneasy dialogue', *Social Science Information* 39(3): 407–420.

Clayton, G. 2012. *Textbook on Immigration and Asylum Law*, 5th edn. Oxford: Oxford University Press.

Coffrey, G., I. Kaplan, R. Sampson, R. Tucci and M. Montagna. 2010. 'The meaning and mental health consequences of long-term immigration detention for people seeking asylum', *Social Science & Medicine* 70(12): 2070–2079.

Cohen, J. 2002. 'Questions of credibility: Omissions, discrepancies and errors of recall in the testimony of asylum seekers', *International Journal of Refugee Law* 13(3): 293–309.

Cohen, J. 2008. '"Safe in our hands"? A study of suicide and self-harm in asylum seekers', *Journal of Forensic and Legal Medicine* 15: 235–244.

Cohen, S. 2003. *No One Is Illegal: Asylum and Immigration Control Past and Present*. London: Trentham Books.

Conley, J. and W.M. O'Barr. 1988. 'Fundamentals of jurisprudence: An ethnography of judicial decision-making in informal courts', *North Carolina Law Review* 66: 467–507.

Conley, J. and W.M. O'Barr. 1990. *Rules vs Relationships: The Ethnography of Legal Discourse*. Chicago, IL: University of Chicago Press.

Conley, J. and W.M. O'Barr. 1998. *Just Words: Law, Language and Power*, 2nd edn. Chicago, IL: University of Chicago Press.

Conley, J. and W.M. O'Barr. 2004. 'A classic in spite of itself: The Cheyenne Way and the case method in legal anthropology', *Law & Social Inquiry* 29: 179–216.

Consterdine, E. 2013. *One Step Forward, Two Steps Back: Evaluating the Institutions of British Immigration Policy Making*. London: Institute for Public Policy Research.

Corcoran, C. 2004. 'A critical examination of the use of language analysis interviews in asylum proceedings: A case study of a West African seeking asylum in the Netherlands', *Speech, Language and the Law* 11(2): 200–221.

Council of Europe. 2016. *Memorandum on the Human Rights of Asylum Seekers and Immigrants in the UK.* Strasbourg: Commissioner for Human Rights.

Couper, K. 1981. 'An elusive concept: The changing definition of illegal immigrant in the practice of immigration control in the UK', *International Migration Review* 18(3): 437–452.

Crawley, H. 2010a. *Chance or Choice? Understanding Why Asylum Seekers Come to the UK.* London: Refugee Council.

Crawley, H. 2010b. '"No one gives you a chance to say what you are thinking": Finding space for children's agency in the UK asylum system', *Area* 42(2): 162–169.

Crock, M. and H. Martin. 2013. Refugee rights and the merits of appeals', *University of Queensland Law Journal* 32: 137–155.

Cunningham, C. 1992. 'The lawyer as translator, representation as text: Towards an ethnography of legal discourse', *Cornell Law Review* 77: 1298–1383.

Cwerner, S. 2004. 'Faster, faster and faster: The time politics of asylum in the UK', *Time & Society* 13(1): 71–88.

Daily Mail Reporter. 2011. 'Anger as more than £12m paid out in legal costs and compensation to immigrants and asylum seekers in just a year', *Daily Mail*, 15 August. Available at: http://www.dailymail.co.uk/news/article-2026206/UKBA-paid-12m-compensation-legal-costs-migrants-year.html (accessed 10 August 2016).

Das, V. 2004. 'The signature of the state: The paradox of illegibility', in V. Das and D. Poole, eds, *Anthropology in the Margins of the State.* Albuquerque, NM: University of New Mexico Press.

Dauvergne, C. 2004. 'Sovereignty, migration and the rule of law in global times', *The Modern Law Review* 67(4): 588–615.

Drewry, G. 1981. 'Lawyers in the UK civil service', *Public Administration* 59: 15–45.

Dunstan, R. 1998. 'United Kingdom: Breaches of Art. 31 of the 1951 Refugee Convention', *International Journal of Refugee Law* 10(1–2): 205–213.

Dunt, I. 2016. 'Secretive legal committee buries ruling against Teresa May', *Politics.co.uk*, 21 April. Available at: http://www.politics.co.uk/blogs/2016/04/21/secretive-legal-committee-buries-ruling-against-theresa-may (accessed 10 August 2016).

Duvell, F. and B. Jordan. 2003. 'Immigration control and the management of economic migration in the UK: Organizational culture, implementation, enforcement and identity processes in the public services', *Journal of Ethnic and Migration Studies* 29(2): 299–366.

ECHR. 2013. *Rule 39 Requests Granted and Refused in 2008, 2009 and 2010, 2011 and 2012 by Responding State.* Available at: http://echr.coe.int/Documents/Stats_art_39_2008_2012_ENG.pdf (accessed 27 July 2016).

Edwards, A. 2003. 'Tampering with refugee protection: The case of Australia', *International Journal of Refugee Law* 15(2): 193–211.

Ellis, J. 2004. 'More than a token gesture: NGOs and trade unions campaigning for a common cause', *Development in Practice* 14(1–2): 248–253.

Epstein, A.L. 1967. 'The case method in the field of law', in A. Epstein, ed., *The Craft of Social Anthropology.* London: Tavistock, pp. 205–230.

Fabienne, P. 2009. 'Rawlsian justice', in P. Anand, P. Pattaniak and C. Puppe, eds, *The Handbook of Rational and Social Choice.* Oxford: Oxford University Press, pp. 433–456.

Fassin, D. 2013. 'The precarious truth of asylum', *Public Culture* 25(1): 39–63.

Felstiner, W. and A. Sarat. 1992. 'Enactments of power: Negotiating reality and responsibility in lawyer–client interactions', *Cornell Law Review* 77: 1447–1495.

Fernandez-Kelly, P. 2007. 'NAFTA and beyond: Alternative perspectives in the study of global trade and development', *Annals of the American Academy of Political and Social Science* 610: 6–19.

Fiddick, J. 1999. *Immigration and Asylum.* House of Commons Research Paper 99/16. London: Home Affairs Section.

Flood, J. 1983. *Barrister's Clerks. The Law's Middlemen.* Manchester: Manchester University Press.

Flynn, D. 2005. 'New borders, new management: The dilemmas of modern immigration policy', *Ethnic and Racial Studies* 28(3): 463–490.

Freeman, G. 2011. 'Comparative analysis of immigration politics: A retrospective', *American Behavior Scientist* 55(12): 1541–1560.

Galanter, M. 1983. 'Reading the landscape of disputes: What we know and don't know about our allegedly contentious and litigious society', *UCLA Law Review* 31(4): 5–69.

Geddes, A. 2003. *The Politics of Migration and Immigration in Europe.* London: Sage.

Gexall, G. 2014. 'Skeleton arguments: If you don't do them properly you won't get paid!', *Civil Litigation Brief*, 11 May. Available at: https://civillitigationbrief.wordpress.com/2014/05/11/skeleton-argument-if-you-dont-do-them-properly-you-wont-get-paid/ (accessed 16 August 2016).

Gherson Immigration. 2013. 'A step in the right direction for UKBA but further regulation required', *Gherson*, 18 January. Available at: http://www.gherson.com/blog/a-step-in-the-right-direction-for-ukba-but-further-regulation-required/ (accessed 8 August 2016).

Gibb, F. 2006. 'Blunders left 210 judges waiting for jobs', *The Times*, 13 November. Available at: http://www.thetimes.co.uk/tto/law/article2214070.ece (accessed 8 August 2016).

Gibb, F. 2008. 'Extra judges drafted in to hear immigration appeals', *The Times*, 15 December. Available at: http://www.thetimes.co.uk/tto/law/article2214070.ece (accessed 8 August 2016).

Gibb, R. and A. Good. 2014. 'Interpretation, translation and intercultural communication in Refugee Status Determination procedures in the UK and France', *Language and Cultural Communication* 14(3): 385–399.

Gibbard, R. 2002. *Whose Land Was It Anyway? The Crichel Down Rules and the Sale of Public Land.* Working Papers in Land Management and Development 01/02. Reading: University of Reading.

Gibney, M. 2008. 'Asylum and the expansion of deportation in the United Kingdom', *Government and Opposition* 43(2): 146–167.

Gilbert, A. and K. Khoser. 2006. 'Coming to the UK: What do asylum seekers know about the UK before arrival?', *Journal of Ethnic and Migration Studies* 32(7): 1209–1225.

Gilboy, J. 1991. 'Deciding who gets in: Decision-making by immigration inspectors', *Law & Society Review* 25: 571–599.

Global Detention Project. 2011. 'United Kingdom Detention Profile', *Global Detention Project.* Available at: http://www.globaldetentionproject.org/countries/europe/united-kingdom/introduction.html (accessed 1 November 2013).

Gluckman, M. 1955. *The Judicial Process among the Barotse of Northern Rhodesia.* Manchester: Manchester University Press.

Good, A. 2004. 'Expert evidence in asylum and human rights appeals: An expert's view', *International Journal of Refugee Law* 16(3): 358–380.

Good, A. 2007. *Anthropology and Expertise in the Asylum Courts.* London: Routledge.

Good, A. 2008. 'Cultural evidence in courts of law', *Journal of the Royal Anthropological Institute* 14(Supplement 1): S47–S60.

Goodwin, C. 1994. 'Professional vision', *American Anthropologist* 96(3): 606–633.

Gower, M. 2010. *The Draft Immigration Bill and Simplification of Immigration Law.* SN/HA/5623. London: House of Commons, Home Affairs Section.

Graham, C. 2003. *The Architectural and Social History of the English Court of Law to 1914.* Aldershot: Ashgate.

Greenslade, R. 2005. *Seeking Scapegoats: The Coverage of Asylum in the UK Press.* Asylum and Migration Working Paper no. 5. London: Institute for Public Policy Research.

Hamlin, R. 2014. *Let Me Be a Refugee: Administrative Justice and the Politics of Asylum in the US, Canada, and Australia.* Oxford: Oxford University Press.

Harvey, A. 1998. 'Researching "the risks of getting it wrong"', in F. Nicholson and P. Twomey, eds, *Current Issues of UK Asylum Law and Policy.* Aldershot: Ashgate, pp. 176–198.

Hepple, B. 1969. 'Immigration Appeal Act 1969', *The Modern Law Review* 32(6): 668–672.

Heyman, J.M. 1995. 'Putting power in the anthropology of bureaucracy', *Current Anthropology* 36(2): 261–287.

Heyman, J.M. 2004. 'Ports of entry as nodes in the World System', *Identities* 11: 303–327.

Hickinbottom, Mr Justice. 2010. 'What makes a good judge', in J. Jowell et al., eds, *Judicial Appointments: Balancing Independence, Accountability and Legitimacy.* London: Judicial Appointments Commission, pp. 55–66.

Hirsch, A. 2010. 'Ministers axe Legal Services Commission to wrest back control of legal aid budget', *The Guardian*, 2 March. Available at: http://www.theguardian.com/uk/2010/mar/03/legal-services-commission-abolished (accessed 16 August 2016).

Hoag, C. 2010. 'The magic of the populace: An ethnography of illegibility in the South African immigration bureaucracy', *PoLAR* 33(1): 6–25.

Hocking, J. 2006. 'Special report on asylum seekers' experiences', *Community Care* (13 April). Available at: http://www.communitycare.co.uk/2006/04/13/special-report-on-asylum-seekers-experiences/#.UxmKifl_vkY (accessed 18 April 2006).

Holiday, Y. 2012. 'CCRC concern over advice given to refugees', *The Law Society Gazette*, 14 June.

Holmes, D. 2016. 'Fascism 2', *Anthropology Today* 32(2): 1–3.

Horne, A. 2006. *Judicial Review: A Short Guide to Claims in the Administrative Court.* Home Affairs Research Paper 06/44. London: Social and General Statistics Section, House of Commons Library.

Human Rights Futures Project. 2011. 'Deportation and the right to respect for private and family life under Article 8 HRA', July. London: Human Rights Futures Project, London School of Economics. Available at: http://image.guardian.co.uk/sys-files/Guardian/documents/2011/10/04/KlugDeportation.pdf (accessed 8 August 2016).

Human Rights Watch. 2010. *Fast-Tracked Unfairness: Detention and Denial of Women Asylum Seekers in the UK.* Available at: https://www.hrw.org/sites/default/files/reports/uk0210webwcover.pdf (accessed 27 July 2016).

Hyde, J. 2016. 'Immigration judges leave in droves as caseload piles up', *The Law Gazette*, 25 February. Available at: http://www.lawgazette.co.uk/news/immigration-judges-leave-in-droves-as-caseload-piles-up/5053832.fullarticle (accessed 10 August 2016).

Hynes, P. 2011. *The dispersal and social exclusion of asylum seekers.* Bristol: The Policy Press.

IAS. 2007. *LSC Accreditation Level I and OISC Level 2 Training Manual Version 2.5.* London: Immigration Advisory Services.

IAS. 2009a. *An Analysis of the March 2009 Zimbabwe Operational Guidance Note (Extended Speaking Notes).* London: Immigration Advisory Services.

IAS. 2009b. *The Use of Country of Origin Information in Operational Guidance Notes.* London: Immigration Advisory Services.

ICAR. 2007a. *Asylum Appeals Process.* Available at: http://www.icar.org.uk/Appeal_Process_Sept2007.pdf (accessed 27 July 2016).

ICAR. 2007b. *The Operation of the Asylum Determination Process.* Available at: http://www.icar.org.uk/The_operation_of_the_asylum_determination_process_June_2007.pdf (accessed 27 July 2016).

ICAR. 2009. *Statistics Paper No. 2: Asylum Decision Making and Appeals Process. March 2009 Update.* Available at: http://www.icar.org.uk/ICAR%20Statistics%20Paper%202%20-%20March%2009%20Update.pdf (accessed 27 July 2016).

ILPA. 2005/2006. *ILPA Annual Report.* London: Immigration Law Practitioners' Association.

ILPA. 2008. *The Detained Fast Track Process: A Best Practice Guide.* London: Immigration Law Practitioners' Association.

ILPA. 2008/2009. *ILPA Annual Report.* London: Immigration Law Practitioners' Association.

ILPA. 2009. *Borders, Citizenship and Immigration Act 2009: Ministerial Statements.* London: Immigration Law Practitioners' Association.

ILPA. 2009/2010. *ILPA Annual Report.* London: Immigration Law Practitioners' Association.

ILPA. 2010. 'ILPA: Proposed Legal Aid Cuts: Why and how to resist them', *Electronic Immigration Network*, December. Available at: https://www.ein.org.uk/ilpa-proposed-legal-aid-cuts-why-and-how-resist-them (accessed 11 August 2016).

Immigration Matters. 2011. '14 year long stay immigration concession to be closed', *Immigration Matters*, 19 July. Available at: http://immigrationmatters.co.uk/14-year-long-stay-concession-to-be-closed.html (accessed 4 August 2016).

Independent Asylum Commission. 2007. Citizens' asylum enquiry hears evidence of trauma caused by "dawn raids"', press release, 6 June. Available at: http://www.independentasylumcommission.org.uk/files/06.06.07.pdf (accessed 8 August 2016).

Independent Asylum Commission. 2008. *Fit for Purpose Yet? Interim Findings.* London: Independent Asylum Commission.

Information Commissioner's Office. n.d. 'Guide to freedom of information'. Available at: https://ico.org.uk/for-organisations/guide-to-freedom-of-information/ (accessed 27 July 2016).

International Association of Refugee Law Judges. 2013. *Assessing Credibility in Refugee and Subsidiary Protection Claims under the EU Qualification Directive: Judicial Criteria and Standards.* Haarlem, the Netherlands: IARLJ.

Jacquemet, J. 2009. 'Transcribing refugees: The entextualization of asylum seekers' hearings in a transidiomatic environment', *Text & Talk* 29(5): 525–546.

James, D. and E. Killick. 2012. 'Empathy and expertise: Case workers and immigration/asylum applicants in London', *Law & Social Inquiry* 37: 430–454.

James, P. and L. Mayblin. 2016. *Factors Influencing Asylum Destination Choice: A Review of the Evidence.* Working Paper no. 04/16/1. Sheffield: University of Sheffield.

Johnston, P. 2005. 'Clarke urges EU to rethink rights laws on deportations', *The Telegraph*, 7 September.

Jones, A. 2001. 'Child asylum seekers and refugees', *Journal of Social Work* 1(3): 253–271.

Jones, C.A.G. 1994. *Expert Witnesses: Science, Medicine and the Practice of Law.* Oxford: Clarendon Press.

Jordan, B., B. Strath and A. Triandafyllidou. 2003. 'Comparing cultures of discretion', *Journal of Ethnic and Migration Studies* 29(2): 373–395.

Jubany, O. 2011. 'Constructing truths in a culture of disbelief: Understanding asylum screening from within', *International Sociology* 26(1): 74–94.

Juss, S. 2007. 'The slow death of citizenship rights', *King's Law Journal* 18: 95–118.

Kafka, Franz. 1925 [1994]. *The Trial.* London: Modern Penguin Classics.

Keith, L. and J. Holmes. 2009. 'A rare examination of typically observable factors in US asylum decisions', *Journal of Refugee Studies* 22(4): 224–241.

Kohli, R. 2005. 'The sound of silence: Listening to what unaccompanied asylum-seeking children say and do not say', *British Journal of Social Work* 36: 707–721.

Latour, B. 2010. *The Making of Law: An Ethnography of the Conseil d'Etat.* Cambridge: Polity Press.

Law Society. 2013. 'Instructing a barrister: New standard contractual terms', 24 January. Available at: https://www.lawsociety.org.uk/support-services/advice/practice-notes/instructing-a-barrister/ (accessed 8 August 2016).

Leech, S. 2006. 'Solicitors "deserting" legal aid', *BBC News*, 5 November. Available at: http://news.bbc.co.uk/1/hi/uk/6115514.stm (accessed 8 August 2016).

Legal Aid Agency. 2013. *Contract Management – Immigration and Asylum Accreditation Scheme: Work Restrictions.* London: Legal Aid Agency.

Leggatt, Sir Andrew. 2001. *Report of the Review of Tribunals, The National Archives.* Available at: http://webarchive.nationalarchives.gov.uk/+/http:/www.tribunals-review.org.uk/leggatthtm/leg-00.htm (accessed 27 July 2016).

Llewellyn, K. and E.A. Hoebel. 1941. *The Cheyenne Way: Conflict and Case Law in Primitive Jurisprudence.* Norman, OK: University of Oklahoma.

London Detainee Support Group. 2009. *Detained Lives: The Real Cost of Indefinite Detention.* London: London Detainee Support Group.

London Detainee Support Group. 2010. *No Return, No Release, No Reason: Challenging Indefinite Detention.* London: London Detainee Support Group.

Long, N. 2004. 'Actors, interfaces and development intervention: Meanings, purposes and powers', in T. Kontinen, ed., *Development Intervention: Actor and Activity Perspectives.* Helsinki: Center for Activity Theory and Developmental Work Research and Institute for Development Studies, University of Helsinki, pp. 14–36.

March, J. and J. Olsen. 1989. *Rediscovering Institutions: The Organizational Basis of Politics.* New York: Free Press.

Mather, L. and B. Yngvesson. 1980–1981. 'Language, audience and the transformation of disputes', *Law & Society Review* 15(3–4): 775–821.

MacAskill, E., J. Glover and V. Dodd. 2005. 'Expulsions illegal, UN tells Clarke', *The Guardian*, 25 August.

McConville, M., J. Hodgson, L. Bridges and A. Pavlovic. 1994. *Standing Accused: The Organization and Practices of Criminal Defence Lawyers.* Oxford: Clarendon Press.

McKee, R. 2006. 'Home Office policies', *Journal of Immigration, Asylum & Nationality Law* 20(4): 289–299.

McKinley, M 1997. 'Life stories, disclosure and the law', *POLAR* 20(2): 70–82.

Meili, S. 2013. 'UK refugee lawyers: Pushing the boundaries of domestic court acceptance of international human rights law', *Boston College International and Comparative Law Review* XXXVI (2): 1123–1148.

Menz, G. 2009. *The Political Economy of Managed Migration.* Oxford: Oxford University Press.

Merrill, J. 2016. 'Theresa May faces Parliamentary investigation over flimsy basis for student deportations', *The Independent*, 23 March. Available at: http://www.independent.

co.uk/news/uk/politics/theresa-may-faces-parliamentary-investigation-over-flimsy-basis-for-student-deportations-a6948796.html (accessed 10 August 2016).

Michener, G. 2011. 'FOI laws around the world', *Journal of Democracy* 22(2): 1–7.

Moore, S.F. 1973. 'Law and social change: The semi-autonomous social field as an appropriate subject of study', *Law & Society Review* 7: 719–746.

Moorhead, R. 2006. 'A challenge to judgecraft', *New Law Journal* 156: 742–746.

Moreno-Lax, V. 2015. *Europe in Crisis: Facilitating Access to Protection, (Discarding) Offshore Processing and Mapping Alternatives for the Way Forward.* Geneva: The Red Cross.

Morris, L. 2002. 'Britain's asylum and immigration regime: The shifting contours of rights', *Journal of Ethnic and Migration Studies* 28(3): 409–425.

Mulcahy, L. 2007. 'Architects of justice: The politics of courtroom design', *Social & Legal Studies* 16(3): 383–403.

Mulcahy, L. 2011. *Legal Architecture: Justice, Due Process and the Place of Law.* London: Routledge.

Mullan, K. 2012. 'Choice of argument on bites of the cherry', *Tribunal Journal* (Spring): 4–8.

Nader, L. 1984. 'A user theory of law', *Southwestern Law Journal* 38: 951–963.

Nader, L. 2002. 'The life of the law: A moving story', *Valparaiso University Law Review* 36: 655–674.

Olsen, J. 1983. 'Organizing political life: What administrative reorganization tells us about government', *American Political Science Review* 77(2): 281–296.

Ordonez, J. 2008. 'The state of confusion: Reflections on Central American asylum seekers in the Bay Area', *Ethnography* 9(1): 35–60.

Overbeek, H. 2002. 'Neoliberalism and the regulation of global labor mobility', *Annals of the American Academy of Political and Social Science* 581: 74–90.

Page, B. 2009. 'British attitudes to immigration in the 21st century', in Bertelsmann Stiftung, Migration Policy Institute, ed., *Migration, Public Opinion and Politics.* Washington, DC: Transatlantic Council on Migration, pp. 130–153.

Painter, C. 2008. 'A government department in meltdown: Crisis at the Home Office', *Public Money & Management* 28(5): 275–282.

Parvin, P. 2007. *Friend or Foe? Lobbying in British Democracy: A Discussion Paper.* London: Hansard Society.

Pellew, J. 1989. 'The Home Office and the Aliens Act, 1905', *The Historical Journal* 32(3): 369–385.

Pettitt, J., L. Townhead and S. Huber. 2008. 'The use of COI in the Refugee Status Determination Process in the UK: Looking back, reaching forward', *Refuge* 25(2): 182–194.

Phelan, M. and J. Gillespie. 2007. *Immigration Law Handbook*, 5th edn. Oxford: Oxford University Press.

Phelps, J. 2016. 'The fast track is dead', *openDemocracy*, 20 May. Available at: https://www.opendemocracy.net/5050/jerome-phelps/fast-track-is-dead (accessed 10 August 2016).

Pirouet, L. 2001. *Whatever Happened to Asylum in Britain? A Tale of Two Walls.* Oxford: Berghahn.

Press Association. 2010. 'Collapsed charity unable to manage its affairs', *The Guardian*, 17 June. Available at: http://www.theguardian.com/law/2010/jun/17/rmj-kenneth-clarke (accessed 6 August 2016).

Ramji-Nogales, J., A. Schoenholtz and P. Schrag. 2007. 'Refugee roulette: Disparities in asylum adjudication', *Stanford Law Review* 60: 295–401.

Rawlings, R. 2005. 'Review, revenge and retreat', *Modern Law Review* 68(3): 378–410.

Rawls, J. 1985. 'Justice as fairness: Political not metaphysical', *Philosophy and Public Affairs* 14(3): 223–251.

Refugee Council. 2006. *Refugee Council Briefing: New Asylum Model.* London: Refugee Council. Available at: http://www.irr.org.uk/pdf/RC_NAM_breifing.pdf (accessed 11 April 2013).

Refugee Legal Centre. 2006. *RLC's Response to the Joint DCA, LSC Consultation Paper, Legal Aid: A Sustainable Future.* London: Refugee Legal Centre.

Rehaag, S. 2008. 'Troubling patterns in Canadian refugee adjudication', *Ottawa Law Review* 39(2): 335–365.

Rehaag, S. 2012. 'Judicial review of refugee determinations: The luck of the draw?', *Queen's Law Journal* 38(1): 1–57.

Rights in Exile Programme. 2016. 'Post-deportation monitoring', *International Refugee Rights Initiative.* Available at: http://www.refugeelegalaidinformation.org/post-deportation-monitoring-network (accessed 27 July 2016).

Robbins, J. 2010. 'Legal aid lawyers facing fight to survive after tendering shakeup', *The Guardian*, 14 July. Available at: http://www.theguardian.com/law/2010/jul/14/legal-aid-lawyers-immigration-shake-up (accessed 16 August 2016).

Roberts, A. 2005. 'Spin control and freedom of information: Lessons for the UK from Canada', *Public Administration* 83(1): 1–23.

Roberts, S. 2009. '"Listing concentrates the mind": The English civil court as an arena for structured negotiation', *Oxford Journal of Legal Studies* 29(3): 457–479.

Robinson, V. and J. Segrott. 2002. *Understanding the Decision-Making of Asylum Seekers.* London: Home Office Research, Development and Statistics Directorate.

Rousseau, C., F. Drepeay, P. Foxen and F. Houle. 2002. 'The complexity of determining refugeehood: A multidisciplinary analysis of the decision-making process of the Canadian Immigration and Refugee Board', *Journal of Refugee Studies* 15(1): 43–69.

Russell, B. and N. Morris. 2008. 'Labour retreats on deportation threat to Zimbabweans', *The Independent*, 13 July. Available at: http://www.independent.co.uk/news/uk/politics/labour-retreats-on-deportation-threat-to-zimbabweans-865060.html (accessed 8 August 2016).

Sarat, A. and W. Felstiner. 1986. 'Law and strategy in the divorce lawyer's office', *Law & Society Review* 20(1): 93–134.

Sassen, S. 2000. 'Regulating immigration in a global age: A new policy landscape', *Annals of the American Academy of Political and Social Science* 570: 65–77.

Sayers, M. and A. Webb. 1990. 'Franks revisited: A model of the ideal tribunal', *Civil Justice Quarterly* 9: 36–50.

Schuster, L. 2000. 'A comparative analysis of the asylum policy of seven European governments', *Journal of Refugee Studies* 13(1): 118–132.

Shah. P. 1999. *Refugees, Race and the Legal Concept of Asylum in Britain.* PhD thesis. London: School of Oriental and African Studies.

Shore, C. and S. Wright, eds. 1997. *Anthropology of Policy: Critical Perspectives on Governance and Power.* London: Routledge.

Silverman, S. 2012. *Return to the Isle of Man: The Implications of Internment for Understanding Immigration Detention in the UK.* Working Paper no. 102. Oxford: Centre on Migration Policy and Society, University of Oxford.

Silverman, S. and R. Hajela. 2012. *Briefing: Immigration Detention in the UK.* Oxford: The Migration Observatory. Available at: http://www.migrationobservatory.ox.ac.uk/sites/files/migobs/Immigration%20Detention%20Briefing.pdf (accessed 27 July 2016).

Singh, A. and F. Webber. 2010. *Excluding Migrants from Justice: The Legal Aid Cuts.* IPPR Briefing Paper no. 7. London: Institute of Race Relations.

Smith, E. 2004. *Right First Time? Home Office Asylum Interviewing and Reasons for Refusal Letters.* Oxford: Medical Foundation for the Care of Victims of Torture.

Somerville, W. 2009. 'Future immigration patterns and policies in the United Kingdom', in Bertelsmann Stiftung, Migration Policy Institute, ed., *Migration, Public Opinion and Politics.* Washington, DC: Transatlantic Council on Migration, pp. 314–329.

Spaulding, N. 2011–2012. 'Facades of justice', *Michigan Law Review* 110: 1067–1082.

Spaulding, N. 2012. 'The enclosure of justice: Courthouse architecture, due process, and the dead metaphor of trial', *Yale Journal of Law and the Humanities* 24: 311–343.

Statham, P. 2003. 'Understanding anti-asylum rhetoric: Restrictive politics or racist publics?', in S. Spencer, ed., *The Politics of Migration: Managing Opportunity, Conflict and Change.* Oxford: Blackwell, pp. 163–177.

Statham, P. and A. Geddes. 2006. 'Elites and the "organized public": Who drives British immigration politics and in which direction?', *West European Politics* 29(2): 248–269.

Sweeney, J. 2007. 'The lure of "facts" in asylum appeals', in S. Smith. Ed. *Applying Theory and Practice: Issues and Questions for Policy Analysis.* Aldershot: Ashgate, pp. 19–35.

Symonds, S. 2008. 'The special immigration status', *Journal of Immigration, Asylum & Nationality Law* 22: 333–347.

The Migration Observatory. 2014. 'Deportations, removals and voluntary departures from the UK', *The Migration Observatory* (June). Available at: http://www.migrationobservatory.ox.ac.uk/briefings/deportations-removals-and-voluntary-departures-uk (accessed 27 July 2016).

Thomas, R. 2005. 'Evaluating tribunal adjudication: Administrative justice and asylum appeals', *Legal Studies* 25: 462–498.

Toal, R. 2008. 'The new "general grounds for refusal"', *Journal of Immigration and Nationality Law* 22(2): 135–146.

Transactional Records Access Clearinghouse. 2009. 'Latest data from immigration courts show decline in asylum disparity', *TRAC Immigration* (22 June). Available at: http://trac.syr.edu/immigration/reports/209/ (accessed 27 July 2016).

Travers, M. 1999. *The British Immigration Courts.* London: Policy Press.

Travis, A. 2002. 'Home office to rewrite Geneva refugee agreement', *The Guardian*, 5 October. Available at: http://www.theguardian.com/uk/2002/oct/05/immigration.immigrationandpublicservices (accessed 10 August 2016).

Travis, A. 2006. 'Asylum seekers forced to return to using supermarket vouchers', *The Guardian*, 20 March. Available at: http://www.theguardian.com/politics/2006/mar/20/immigrationandpublicservices.immigration (accessed 10 August 2016).

Travis, A. 2007. 'Warning on shifting asylum seekers to dangerous areas is revealed', *The Guardian*, 16 March.

Travis, A. 2008. 'Ministers aim to block high court appeals by failed asylum seekers', *The Guardian*, 22 August. Available at: http://www.theguardian.com/politics/2008/aug/22/immigrationpolicy.immigration (accessed 8 August 2016).

Travis, A. 2010. 'Home Office to lift ban on deporting failed asylum seekers to Zimbabwe', *The Guardian*, 14 October. Available at: http://www.theguardian.com/uk/2010/oct/14/asylum-seekers-home-office-lifts-zimbabwe-deportation-ban (accessed 8 August 2016).

Travis, A. 2013. 'UK Border Agency to be abolished, Theresa May announces', *The Guardian*, 26 March. Available at: https://www.theguardian.com/uk/2013/mar/26/uk-border-agency-broken-up (accessed 4 August 2016).

Trish, L, 2013. 'Decision making conditioned by radical uncertainty: Credibility assessment at the Australian Refugee Review Tribunal', *International Journal of Refugee Law* 25(3): 502–534.

UK. 2004a. *Summary of Responses to the Consultation Paper 'Proposed Changes to Publicly Funded Immigration and Asylum Work'*. London: Department of Constitutional Affairs.

UK. 2004b. *The Asylum and Immigration Tribunal: The Legal Aid Arrangements for Onward Appeals*. London: Department of Constitutional Affairs.

UK. 2005a. *A Fairer Deal for Legal Aid*. Cm 6591. London: Department of Constitutional Affairs.

UK. 2005b. *Asylum Statistics UK 2004: Home Office Statistical Bulletin 13/05*. London: Home Office.

UK. 2006a. *Eritrea: 'Evangelicals: Unregistered Christian Churches'. Country of Origin Information Report*. London: Home Office.

UK. 2006b. *House of Commons Select Committee on Home Affairs: Fifth Report*. July. London: The Stationery Office.

UK. 2007a. 'Examination of witnesses (Questions 174–179)', *Select Committee on Constitutional Affairs: Minutes of Evidence*, 30 January. Available at: http://www.publications.parliament.uk/pa/cm200607/cmselect/cmconst/223/7013002.htm (accessed 8 August 2016).

UK. 2007b. *Home Office Departmental Report*. Cm 7096. London: Home Office.

UK. 2007c. *The Creation of the Ministry of Justice: Sixth Report of Session 2006–07*. HC 466. London: House of Commons Constitutional Affairs Committee.

UK. 2008a. *Operational Guidance Note: Ethiopia*. London: Home Office.

UK. 2008b. *The Economic Impact of Migration, Volume 1: Report*. HL 82-I. London: The Stationery Office.

UK. 2008c. *TSol Business Plan, 2007–2008*. London: Treasury Solicitor's Department.

UK. 2008d. *UKBA Business Plan 2008–2011*. London: Home Office.

UK. 2009. *Management of Asylum Applications by the UK Border Agency*. London: The Stationery Office.

UK. 2010a. *Asylum: Getting the Balance Right? A Thematic Inspection*. London: Office of the Independent Chief Inspector of the UKBA.

UK. 2010b. *Joint Presidential Guidance Note No. 2 of 2010: Child, Vulnerable Adult and Sensitive Appellant Guidance*. London: Tribunals Judiciary. Available at: https://www.judiciary.gov.uk/wp-content/uploads/2014/07/ChildWitnessGuidance.pdf (accessed 10 August 2016).

UK. 2010c. *Practice Directions: Immigration and Asylum Chambers of the First-Tier Tribunal and the Upper Tribunal*. London: Tribunals Judiciary. Available at: http://www.judiciary.gov.uk/wp-content/uploads/JCO/Documents/Practice+Directions/Tribunals/IAC_UT_FtT_PracticeDirection.pdf (accessed 8 August 2016).

UK. 2010–2011. *Home Office Annual Accounts*. London: Home Office.

UK. 2011a. 'Draft First-Tier Tribunal (Immigration and Asylum Chamber) Fees Order 2011', *Hansard*, 14 September 2011, available at: http://www.publications.parliament.uk/pa/cm201012/cmgeneral/deleg3/110914/110914s01.htm (accessed 8 August 2016).

UK. 2011b. *Public Opinion and Immigration: Policy Briefing*. London: All-Party Parliamentary Group on Migration.

UK. 2011c. *The Use of Country of Origin Information in Deciding Asylum Applications: A Thematic Inspection (Oct.–May 2010)*. London: Office of the Independent Chief Inspector of the UKBA.

UK. 2012a. *User Guide to Home Office Immigration Statistics*. London: Home Office.

UK. 2012b. *An Inspection of the UK Border Agency's Handling of Legacy Asylum and Migration Cases*. London: Office of the Independent Chief Inspector of the UKBA.

UK. 2012c. 'Border Agency's backlog spiralling out of control say Home Affairs Committee' (8 November). London: House of Commons Constitutional Affairs Committee.

UK. 2012d. *Asylum Process Guidance: Detained Fast Track Processes*. London: Home Office.

UK 2012e. *Home Affairs Committee – Fourth Report: The Work of the UK Border Agency* (October–December). HC 616. London: The Stationery Office.

UK. 2013a. 'Attorney General's civil panel counsel: Appointments, membership lists and off panel counsel'. Available at: https://www.gov.uk/attorney-generals-panel-counsel-appointments-membership-lists-and-off-panel-counsel (accessed 27 July 2016).

UK. 2013b. 'Attorney General's civil panel counsel: Practical information'. Available at: http://www.tsol.gov.uk/attorney_generals_panel_of_counsel.htm (accessed 6 August 2016).

UK. 2013c. *Detained Fast Track Processes*, Version 5. London: UKBA. Available at: https://www.gov.uk/government/uploads/system/uploads/attachment_data/file/257435/detained_fast_processes.pdf (accessed 27 July 2016).

UK. 2013d. *Judicial Review Statistics 2007–2013*. London: Ministry of Justice.

UK. 2014a. *Asylum Process Guidance Note: Conducting the Asylum Interview*, Version 5.0, March. Available at: https://www.gov.uk/government/uploads/system/uploads/attachment_data/file/298853/Asylum_interview_policy_guidance_v_5.pdf (accessed 21 August 2014).

UK. 2014b. 'Experts – overriding duty to the court', 'Part 35 – Experts and Assessors', *Civil Procedure Rules*. London: Ministry of Justice. Available at: http://www.justice.gov.uk/courts/procedure-rules/civil/rules/part35#IDASLICC (accessed 8 August 2016).

UK. 2014c. *Ministry of Justice and Legal Aid Agency: Implementing Reforms to Civil Legal Aid*. HC 784. London: National Audit Office.

UK. 2015a. *Have Changes to Legal Aid in England and Wales since 2013 Created More 'Advice Deserts'*? Commons Briefing Papers SN06273. London: House of Commons Library.

UK. 2015b. *Immigration and Asylum: Changes Made by the Coalition Government 2010–2015*. SN/HA/5829. London: House of Commons Library.

UK. 2015c. 'Part 52 – appeals', *Rules & Practice Directions*. London: Ministry Of Justice. Available at: http://www.justice.gov.uk/courts/procedure-rules/civil/rules/part52 (accessed 8 August 2016).

UK. 2015d. *Upper Tribunal Immigration and Asylum Chamber Guidance Note 2011 No. 2*. London: Tribunals Judiciary. Available at: https://www.judiciary.gov.uk/wp-content/uploads/2014/01/guidance-note-2001-no-2-reporting-decisions-july-2015.pdf (accessed 10 August 2016).

UK. 2016a. *A Guide to Bringing a Case to the Supreme Court*. London: Registry of the Supreme Court of the United Kingdom. Available at: https://www.supremecourt.uk/docs/a-guide-to-bringing-a-case-to-the-supreme-court.pdf (accessed 8 August 2016).

UK. 2016b. 'MoJ consultation: Appeals to the Court of Appeal, proposed amendments to Civil Procedure Rules and Practice Direction', 20 May. London: Courts and Tribunals Judiciary. Available at: https://www.judiciary.gov.uk/publications/moj-consultation-appeals-to-the-court-of-appeal-proposed-amendments-to-civil-procedure-rules-and-practice-direction/ (accessed 10 August 2016).

UK. 2016c. *Processing Children's Asylum Claims*, Version 1. London: Home Office. Available at: https://www.gov.uk/government/uploads/system/uploads/attachment_data/file/537010/Processing-children_s-asylum-claims-v1.pdf (accessed 4 August 2016).

UNHCR. 1998. *Note on Burden and Standard of Proof in Refugee Claims* (16 December). Geneva: Office of the High Commissioner for Refugees.

UNHCR. 2006. *Quality Initiative Project: Key Observations and Recommendations, September 2005–February 2006*. London: Office of the UN High Commissioner for Refugees. Available at: http://www.unhcr.org/4e11b2fa9.pdf (accessed 4 August 2016).

UNHCR. 2013. *Beyond Proof: Credibility Assessment in EU Asylum Systems*. Geneva: European Refugee Fund of the European Commission.

Verkaik, R. 2006. 'Crime statistics "were distorted by politics"', *The Independent*, 13 February.

Vincenzi, C. 1992. 'Extra-statutory ministerial discretion in immigration law', *Public Law* 2 (Summer): 300–321.

Vitus, K. 2010. '"Waiting time": The de-subjectification of children in Danish asylum centres', *Childhood* 17(1): 26–42.

Wagner, A. 2011. 'Secret foreign nationals detention policy was "serious abuse of power"', *UK Human Rights Blog*, 23 March. Available at: http://ukhumanrightsblog.com/2011/03/23/secret-foreign-nationals-detention-policy-was-serious-abuse-of-power/ (accessed 8 August 2016).

Walby, K. and M. Larsen. 2011a. 'Access to information and Freedom of Information requests: Neglected means of data production in the social sciences', *Qualitative Inquiry* 18(1): 31–42.

Walby, K. and M. Larsen. 2011b. 'Getting at the Live Archive: On access to information research in Canada', *Canadian Journal of Law & Society* 26(3): 623–633.

Wedel, J., C. Shore, G. Feldman and S. Lathrop. 2005. 'Towards an anthropology of public policy', *Annals of the American Academy of Political and Social Sciences* 600: 30–51.

White Ryland Solicitors. 2006. *Legal Aid for Asylum and Immigration: An Unsustainable Future. Response to the DCA Consultation Paper*. London: White Ryland Solicitors.

Whitehead, T. 2005. '1 in 4 terror suspects are asylum seekers', *The Express*, 22 August.

Wintour, P. 2005. 'Quitting UN agreement on refugees "not feasible"', *The Guardian*, 26 January. Available at: http://www.theguardian.com/society/2005/jan/26/asylum.immigrationasylumandrefugees (accessed 10 August 2016).

Wintour, P., M. White and A. Travis. 2005. 'Judges to be told to act on deportations', *The Guardian*, 12 August.

Woolf, H. 1998. 'Judicial review: The tensions between the executive and the judiciary', *Law Quarterly Review* 114: 579–593.

Yeo, C., ed. 2005. *Country Guideline Cases: Benign or Practical?* London: Immigration Advisory Services.

Yeo, C. 2010. 'New tribunal rules and procedure', *Free Movement*, 17 February. Available at: https://www.freemovement.org.uk/new-tribunal-rules-and-procedure/ (accessed 8 August 2016).

Young, R. 1990. 'The effectiveness of representation at tribunals', *Civil Justice Quarterly* 9: 16–23.

Index

Taylor & Francis eBooks

eBooks
from Taylor & Francis

Helping you to choose the right eBooks for your Library

Add to your library's digital collection today with Taylor & Francis eBooks. We have over 50,000 eBooks in the Humanities, Social Sciences, Behavioural Sciences, Built Environment and Law, from leading imprints, including Routledge, Focal Press and Psychology Press.

REQUEST YOUR FREE INSTITUTIONAL TRIAL TODAY

Free Trials Available
We offer free trials to qualifying academic, corporate and government customers.

Choose from a range of subject packages or create your own!

Benefits for you

- Free MARC records
- COUNTER-compliant usage statistics
- Flexible purchase and pricing options
- All titles DRM-free.

Benefits for your user

- Off-site, anytime access via Athens or referring URL
- Print or copy pages or chapters
- Full content search
- Bookmark, highlight and annotate text
- Access to thousands of pages of quality research at the click of a button.

eCollections

Choose from over 30 subject eCollections, including:

- Archaeology
- Architecture
- Asian Studies
- Business & Management
- Classical Studies
- Construction
- Creative & Media Arts
- Criminology & Criminal Justice
- Economics
- Education
- Energy
- Engineering
- English Language & Linguistics
- Environment & Sustainability
- Geography
- Health Studies
- History
- Language Learning
- Law
- Literature
- Media & Communication
- Middle East Studies
- Music
- Philosophy
- Planning
- Politics
- Psychology & Mental Health
- Religion
- Security
- Social Work
- Sociology
- Sport
- Theatre & Performance
- Tourism, Hospitality & Events

For more information, pricing enquiries or to order a free trial, please contact your local sales team: **www.tandfebooks.com/page/sales**

www.tandfebooks.com

For Product Safety Concerns and Information please contact our EU representative GPSR@taylorandfrancis.com
Taylor & Francis Verlag GmbH, Kaufingerstraße 24, 80331 München, Germany

www.ingramcontent.com/pod-product-compliance
Ingram Content Group UK Ltd.
Pitfield, Milton Keynes, MK11 3LW, UK
UKHW011009180926
475701UK00004B/640
* 9 7 8 0 3 6 7 2 6 6 3 7 0 *